Staffordshire Figures

History in Earthenware

1740-1900

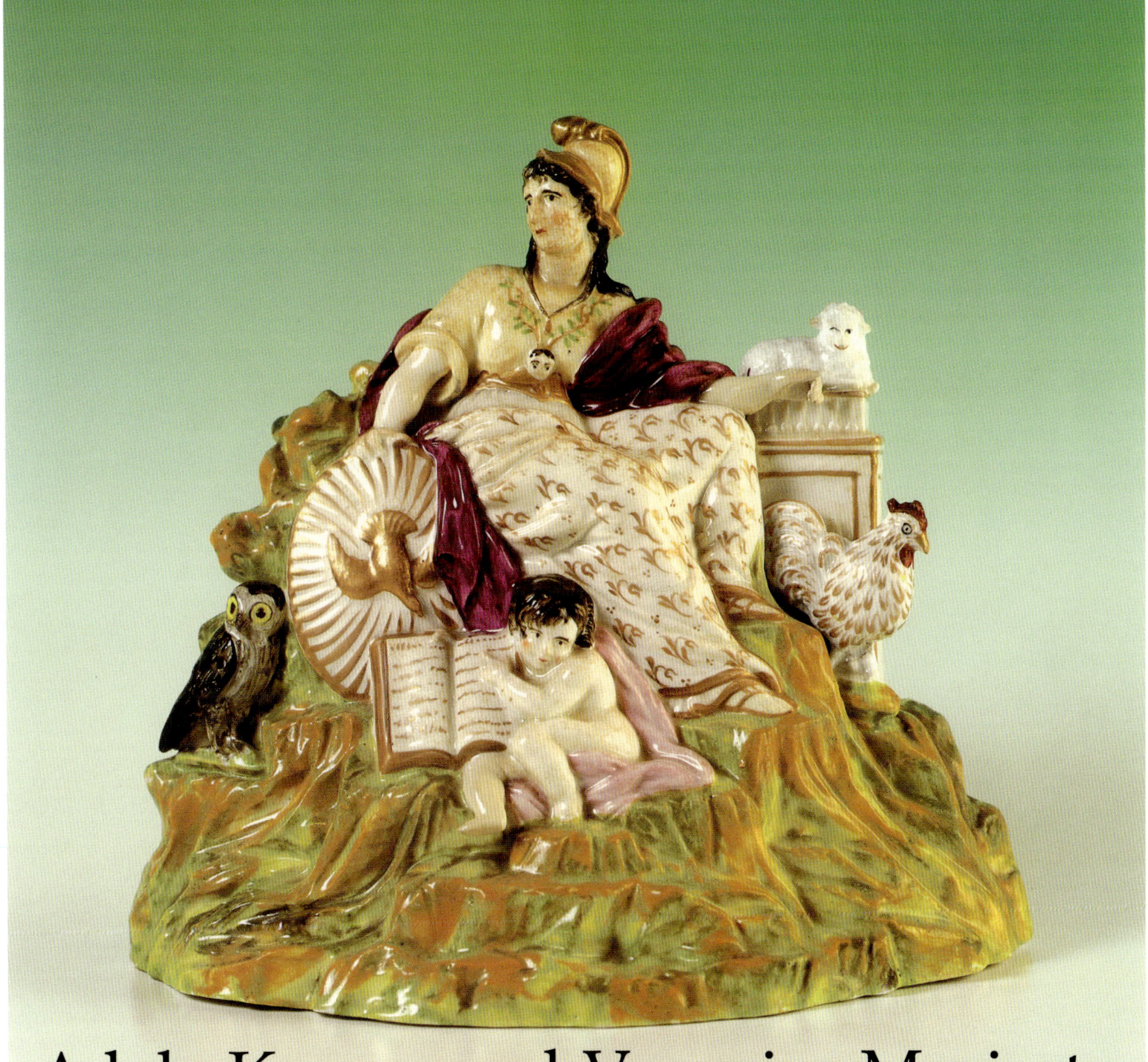

Adele Kenny and Veronica Moriarty

Schiffer Publishing Ltd®

4880 Lower Valley Road, Atglen, PA 19310 USA

Dedication

This book is lovingly dedicated to the memory of the authors' parents: Adele Mary Petro Kenny and William John Kenny Jr., Veronica Anne Margaret Moriarty and Dennis Dunne Moriarty.

Library of Congress Cataloging-in-Publication Data

Kenny, Adele, 1948-
Staffordshire figures : history in earthenware, 1740-1900 / by Adele Kenny, Veronica Moriarty.
p. cm.
ISBN 0-7643-1917-5
1. Staffordshire pottery--Collectors and collecting. 2. Pottery figures--England. I. Moriarty, Veronica. II. Title.
NK4087.S6 K434 2004
738.8'2'094246075--dc22

2003018181

Designed by Mark David Bowyer
Type set in ZapfCalligr BT / Dutch 801 Rm BT

ISBN: 0-7643-1917-5
Printed in China
1 2 3 4

Published by Schiffer Publishing Ltd.
4880 Lower Valley Road
Atglen, PA 19310
Phone: (610) 593-1777; Fax: (610) 593-2002
E-mail: Info@schifferbooks.com
Please visit our web site catalog at **www.schifferbooks.com**
We are always looking for people to write books on new and related subjects. If you have an idea for a book, please contact us at the above address.

This book may be purchased from the publisher.
Include $3.95 for shipping.
Please try your bookstore first.
You may write for a free catalog.

In Europe, Schiffer books are distributed by
Bushwood Books
6 Marksbury Avenue
Kew Gardens
Surrey TW9 4JF England
Phone: 44 (0) 20 8392 8585
Fax: 44 (0) 20 8392 9876
E-mail: Bushwd@aol.com
Free postage in the UK. Europe: air mail at cost.

Contents

Acknowledgments

The authors gratefully acknowledge Denise Sater (Editor of *Antiques & Auction News*) and Michael Kerr (Publisher of *The Antiquer*, *The Antiques News,* and *New York City's Antiques News*) for their kind permission to use versions of, and excerpts from, articles that first appeared in their publications. Gratitude for use of photographs is extended to the Ballarat Fine Art Gallery, Victoria, Australia; Susan Bishop and Darcy McGroarty (Bishop and Daughter Antiques, www.bishopantiques.com); to Roy W. Bunn (Roy W. Bunn Antiques, www.roywbunnantiques.co.uk); to John and Barbara Gair (Castle Antiques, www.castleantiques.freeserve.co.uk); to S. J. Hales Auctioneers (www.sjhales.com); to Jonathan Horne (Jonathan Horne Antiques, Ltd., www.jonathanhorne.co.uk); to Marie Gartside (Knight's Antiques, www.knights-antiques.com); to Nick Harding (www.staffordshirefigures.com), to David, Jeni, and Ben (Madelena Antiques, www.madelenaantiques.com); to Jane and Fred McClafferty (Jane McClafferty Antiques, www.janemcclaffertyantiques.com); to Zane Moss (Zane Moss Antiques, www.zanemossantiques.com); to Gillian and David Nash (Kellerton Ceramics, www.kellerton.com); to Nick and Gail Young (Grayling's Antiques, www.Staffordshire-Figures.com); and to Tracy at Golden Age Antiques, Hertfordshire. England. The authors gratefully acknowledge Robert Buczynski (Royal Treasures Antiques, Inc., Cherry Street, Rahway, New Jersey) for his sketches, and Kenneth Lay and Peter Leaver (Kenneth Lay Antiques, High Street, Prahran East, 3181, Victoria, Australia) for providing access to their extensive stock and collection of Staffordshire figures. Thanks also go to Marla W. Chaikin (William Charles Antiques, Monmouth Beach, New Jersey), to Anita L. Grashof (Gallerie Ani'tiques, Scotch Plains, New Jersey), and to David P. Willis (David P. Willis Antiques, Inc., Plainfield, New Jersey). The authors extend special thanks to their editor, Ginny Parfitt, to all the Schiffer staff, to Alex Pinto for his unfailing friendship, and, *last but far from least*, to Garry Taylor and Bob Fiorellino for their encouragement, support, patience, and understanding.

Introduction

Imagine the gilded age of a nation expressed in many thousands of earthenware figures, each with its own story to tell, each with a corresponding narrative that informs subsequent generations of the cultural, social, religious, and political life of its time. Imagine the panorama of eighteenth and nineteenth century Britain – decades of progress and change – and the development of a glorious empire with a presence that was felt throughout the world. Imagine the historic national and international events that shaped British history – the pageant of a storied realm – and add to it the everyday dramas, interests, pastimes, and occupations of England's people. It sounds exciting and it is – this is what Staffordshire's earthenware figures are all about! They were unique as a chronicle of their own place in time, and they remain unique today as a figural history. No other medium has served with such vitality and accuracy in recording the essence of a people and an empire as the art of the Staffordshire pottery figure. Staffordshire figures are the potters' unparalleled legacy: one of confidence, courage, innovation, and dawning humanitarianism. We, grateful inheritors, have much to learn about Britain's history, and what better tutors are there than the figures themselves?

Functional pots made in Britain during the early Bronze Age from a series of coils and low-fired in a bonfire because kilns were unknown at the time. The smaller beaker has been incised with a five-pronged comb, probably made from bone. The larger urn was found at Tregiffan, St. Buryan, Cornwall and is typical of the pottery produced in England's southwest during the early Bronze Age. *Courtesy of Jonathan Horne (Antiques) Ltd.*

Although no one knows when the first pots were made in Britain, when the first kilns and potters' wheels were introduced, or when glazing was first used, archaeological findings confirm that pottery making existed in Britain as early as the Bronze Age. The Romans created pottery in England, and by the fourteenth and fifteenth centuries functional wares were made in and around British abbeys. Independent potters produced red stonewares by the 1690s, and the late seventeenth and early eighteenth centuries saw improvements in stoneware, the addition of Chinese-and Continental-style enameling, and the introduction of lead glazing. Beginning around 1740, the potters of North Staffordshire began to add decorative figures to their repertoire of utilitarian ceramic wares. The early figures were generally simple, often clever, and sometimes humorous.

Rare and important slipware coronation charger signed "William Talor" and dating to circa 1675. The red earthenware dish has been coated on the upper side with white slip, and the decoration has been trailed over in different colored slips. This dish most likely portrays the coronation of Charles II in 1661. According to Jonathan Horne, two contenders for making this dish are William Talor (baptized August 1624 at Burslem) and William Talor (baptized December 1632 at Wolstanton). 16.75". Value: $30,000-$40,000. *Courtesy of Jonathan Horne (Antiques) Ltd.*

Large earthenware mug made in Staffordshire featuring a bulbous shape with stylized tulip decoration. 7". Circa 1695. Value: $8000-$10,000. *Courtesy of Jonathan Horne (Antiques) Ltd.*

Large, two-handled posset pot made in Staffordshire, decorated with three colors of slip, and inscribed "The best is not too good for you ET04," a common inscription usually found on late seventeenth century examples. 5.50". Circa 1704. Value: $15,000-$20,000. *Courtesy of Jonathan Horne (Antiques) Ltd.*

Ongoing experimentation led to the use of underglaze oxide decoration, overglaze enamels, creamware, and the satiny pearl-like finish of pearlware. Some of the earliest figures and groups reflected the potters' innovative and artistic pursuits. Most, in keeping with Staffordshire's cottage industry and folk art origins, were crudely rendered but wonderfully appealing in their naïve charm. None was, by any standard, equal in detail and finesse to the expensive and more sophisticated British and Continental porcelains they were intended to imitate. All, however, represented significant technical achievements on the part of the Staffordshire potters who chose to work in the more difficult medium of pottery. Figure production began with the market potentials of providing an affordable alternative to expensive porcelains, and the potters were spot on. Staffordshire figures found their way into nineteenth century homes across Britain, throughout her colonies, and around the world. More importantly, the potters created an earthenware idiom that has undoubtedly exceeded their wildest dreams of future collectibility.

Late eighteenth century creamware ewe, recumbent on a green base. 4". Value: $1000+. *Courtesy of Zane Moss Antiques.*

By the beginning of the nineteenth century, victories over the French, the Prince Regent's flamboyant character and fashionable tastes, and a growing market economy contributed to a national sense of well-being. The Staffordshire potters accommodated high spirits and humble purses with the introduction of low-cost figures decorated in bright enamels and underglaze colors that enabled even the less affluent members of society to achieve a sense of decorative prosperity and a veneer of learnedness in their homes. By the time Victoria became queen, Britain had passed every test of the Industrial

Revolution with high marks, and the Staffordshire potters had secured Britain's dominance in the world ceramics trade. Buttressed by interest in progress and a preoccupation with the "here and now," mass production of earthenware figures that reflected the people and events of their time had begun in earnest. Early and mid-Victorian figures maintained the integrity of Staffordshire craftsmanship to some extent and remained true to the traditional folk art quaintness that was a hallmark of local style.

Portrait figure of Queen Victoria (fronted by miniature dog figures). 17.50". Mid-Victorian. Value: $500-$1000. *Courtesy of Anita L. Grashof, Gallerie Ani'tiques.*

There was nothing serendipitous in the potters' choice of subject matter – they were keen businessmen with their fingers on the pulse of the buying public. Always resourceful and ever enterprising, the Victorian potters' primary objective was to turn a profit rather than to create art. However, whether they intended to or not, they succeeded in producing an earthenware record of their era that has become a singular extension of earlier British folk art. The potters' inventory ran the gamut of human experience and included sinners and saints, orphans and clowns, royalty and rogues; they infused their craft with a humble vitality and a conspicuous immediacy that suggested the daily lives, interests, dreams, and aspirations of the people who purchased them. By Victoria's time, an age in which ornamentation mirrored success, Staffordshire figures on the mantelpiece were tangible reminders of achievement.

Couple in traditional Welsh costume. 10". Circa 1850. Value: $500-$1000. *Courtesy of Susan Bishop and Darcy McGroarty, Bishop and Daughter Antiques.*

Woman in Welsh costume. 9". Circa 1850. Value. $500-$1000. *Courtesy of Susan Bishop and Darcy McGroarty, Bishop and Daughter Antiques.*

Most figures and groups reflect the potters' response to history and their successful efforts to remain current with the issues and news of their time. Throughout the Victorian Era, portrait figures and groups were produced in huge numbers, and the potters' roster included a comprehensive range of personalities who either had been or were currently making headlines. In addition, local persons of interest like Old Parr (who reputedly lived to the ripe old age of 152) and the last woman to speak Cornish were not left out, along with scores of figures that were crafted to represent various aspects of the average person's life.

"Old Parr." Thomas Parr (not the famous nineteenth century potter!) was the oldest man to have ever lived in England who died at the incredible age of 152 years and nine months. Old Parr, a farmer for most of his life, was buried in Westminster Abbey (by order of King Charles I) beside royalty and other celebrity dead. The inscription on his small white marble gravestone in the center of the South Transept reads: THO: PARR OF YE COUNTY OF SALLOP. BORNE IN AD: 1483. HE LIVED IN YE REIGNES OF TEN PRINCES VIZ: K.EDW.4. K.ED.5. K.RICH.3. K.HEN.7. K.HEN.8. K.EDW.6. Q.MA. Q.ELIZ. K.JA. & K.CHARLES. AGED 152 YEARES. & WAS BURYED HERE NOVEMB. 15. 1635. Most information about Parr was recorded in John Taylor's 1635 pamphlet entitled "The Old, Old, Very Old Man or the Age and Long Life of Thomas Parr." The son of John Parr of Winnington near Shrewsbury in Shropshire, Thomas married Jane Taylor, his first wife, in 1563 when he was 80 years old. They had a son and a daughter (both died in infancy). At the age of 100 he did penance (standing draped in a white sheet in his parish church and is depicted as such with the potter's slight embellishment of making the sheet orange) for being unfaithful to his wife and for fathering a child by Katherine Milton. Documents in the parish register confirm that after Jane's death he married Jane Lloyd (in 1605 at the age of 122). Old Parr's likeness was used during the nineteenth century as advertising for patent medicines promoting longevity and it is from this later promotional source that Thomas Parr, the potter, most probably drew his inspiration. 10". Circa 1850. Value: $1000+.

Staffordshire's potters not only celebrated British royalty, but also made portrait figures of the royals and leaders of other nations. Geographic locations, and people of various nationalities, were memorialized in earthenware as well. North Wales and Scotland were well represented in a range of figures (including Robert Bruce, William Wallace, and Rob Roy), and Ireland was remembered with portrait figures of notables like Lord Edward Fitzgerald, Henry Jez McCracken, Daniel O'Connell, Charles Stewart Parnell, William and Lucy O'Brien, and Theobald Wolfe Tone. International newsmakers like Hungary's Lajos (Louis) Kossuth, numerous French citizens from Napoleon Bonaparte to naval hero Jean Bart, and even the more exotic Sultans of Turkey (Abd-ul-Mejid and Abd-ul-Hamid II) had their portraits made by the potters. Americans were commemorated in numerous portrait figures; among them were George Washington, Benjamin Franklin, Abraham Lincoln, Thomas Jefferson, John Brown, the Cushman sisters, Moody and Sankey, and even characters from Harriet Beecher Stowe's *Uncle Tom's Cabin*. Like the latter, numerous figures and groups recorded the literature, art, and other entertainments that were enjoyed during sixteen decades of figure production.

Large figure of Scottish hero Rob Roy. 17.50". Mid-Victorian. Value: $500-$1000. *Courtesy of Anita L. Grashof, Gallerie Ani'tiques.*

Portrait figure of American abolitionist John Brown depicted with two slaves and made to commemorate Brown's 1859 death at Harper's Ferry. 11.50". Value: $500-$1000. *Courtesy of Susan Bishop and Darcy McGroarty, Bishop and Daughter Antiques.*

Criminals, whose nefarious deeds were hot news, comprised an earthenware rogues gallery that was more inclusive than Madame Tussaud's famous Chamber of Horrors. The potters' depictions of criminals and crime scenes were purchased with the same enthusiasm as figures of Biblical personalities, important religious leaders and preachers, military and naval luminaries, and heroes and heroines of the time. It is amusing to imagine that figures of murders were placed on Victorian mantles beside figures of Christ, the apostles, or contemporary fire and brimstone preachers.

We would be remiss if we neglected to comment on the potters' sense of humor as evidenced in figures like *Roger Giles*, depicted squatting with his backside bare in response to an advertisement that read "...newlayde heggs [new laid eggs] by me Roger Giles" (Harding, Book Two, p. 293). As already noted, the potters were keen observers of their times, and opportunities for social commentary were rarely passed up. Often their wit and playfulness were expressed in satirical groups that were a ceramic form of indictment against the injustices and absurdities they perceived in their world as depicted in groups like *The New Marriage Act* and *The Tithe Pig*.

With limited exceptions, very few "stones" were left unturned, and the number and variety of Staffordshire figures is so immense that it is nearly incomprehensible. Sustaining any product's marketability over time is no small task, but the potters remained eminently successful for about a century and a half before the pressures of commercialism, competition, and, finally, waning consumer interest took their toll late in the nineteenth century.

Placed on a mantle beside figures of criminals like William Corder, these outstanding examples of Staffordshire's religious figures would clearly suggest the diverse and pervading interests of nineteenth century purchasers. *Above:* 12.25" enameled figure of a flaming altar. Value: $7500-$8500. *Right:* 9.50" enameled group titled "CHRIST'S AGONY," also inscribed "FATHER LET THIS CUP PASS." Value: $7000-$8000. Both date to circa 1830. *Courtesy of Jonathan Horne (Antiques) Ltd.*

The notorious Red Barn at the left and murderer William Corder with victim Maria Marten at the right (see Chapter Fifteen for details on the Corder-Marten murder). The Red Barn: 7.50", circa 1828; $3000-$3500. Corder and Marten: 8", circa 1828; $4000-$4500. Both examples bear impressed titles within elliptical panels above relief-molded swags; the Red Barn is set on a table base with pearl-beaded feet, and the Corder-Marten group stands on a ridge-footed table base (see Chapter Five for details on table base figures). *Courtesy of Jonathan Horne (Antiques) Ltd.*

The Staffordshire figures used to illustrate this work are those to which collectors may hope to aspire in their own collections. Very rare figures, usually beyond the scope of the everyday collector and usually found only in museums and extraordinary collections, have been included when deemed to be absolutely necessary to enhance the readers' appreciation of the text. Figures exhibiting damage and repairs have been included as they represent the true "survivors" of Staffordshire pottery; a century or so ago someone cared enough to keep them, and we care enough now not to let damage detract from our appreciation of the potters' art.

The values we have listed are for figures in good condition (despite possible damages in the examples illustrated) and reflect recent international market trends based on prices provided by dealers, collectors, recently published value guides, and Internet auctions. Our values are *not* intended to set prices but only suggest current ranges, and are included in photo captions.

Because prices vary and change, neither the publisher nor the authors assume responsibility for losses incurred as a result of consulting values printed herein. With Staffordshire figures, as with other antique collectibles, the maxim that "value is what anyone is willing to pay" applies regardless of set prices and book values. Purchase of any antique begs the question, "Did you get a good deal?" Our experiences as collectors have taught us that if a particular figure is bought at a price that's right for us, and if it makes us smile, then the deal was indeed very good.

Much has been written about Staffordshire figures, including specialized studies of particular categories and large catalogs of known figures. There are several standard references in the field including P. D. Gordon Pugh's classic *Portrait Figures of the Victorian Era*, Pat Halfpenny's *English Earthenware Figures 1740-1840*, and Adrian and Nick Harding's more recent three-volume *Victorian Staffordshire Figures 1835-1875*. This reference does not pretend to impersonate these or any other works, nor is it intended to be a catalog or a picture book. Rather, our goal has been to provide a social, cultural, religious, and economic context for the various types and classes of figures that were produced through a period that spanned the years from 1740 through 1900.

Spill vase group depicting a boy, girl, and deer. 7". Mid-Victorian. Value: $500-$1000. *Courtesy of Marla Chaikin, William Charles Antiques.*

Our illustrations offer a *representative sampling* (please note the emphasis!), and we direct our readers to the references cited for additional illustrations. New archaeological evidence and documentary findings are discovered each year, and because previously unrecorded figures and groups continue to surface, no Staffordshire text can ever be all-inclusive. We have attempted to be as comprehensive as possible in including the best known and best loved figures and groups, and those that are generally available for purchase. Most importantly, our goal has been to infuse this book with the "real life" of the people and times we have written about.

We have begun with a section that introduces the potters and modelers whose unique talents, perceptions, and vision were the "gears" that moved the "wheels" of Staffordshire figure production. We have followed with chapters that include the most interesting and popular figure classes, types, and categories and have included miscellaneous figures when they fit an appropriate historical framework.

We ask our readers to please note that each chapter is complete in itself – a study of the specific content area that may be read and enjoyed individually or as part of the larger whole. We have designed the chapters with an understanding that some readers (collectors, designers, historians, museum curators, students) may have particular interests and will wish to focus on chapters that relate to their areas of concentration. In addressing that consideration, readers may encounter some repetition, which was necessary in order to maintain the historical integrity of the separate, yet intrinsically related, topics. For this, we beg the indulgence of "cover-to-cover" readers. Hundreds of thousands of figures and groups were produced and many either cross categories or defy specific categorization. Accordingly, we note that some figures and groups "fit" comfortably in more than one chapter. In general, the "stuff" of life often defies compartmentalization, and the potters were true to life. Hence, readers will find some figures and groups discussed in one chapter and illustrated in another. We have cross-referenced the most important of these.

Believing, as we do, that Staffordshire figures comprise a unique and important history in earthenware, we have written our book from the historical perspective of the lifestyles, interests, and emotions of the people who made, purchased, and lived with these wonderful figures during the heyday of their production. This, then, is a book about Staffordshire figures, but it is equally a book about people. Writing it has been a labor of appreciation and respect and a way of honoring the potters and pottery workers who left us an incredible earthenware legacy. The potters' *history-in-the-making* has become our *history-in-the keeping*. Together, we share with generations of Staffordshire collectors – past, present, and future – a remarkable continuum of stewardship and study. We wish you Happy Reading!

–Adele Kenny
Fanwood, New Jersey, USA

–Veronica Moriarty
Ballarat, Victoria, Australia

Group known as "The Dandies," the Internet auction of which initiated correspondence and a special friendship between the authors (very "dandy" indeed). 6.25". Early 19th century. Value: $500-$1000.

Chapter One
The Potteries

Although the Industrial Revolution and the consequent drift of workers to towns dated effectively from the latter part of the eighteenth century, North Staffordshire maintained an essentially agrarian character. Advancements in technology and transportation, however, contributed to the region's inevitable industrialization. Originally, seven small villages – Stoke-on-Trent, Tunstall, Hanley, Fenton, Burslem, Shelton, and Longton – spread over Staffordshire moorland rich in marls, coal, and clay and became, over the course of two centuries, the center of a world-renowned ceramics industry. By the 1850s, that industry became Staffordshire's undying focus and fame. Known as *The Potteries*, the district covered an area of some nine miles and contained a largely working class population of 70,000 people. The people were hard working, unaccustomed to luxury, and poorly educated. While a dramatic shift from its cottage industry origins to a thriving and lucrative factory business was keenly felt in Staffordshire by the mid-nineteenth century, the rising middle class and the increasingly affluent nobility were the main beneficiaries of this prosperity.

The Staffordshire figures with which collectors are most familiar came about as byproducts of the Industrial Revolution when the primary concern of every pottery, or "pot bank," was to make money. Although figures were hand made and individually decorated, they were produced through "production line" methods, as commercial viability was a priority. In an attempt to attain this commercial viability the welfare of the pottery workers was frequently ignored, for workers were always in ready supply as a result of the social dislocation wrought by the Industrial Revolution.

Country house and estate from the 18th century in North Staffordshire today. Pockets of the region remain, at least superficially, much as they must have appeared to the potters.

North Staffordshire in the 21st century retains much of its heritage and beauty as demonstrated in this misty, early morning scene taken only a few miles from the heavily industrialized city of Stoke-on-Trent, once the center of "The Potteries."

An agrarian vista: views across fields to a small village with a church steeple that still beckons to the faithful as it did to the potters for centuries.

Numerous china and figure making concerns operated in Staffordshire throughout the late eighteenth and early nineteenth centuries. Many firms were small, and production of the items collected today was highly competitive. Specialist figure making concerns were apparently small, some containing as little equipment as a single making oven and one enameling kiln (Halfpenny, 13). The majority of the workers in these factories came from impoverished families for whom the threat of starvation was frighteningly real. For some, the disgrace of a workhouse was the only alternative to long hours and meager pay in the potteries. While some of the larger and more prosperous potteries provided better environments for their workers, most were small concerns with limited work forces. Long hours and abysmal conditions were standard. In general, the masters extended few considerations to their employees. Trade unions were not yet firmly established in the backwoods of Staffordshire, and the existing system was perpetuated by the masters' greed and the workers' fear of dismissal as contracts were made on an annual basis and the threat of non-renewal was always present.

An image of North Staffordshire with which the potters of the 19th century would have been more familiar: bottle ovens dominate the yard of the Gladstone Pottery, the only remaining example of a 19th century pottery in the region.

Despite attempts at local reform by some enlightened and humanitarian factory owners like Enoch Wood, the Staffordshire pottery workers' lives were brutal, and like those of contemporaries employed in other industries, inevitably shortened by the appalling conditions under which they toiled. In the potteries, the air was filled with dust, food was scarce, and sanitary conditions ranged from poor to virtually nonexistent. Toilet facilities were crude and rarely private. An 1842 report entitled "Report of the Royal Commission on Children's Employment in Industry" compiled by Samuel Scriven, Esq., cited *"In eight cases out of ten the places of convenience are indecently and disgustingly exposed and filthy, girls pass through the hovels where the lowest classes of men and boys work. The shed (toilet area) is crudely partitioned and exposed to the gaze of half of the men."*

A typical workday began as early as four or five in the morning and concluded as late as ten o'clock at night. Many of the workers were children as young as seven years old. Women and children did most of the tedious decorating in dark and damp workshops and received as little as one or two shillings per week. Wages were often paid by the piece in scrip that could only be exchanged for cash at local pubs, owned, in some cases, by the pottery bosses and often of the lowest description. The bottle's temptations were strong, and drunkenness was widespread among male laborers.

Artist's sketch of a typical bottle kiln of the type used in North Staffordshire during the 18th and 19th centuries. It has been estimated that there were once over 2000 bottle kilns in Staffordshire that rose from the landscape in every direction. The kilns were arranged in groups or in rows with no particular plan. Larger potteries had as many as twenty-five kilns, while the smallest potbanks operated with only one. *Courtesy of Robert Buczynski.*

Pottery workers have been described as generally sickly, prone to consumption (a chief cause of death), asthma and other pulmonary diseases, rheumatism, indigestion, constipation, piles, and fistula – the results of working with toxic materials, the dust filled environment, overheated rooms, exposure to cold in winter, lack of exercise, and poor nutrition. Many of the workers spent up to sixteen hours a day in small rooms that were damp, dark, dirty, too hot or too cold, and badly ventilated. Children who worked in highly heated rooms often walked home half-clothed in the cold night air. One of the greatest hazards lay in the glazing process, which was integral to pottery production and required hand dipping. The glazes contained both lead and arsenic that were absorbed through the skin. Dippers, who dipped each ceramic item into a glazing tub, often suffered from bleeding fingers that made absorption of the lead and arsenic quick and unavoidable. In addition, long hours over the tubs resulted in saturation of their clothing. Paralysis of the fingers and hands, epilepsy, and other nervous disorders were common. Colorers were equally susceptible to toxins. Metallic oxides used to color pottery required application of powders that were constantly inhaled. An illness called painter's colic developed rapidly, and paralysis of the limbs usually appeared within five or six years, leaving the worker unfit for any kind of labor. In the biscuit oven, wares were placed in pulverized flint. When they were removed, women and children called scourers cleaned them, inhaling the powder in the process and increasing their susceptibility to a disease called phthisis. Many boys less than thirteen years of age were employed as runners and, without shoes or stockings, ran repeatedly between a plate maker and a stove. A good plate maker could produce over three hundred plates per day, each of which kept a single child literally "on the run."

Scriven's report provides a comprehensive description of conditions in the potteries, reports from medical practitioners in the district, and statements by workers. Child labor laws, notably the Factory Act of 1844, were aimed to protect and educate young workers, but conditions in Staffordshire changed slowly. Attempts to provide academic and religious education were put forward through the establishment of day and Sunday schools, but Scriven notes that about three-fourths of the population remained illiterate. He attributes this to several facts. The first and most significant was that children were sent to work at an early age, often for 15 or 16 consecutive hours with only brief periods of rest for meals – a half hour for breakfast and one hour for dinner. Scriven also cites the indifference of parents and the fact that most academic schools required tuition that families could not afford. Children who worked as runners, dippers, scourers, and throwers – monotonous and arduous occupations – had little time or energy for normal childhood play or formal education.

Of the numerous worker statements in Scriven's report, George Burton, aged nine, states that he does not know how much payment he receives because it all goes to his father; he cannot read or write although he attended Sunday school. He says, *"I feel cold on coming out of the oven; 'tis very hot there; I get very thirsty... This is all the clothes I got; I have no change at home for Sunday."* Scourer Fanny Wood, aged thirty-three, states: *"...everyone that works in this place suffers more or less with coughs, and we are all stuffed up; we have known a great many deaths from it."* And, Samuel Broster, aged thirty-three, sums up with: *"I call 40 old."* Pottery workers like these, and thousands who remain anonymous, speak to us and to all future collectors through their legacy of earthenware figures. They were people of the earth who worked with the earth's materials. In the words of a Staffordshire potter long forgotten, *"No art with potters can compare/We make our pots of what we potters are."*

Portrait of a pottery worker: John Brooks (born circa 1810) in Staffordshire, England; worked in the potteries as a youth and young man; married Mary Ann Eliza Reynolds on March 26, 1837 (the year Victoria acceded to the throne); traveled by ship to the United States during the 1850s and settled in Brooklyn, New York; his son, Joseph Henry Brooks fought and died in the American Civil War. (John Brooks was Adele Kenny's paternal great, great grandfather.) *Courtesy of Robert Buczynski, from an original cabinet photo.*

Chapter Two

Meet the Makers and Modelers

Numerous potteries operated in Staffordshire throughout the eighteenth and nineteenth centuries. Some employed hundreds of workers, while others were small and had skeleton staffs of a dozen or less. With the exception of a few luminaries, the little we know about the majority of potters comes to us through listings in contemporary trade directories like Pigot's and Allbut's. In many cases, potting was a family affair – fathers and sons, husbands and wives, and other family members often worked together in family businesses. Alternatively, younger family members learned from their pottery patriarchs and went on to open potworks of their own. Potting families also intermarried, and there was a fairly consistent exchange of trade "secrets" and formulas. Because competition was intense, there was also a substantial amount of "pottery plagiarism," and there exist some fascinating tales of industrial espionage.

Many potworks, or potbanks, commenced operation and closed within a short time and, while a few specialized in figure making, many more produced other wares along with earthenware figures in order to remain financially solvent. A figure-making pottery's success ultimately depended upon the skills of the modeler or modelers employed to create the original figure molds. Except in rare cases where a potting family included an artist/modeler, most potteries did not hire full-time modelers; instead, molds were purchased from traveling freelancers. It is interesting to note that Pigot's directory recorded fifteen freelance modelers in Staffordshire by 1841, some of whose names also appear on toy or small ceramic figure makers' lists (for example, Joshua Walton and Henry Mills). Also interesting is the fact that self-employed tradesmen like modelers were known to work a specific number of days for a specific manufacturer each week (Halfpenny, 13). This allowed modelers to work for more than one master during a given week. It has also been suggested that perhaps independent modelers had stock patterns from which various figure makers chose, thus obviating attribution of any particular figure on the basis of style alone (Halfpenny, 13), something that has proven the subsequent bane of modern pottery collectors and researchers attempting to attribute figures and modeling techniques.

As the Hardings point out, the modelers were the real artists of the potteries – without them, there would have been no figures to pot. Sadly, there is little record of the modelers, except in a few rare cases where they signed their original molds (Harding, Book Three, 15). At a time when even factory marks were largely ignored, it is easy to understand why the majority of modelers remain anonymous or obscure. Some records of modelers' duties from larger factories exist. In 1843, Edward Keys was a forty-four year old modeler who had worked in the potteries for thirty-three years and recorded his duties working from a small room at a potbank, *"My duty is to make models to pattern, from drawings, sometimes from taste: they go from me to the mould makers."* Key's information provides an interesting and useful insight into how figures were created and also reveals that the art of the potters was no mere copyist's exercise, but also gave the potter the opportunity to create original artworks.

The following list includes a sampling of potters, potting families, and potworks. A few of the known modelers have been included.

Note: Some of the following have been excerpted and adapted from *Staffordshire Animals, A Collector's Guide to History, Styles, and Values* (Chapter 5 and Appendix I).

Adams, William – Burslem and Cobridge; made figures during the early nineteenth century; died 1831.

Adderley, John – Longton; continued production of figures, ornaments, china tea and other services in the old style of Sampson Smith at the Sutherland Works on Barker Street following Smith's death in 1879.

Alpha and Tallis Factories/Modelers – Various Victorian-era figures are catalogued as having been made by the Alpha and Tallis factories. Thomas Balston proposed these names, and considerable research and commentary have evolved subsequent to his pioneer studies. Alpha figures (circa 1845-1851) were remarkably well modeled and decorated. They were designed and decorated in the round and each required several mold parts. When titled, Alpha figures are distinguished by indented capitals with some few titled in gilt script (Harding, Book Three, 15). Tallis figures, the first of which date to around 1849, include a portrait gallery of Shakespearean characters. Importantly, through study of engravings and lithographs of the time, many of these have been identified as portraits of the actors and actresses who played various Shakespearean roles on the stage and are not mere depictions of Shakespeare's characters. The distinguishing features of Tallis figures identified by Balston correspond to "theater" figures first identified by Raymond Mander and Joseph Mitchenson in 1944. Recent Staffordshire scholarship has attributed the production of the Tallis figures to Thomas Parr due to similarities in modeling and decoration evident between this group and acknowledged Parr figures. The derivation of figures from an immediately recognizable "fine art" source is also typical of Parr's work, as many of his figures were adapted directly from paintings, prints, and sculptures.

Alpha and Tallis figures have received much attention and whole books might be devoted to their distinguishing characteristics and the potters by whom they may have been made. (For additional information see Thomas Balston's studies of Alpha and Tallis figures in *Staffordshire Portrait Figures of the Victorian Age* and *Supplement to Staffordshire Portrait Figures of the Victorian Age* and to P. D. Gordon Pugh's standard reference for portrait figures, *Staffordshire Portrait Figures of the Victorian Era*.)

Astbury, John – A tombstone in the churchyard of Stoke Parish in Shelton bears the following words, "*John Astbury the Elder of Shelton, Potter who departed this life March 3rd 1743, age 55.*" (Turner, 40)

Astbury was born in 1688 and was christened on May 14, 1690 (Turner, 40). Unfortunately, little more is known of his life. According to Simeon Shaw, Astbury was responsible for introducing Devonshire white clays and ground (calcined) flints into the earthenware body. Shaw also contends that it was Astbury who infiltrated the Elers brothers' factory under the guise of a mentally deficient worker and absconded with enough secret information to start his own potting firm. None of Astbury's wares was marked and, as Pat Halfpenny points out (in *English Earthenware Figures 1740-1840*), the "Astbury" mark, when seen, may belong to other family members, including John's son Thomas, Thomas II, Joshua Astbury (Thomas's nephew) and Richard Meir Astbury (Joshua's son), but definite attribution cannot be proved.

Pat Halfpenny notes that the generic term "Astbury," based on John Astbury's name, governs understanding of the wares which, attributed to John Astbury and dated to the early 1740s, were most likely produced at a later date. There is no documentary evidence to prove that the Elder Astbury was responsible for the figures traditionally credited to him. Ms. Halfpenny notes further that the "Astbury" designation was introduced during the twentieth century to accommodate dealers and collectors, and proven twentieth century copies exist (Halfpenny, 19-23).

Typical pieces called "Astbury-type" include tea wares and various useful items. The subject matter of so-called "Astbury-style" figures is generally modest and tends to reflect aspects of mid-eighteenth century life. Tradesmen are seen, but the most well known figures are a variety of musicians playing instruments. The bases of these figures were often made from red clays but the bodies are normally light in color (made with white clays from Devon and Dorset mixed with flint to produce a cream-colored earthenware). Figures of this type were made by hand and by press-molding. Usually, the bodies and bases were molded separately. The limbs were solid and many have hand-modeled details. Colored slips were sometimes used for eyes and costume details and white dots of slip were often used to decorate the musical instruments. Most frequently, the figure was fired to biscuit state and decorated in streaks with colored metal oxides (manganese brown, copper green, iron yellow, or cobalt blue) before lead-glazing and a second firing. Ms. Halfpenny comments that the range and variety of this class of figure has led leading authorities to suggest that various potters created the pieces, which may have been produced over a period of twenty years and not during the early 1740s, before John Astbury's death in 1743 (Halfpenny, 19-20; for additional information, see Pat Halfpenny, *English Earthenware Figures 1740-1840, pages 19-29*).

Important mid-18th century figure of a mounted cavalryman made from colored clays and decorated with underglaze colors (soldier figures were popular at the time of the '45 Rebellion). Although the term "Astbury-type" is commonly used today to describe figures of this sort, there is no evidence to confirm that Astbury made this type of ware. 8.25". Circa 1745. Value: $10,000-$15,000. *Courtesy of Jonathan Horne (Antiques) Ltd.*

Astbury, Richard Meir (see entry for John Astbury).

Astbury, Thomas (see entry for John Astbury).

Baddeley, William – Hanley, late eighteenth and early nineteenth centuries; worked at the Eastwood Pottery and sometimes used an impressed "EASTWOOD" mark.

Baggaley, George – Hanley, circa 1851; toy and ornament maker.

Baguley, C. – Hanley, circa 1815-1820; produced small figures and groups.

Bailey & Batkin – Longton, circa 1823; made figures and busts; much lustered work.

Barker, Sutton & Till – Burslem, circa 1834-1843; William Barker, James Sutton, and Thomas Till were partners at the Sytch Pottery; Till was the only owner by 1850, and the firm later became Thomas Till & Sons; produced chimney ornaments and other wares; William Barker & Son is listed for 1851.

Beech, William and Jane – Burslem, 1834-1873; operated the Bell Works and produced chimney ornaments, etc.; Jane continued after William's death.

Bennet, John – Burslem, mid-1860s; earthenware ornament maker.

Bentley, H. – Hanley; little is known of this potter or modeler whose impressed mark appears on the back of a bust of Benjamin Caunt made in 1844.

Beswick, John – Longton, circa 1895; owner of two potteries, the second of which was the Britannia Works in High Street (established 1896); produced a wide range of chimney ornaments with special emphasis on dogs, cats, and other animals; the firm continued as John Beswick Ltd; modern animal figures are marked and numbered.

Beta Factory/Modeler – Figures with distinctive facial features and unique back-of-figure designs consisting of indented lines in random patterns have been suggested as having been designed by the "Beta Factory Modeler" (Harding, Book Three, 17). According to the Hardings, this modeler specialized in groups of a patriotic character and was very prolific.

Bevington & Son – Hanley, 1860s; toy makers.

Birch, Joseph – Hanley, 1851; toy and ornament maker.

Boot, Jonathan – Cobridge, 1800-1802; manufactured toys and figures.

Booth, Richard – Shelton and Hanley, early 19th century; died in 1842; toy maker.

Booth, Thomas – Burslem 1860s; toy maker.

Bott & Bond – Recorded from 1807; Mr. Bond continued with other partners after Mr. Bott died in 1811; although there is no documentary evidence, products are said to have included busts, figures, painted vases, and luster wares; two silver luster decorated bulb pots are the only known examples.

Bott & Co. – Longton; the only figure known from this company is a portrait bust of William Shakespeare.

Boulton, C. B. – Hanley, circa 1851; image toy maker.

Brammer, Thomas – Daisy Bank, Lane End; figure maker; listed 1830. Turner notes that Thomas died early in the 1830s; his wife Elizabeth continued potting until around 1835.

Brown, Henry – High Street, Lane End; figure maker; listed 1828/9.

Brownfield, William (& Sons) – Cobridge, 1864-1890; figure makers.

Carr, John (or J. C. Carr) – A well-executed figure of Admiral Sir Charles Napier (from the Pugh collection, housed in the City Museum and Art Gallery, Stoke-on-Trent) is signed on the base "John Carr 1857." As the Hardings point out, there are no records to document the name in any known Staffordshire records, and it may be assumed that John Carr was an independent modeler who was not a member of the Carr family (Harding, Book Three, 15). Also recorded are signed figures of Whippets and hares that demonstrate established hallmarks of the Parr Factory and are inscribed "J.C. Hanley June 30 1854" in a script that corresponds to the Napier figure signature. The Hardings suggest that the same John Carr modeled the Whippets and Napier and apparently worked for at least two different factories (Harding, Book Three, 15).

Cartledge, Hugh – Burslem, until the mid-1820s; figure maker.

Cooper, Thomas (T. Cooper & Co.) – Hanley, circa 1845-1865; figure makers.

Copeland & Garrett – Stoke, 1833-1847; Messrs. Copeland and Garrett took over the Spode works in 1833 and produced a variety of superior quality porcelains, earthenwares, and Parian wares; several fine porcelain figures are recorded.

Copestick, Daniel – Lane Delph, 1817-1830; earthenware toys.

Cutts, John (& Co.) – Hanley, 1820-1850; figure makers.

Dale, John – Burslem, early nineteenth century; a rather "mysterious" potter of whom little is known; an extremely rare figure of a guitar player with bocage (circa 1825) bearing the impressed John Dale of Burslem mark is recorded by Geoffrey Godden and illustrated in *An Illustrated Encyclopedia of British Pottery and Porcelain*, page 114. Pat Halfpenny notes that "Dale" is a common name in the Potteries and known information may refer to one or more persons of the same name; Ms. Halfpenny further notes that John and William Dale were involved in partnerships with George and Samuel Poulson and with Stevenson and Godwin during the early 1800s; a child named John Dale is recorded to have been born to John and Hannah Dale and christened on May 8, 1791; the trade directories for 1818 list a John Dale and it is known that a John Dale produced figures around 1825; no other documentary evidence exists.

Dale, William – Hanley; toy and ornament maker around 1851.

Doulton & Co. – Burslem, from 1877; made figures, Toby Jugs, and character items.

Dudson, James – Hanley; the Dudson family was established as a potting family around 1800; their Hope Street works was begun around 1809 and is still standing; Thomas Dudson ran the factory at first and then with his two sons; the elder son, James, took over in 1845; despite little documentary evidence, it may be supposed that figure production was a relatively small part of the business. Geoffrey Godden notes that Dudson was the only potter known to have exhibited image toy figures at the International Exhibitions of 1851 and 1862 (Godden, *Antique China and Glass*, 29). The Dudson pottery operated as J. T. Dudson from 1888-98 when it became Dudson Bros. Ltd.

Elers, John Phillip & David – Bradwell Wood, Burslem; 1693-1698, Dutch potters who produced pottery in imitation of Chinese ceramics and helped introduce new production techniques and standards to the region of Staffordshire.

Elkin, Richard – Burslem; toy maker during the mid-1830s.

Ellis, James – Shelton, 1818-1830; produced earthenware figures and toys.

Edge, Daniel – Burslem, listed at Waterloo Road in 1830.

Edge, Timothy – Burslem, presumably working around 1830.

Edge & Grocott – 1820s; Samuel Grocott worked in Tunstall from 1822 until 1828; there is no documentary evidence to support a partnership between Samuel Grocott and either Timothy or Daniel Edge (of Burslem), but a few marked Edge & Grocott figures exist and a partnership with one of the Edges was probably short-lived.

Edwards of East Vale – Recorded in Haggar's *Staffordshire Chimney Ornaments* as a modeler employed by Sampson Smith (Harding, Book Three, 15).

Godwin, Thomas & Benjamin – Burslem; began as partners around 1809-1811 in Navigation Road and worked together until Benjamin's death in 1833; Thomas continued alone; not considered figure makers but known to have supplied several models to a London retailer in 1823.

Greatbatch, William – William Greatbatch operated a potworks in Fenton between 1762 and 1782 with figures seeming to represent a small percentage of his work. Reconstructed fragments recovered from his site form the base of a female figure with a lion at her feet and a cornucopia in the foreground, the biscuit creamware head of a bird, and a swan. Also excavated was a particularly striking cream-colored earthenware wing (of an as yet unidentified exotic bird) with overglaze enamel-painted tips (Halfpenny, 48-49). Greatbatch went bankrupt in 1782.

Green Factory/Modeler – The Hardings have identified a modeler whose work was of a consistently high standard and distinguished by comprehensive coloring, slightly Oriental facial features, plumed hats, separate molds, and vibrant green or, alternatively, vibrant yellow/gold bases. Most "Green" figures are decorative but include portraits of the Princess Royal and Prince of Wales in a pony cart and religious figures of Rebekah at the Well, Samuel Anointing David, and Joseph and Mary (Harding, Book Three, 16-17).

Griffiths, Thomas – Longton; known to be a figure maker in 1850.

Hall, John and Ralph – Burslem and Tunstall, circa 1800-circa 1825; produced image toys at two potteries, one in Burslem and one in Tunstall; many figures were designed in the Walton School style. (See Hall mark illustrated in Chapter Five.)

Hall, Samuel – First recorded in 1818 as a potter at New Hall Street in Shelton; listed as an earthenware toy maker in 1822, china and earthenware toy maker in 1834, and china toy manufacturer in 1841.

Harrison, John – Tunstall, around 1828; made toys and blackware.

Heath, John – Sitch Lane, Burslem, in business for ten or twelve years; earthenware toy manufacturer.

Heath, Thomas – Shelton, recorded in Allbut's in 1800 as a modeler, along with Peter Stephan of Shelton and Ralph Johnson of Burslem (Halfpenny, 15); Thomas Heath's daughters were married to Felix Pratt, James Neale, and Humphrey Palmer (Turner 107). A Thomas Health is also recorded as manager of the Lakin & Poole manufactory in circa 1795 (Halfpenny 151).

Hilditch, John – Lane End, circa 1800-circa 1845; operated a pottery at Lane End in 1818 with a partner named Martin; later owned Hilditch & Son and then Hilditch & Hopwood; manufactured various image toys.

Hobson, Ephraim – Cobridge, early nineteenth century; black Egyptian and earthenware toy manufacturer, listed in Pigot & Co. *Directory* in 1818.

Holland, Thomas – Church Street, Burslem, 1818-1830; modeler and toy maker.

Hood, George – Tunstall and Burslem; suffered irreversible business losses at his pottery in Tunstall and took over John Walton's factory in Navigation Road (John Walton was his father-in-law); Hood has been remembered mainly through reference to "G. Hood," presumably George Hood, in the memoirs entitled *When I was a Child* written from the unique perspective of a worker who was employed by Hood in Burslem after the Tunstall loss. Hood's works were described as derelict, "rusty and grim," where various figures were produced and only about twelve workers were employed; the *Staffordshire Advertiser* of January 1848 records Hood's death at the age of sixty-eight.

Jones, Hannah – George Street, Hanley, listed 1822, 1830; figure maker.

Kent, William – Burslem, from 1878; probably entered the trade with left-over molds, which included marked Walton figures; a well-known manufacturer of all varieties of figures and ornaments; used molds that still exist today (some were obtained from William Machin whose source of the molds is unknown). A partnership between William Kent and Gaskell and Parr in Burslem terminated in 1878 when Kent built a pottery at Auckland Street in Burslem where he traded under the name Kent & Parr until 1894 when the works became known as William Kent. In 1944 the manufactory became William Kent (Porcelains) Ltd. and produced figures until 1962. William Kent is well known to collectors because a number of his company's illustrated catalogs still exist. The Kent firm, established around 1878, apparently acquired a number of old molds from which figures were produced until 1962 when the business closed. After that time, some of the Kent molds were passed on to other twentieth century companies. Among the molds used by the Kent firm were marked Walton pieces and models known with an earlier Enoch Wood mark. Some of the Kent pieces were marked with the Staffordshire Knot and the words "Olde Staffordshire Ware" (often abraded which contributes to dating confusion); however, the greatest number was unmarked (Halfpenny, pp. 278, 284, 286-89). William Kent's company issued color catalogs of their figures until 1955; these include figures not originally made by Kent & Parr and many that were made from molds acquired by Kent when other potteries went out of business. Earlier Kent figures are superior in quality to those made later in the pottery's history, not so much in the quality of the modeling and molding but in the quality of decoration, which, by the 1880's-90s became inferior to well colored earlier pieces.

Twentieth century Kent mark, circa 1944-62; Godden mark #2272.

Keys, Edward and Samuel – Former Derby Factory modelers recorded in an 1834 Staffordshire directory as modelers in Stoke Lane and Upper Cliff Bank (Halfpenny, 15).

Lakin & Poole – Hanley, 1791-1796; a partnership of brief duration; produced distinctive figures that were probably a small part of their trade in comparison to tea and tablewares.

Lancaster & Sons – Hanley, late nineteenth and early twentieth centuries; produced a variety of figures including large dog models; the firm became Lancaster Ltd.

Lawton, Daniel – Chapel Lane, Burslem; specialist figure maker; listed 1828/9, 1830.

Lees, Thomas – Sneyd Green; specialist figure maker; listed 1822.

Littler, William – 1750-1760; Brownhills and Longton Hall; salt-glazed figure maker.

Lloyd, John – John Lloyd (1805-1850) potted in Shelton, Hanley from circa 1834 until his death in 1850. His wife, Rebecca, who kept the firm in operation until 1852, assisted him. Although most of Lloyd's work is unmarked, a few extremely rare marked Lloyd figures have been recorded. Dog figures bearing the impressed Lloyd mark are illustrated in Clive Mason Pope's *A-Z of Staffordshire Dogs*, page 85, and Geoffrey Godden shows marked Lloyd figures *An Illustrated Encyclopedia of British Pottery and Porcelain*, page 200.

Rare impressed Lloyd Shelton mark, circa 1834-52; Godden mark #2389; Godden notes that an initial may appear before the surname on some pieces. *Courtesy of Robert Buczynski.*

Locker, John – Tunstall, early nineteenth century; toy maker.

Machin, William – Hanley, around 1875-1911; first listed at Percy Street and after 1884 at the Dresden Works on George Street; produced figures and toys.

Marsh, Jacob – First known in 1793 as a specialist enameller; by 1805, listed as an earthenware manufacturer in Burslem; left Burslem in 1806 and moved to Fenton (Lane Delph) and rented a potworks; built a new factory on the border of Fenton and Longton (Lane End) in 1818; no documentary evidence of the type of wares produced; only one marked figure is known.

Maskery, Maria – Hanley; toy maker listed during the mid-1830s.

Massey, Nehemia – Burslem, around 1834-1866; figure maker.

Maybury, Alfred – Hanley, 1850s; toy maker.

Mayer, Samuel – Piccadilly, Shelton; specialist figure maker; listed 1830.

Mayer, Elijah (& Son) – Hanley, well-known potting family; Elijah from around 1787 to 1813, Samuel from 1830-1835, and Thomas from 1834-1846.

Meli, Giovanni – Noted in Haggar's *Staffordshire Chimney Ornaments* as a Sicilian modeler who worked in Rome Street, Stoke from around 1845-65 and who made the molds for Sampson Smith's baroque-type figures (Harding, Book Three, 15).

Mills, George – Hanley, circa 1846; toy maker.

Mills, Henry – Hope Street, Shelton; figure maker and modeler; listed 1830; in business until circa 1850.

Minton – Although Minton's was one of the largest potteries and employed over 1500 recorded employees, there is no documentary evidence that the firm produced the standard type of figures. Pottery figures similar to those produced in Parian or bisque by Minton's have been identified, and Minton's first figure design book includes drawings of several portrait figures, including John and Charles Wesley (Pugh, 21).

Pearlware figural vase decorated in enamel colors and bearing the impressed "Neale & Co." mark. 8.75". Circa 1790. Value: $2000-$2500. *Courtesy of Jonathan Horne (Antiques) Ltd.*

Neale & Palmer (Humphrey Palmer, James Neale, and Robert Wilson) – James Neale of Hanley worked in the Wood tradition and created distinctive enamel-painted pieces. Interestingly, Neale was not a potter and, although some sources state that he was a warehouseman or London agent, Pat Halfpenny notes in personal correspondence that his position was much more elevated as he owned a china business in London where in 1763 he is recorded as having sold goods for Wedgwood. By 1767, Neale was working in St. Paul's Churchyard and had established a connection with Humphrey Palmer, a potter at the Church Works in Hanley (Halfpenny, 140). Neale was a successful businessman, but Palmer apparently lacked the skills needed for commercial prosperity and by 1778, Palmer was in such financial distress that Neale assumed control of Palmer's firm (Halfpenny, 140).

From around 1781, the firm traded as James Neale & Co., probably from the time that Robert Wilson became Neale's partner and Neale returned to London to work with other partners in the retail aspect of their business. Enoch Wood, who had been associated with Palmer, very likely continued at the Church Works until he and Ralph Wood II became partners in 1783, and it may be that the famous Enoch Wood bust of Wesley was modeled during Wood's last years with Neale & Co. Although Neale & Co. operated at least as early as 1781, their production dates are usually set at 1785-1790. Around 1790-1791, Robert Wilson became owner of the firm. The factory was expanded and Robert's son, David, came into the business. Robert Wilson died in 1801 and David's son, David, Jr., became a partner. By 1820 the company had closed. While larger figures are recorded, Neale & Wilson figures are usually small in size, well executed, and characterized by fine modeling with greater detail than is seen in many other enameled pieces. Among the most well known are the "Four Seasons" figures, some of which are marked and have subject titles impressed beneath the base. Some of the superior pieces were decorated with additional gilding (Halfpenny, 140-151).

Parr Family – Among the eminent Victorian-era figure-makers who produced earthenware figures were the Parrs who represent a long line of important potters and partnerships: Richard Parr (circa 1828-1835), Thomas Parr (1852-1870), William Parr (circa 1860), Edward Parr (1860-1864), and John Parr (circa 1870-1879). A pottery located at 34 Church Street, Burslem was opened by Thomas Parr in 1852 and continued under his name until 1870 when the name and address reverted to John Parr at Wellington Street. Thomas Parr's mid-Victorian figures are noted for their characteristically fine modeling in the round and well-executed decoration.

After 1880 the Parr factory went into partnership with William Kent to form the company "Kent & Parr."

Pattison, James – Lane End, around 1818-1830; probably related to Alfred Pattison (who marked some figures) and to John Pattison.

Pattison, John – Longton, early 1800s; produced earthenware toys; a potter of whom little is known; marked a rare figure of Venus with his name and the year 1825.

Pinder, Bourne, & Hope – Succeeded Enoch Wood and used a number of his molds (from about 1846).

Plant, Benjamin – Lane End; listed as a pottery worker in 1818 and as a potter's presser in 1822; probably responsible for a large lion figure (several versions) inscribed with his initials or "Benjamin Plant, Lane End."

Poole, George – Hanley, 1802; toy maker.

Poole and Unwin (eee entry for Unwin).

Pratt, William, Felix, and Richard – Felix Pratt was the son of the eighteenth century Lane Delph potter William Pratt. After William's death, Felix followed in his father's footsteps and produced various wares. "Prattware" is a collector's term that generates confusion between the hollow wares produced by the Pratt factory and the figures labeled "Pratt" by today's collectors. Technically, the underglaze-painted figures described as "Prattware" or "Pratt-type" were made from about 1780 until 1840 from white Dorset and Devon clays. The figures were modeled and fired to biscuit temperature then sponged or painted by brush with a restricted range of colors before they were dried, dipped into a liquid pearl glaze, and refired. The characteristic shades of yellow, blue, green, purple, brown, and black were derived from metal oxides and were limited because they were the only colors able to withstand the heat of glaze firing. The production process was relatively simple and inexpensive, especially when compared to processes like overglaze enameling. Numerous figures of the so-called "Pratt" type were made at various sites, including Staffordshire, Yorkshire, Liverpool, Sunderland, and elsewhere. Some of the figures were produced in uncomplicated two-part molds and others were designed with supplemental mold parts that required more complicated assemblies. Collectors should be aware that there is absolutely no evidence that the Pratt factory ever produced figures and none can be attributed to Felix on any grounds (Halfpenny, 110-107 and personal communications).

Felix Pratt established his own firm in 1810 and formed a partnership with his brother Richard in 1818. The F & R Pratt (& Co) (Ltd) firm continued in Fenton until the twentieth century (Godden, *An Illustrated Encyclopedia of British Pottery and Porcelain*, 266).

Recumbent cow decorated in "Pratt-type" colors on a green base. 5.75" (length), 4.25" (height). Late 18th century. Value: $1000+. *Courtesy of Jane McClafferty Antiques.* ***[[Could this possibly be a sheep?]]***

Ridgway, James – Hill Street, Hanley; figure maker; listed 1822.

Ridgway & Robey – The Ridgway family of Shelton is one of long-standing and noteworthy accomplishment in The Potteries. During the nineteenth century, the Ridgways produced fine earthenwares and porcelains. Consisting of several generations of potters, the family concentrated their production in two potteries, the Bell Works (1792) and Cauldon Place (1802). In 1792, brothers Job and George Ridgway potted from the Bell Works at Shelton and remained in partnership until 1802 when Job built the Cauldon Place works, also at Shelton. Job's sons, John and William, joined the company and succeeded their uncle, George Ridgway, at the Bell works. William remained at the Bell works until 1848. In 1830, John joined his father at Cauldon Place and was later appointed potter to Queen Victoria (his standard mark includes the Royal Arms with the initials "J. R." placed small beneath the central arms motif). In 1840, "& Co" was added. John Ridgway & Co. remained in operation until 1855 and was followed by Ridgway, Bates, & Co. Ultimately, the firm passed to Brown-Westhead, Moore, & Co. (1862) and to Cauldon Ltd. (1905) (Godden, *An Illustrated Encyclopedia of British Pottery and Porcelain*, 271).

A short-term partnership between William Ridgway and Ralph Mayer Robey is recorded in the *Hanley Rate Books* of 1837-39, and portrait figures depicting characters from Charles Dickens's *Nicholas Nickleby* appear with the printed mark "Published June 15, 1839,/By Ridgway & Robey/Hanley..."(Godden mark #3298). It is likely that other figures were produced while Ridgway and Robey worked together (Pugh, 17).

Riley, John and Richard – Burslem, around 1796-1828; toy makers.

Sale, William – Hanley, mid-1860s; figure maker.

Salt, Ralph – Ralph Salt was born in 1782 and potted at Miles Bank, Hanley before moving to Marsh Street, Shelton (1829-1841). He was a partner in a Hanley decorating firm before March of 1816, at which time the *Staffordshire Advertiser* records the termination of his partnership with Joseph Gould and Charles Massey. Salt and Massey continued to work together in New Street, Hanley; however, within about two months Salt moved to his own business. He is listed in 1822-23 as a "lusterer, enameller, & figure maker" (*Newcastle & Pottery General and Commercial Directory*). By 1829, he had moved to Marsh Street in Shelton where he worked until 1841. Salt specialized in figures, earthenware and porcelain, and died on November 28, 1846, only five years after his retirement (Halfpenny, 234-237).

Ralph Salt mark, circa 1820-46; Godden mark #3450. Courtesy *of Robert Buczynski.*

Salt's figures are similar to John Walton's but are generally more crudely rendered and titles are sometimes misspelled (Halfpenny, 237). Some of Salt's pieces are marked with his name in capital letters, sometimes within a scroll much like Walton's. He is noted for his animal models that include sporting dogs, sheep, rams, ewes, and lambs (Bedford, 37-38).

It has been suggested that Ralph Salt's son, Charles, kept the business in operation after his father's death but no documentary evidence of this has been found. In fact, the *Staffordshire Advertiser* of April 1841 (the year Ralph retired) carried a notice that referred to the auction of his property (Halfpenny, 235-237). (See Salt mark illustrated in Chapter Five.)

Sandland, T. H. – Among the late Victorian-era animal figures, examples marked "T. H. Sandland" are sometimes seen along with similarly marked portrait figures of Edward VII, Queen Alexandra, and others. The Sandland mark sometimes appears with the word "copyright" and a date (usually Dec. 10 or Dec. 20, 1901). These marks apparently refer to a copyright date and, according to P. D. Gordon Pugh, although T. H. Sandland's name is not listed among the Staffordshire potters of his time, a Thomas Henry Sandland is known to have been a designer (modeler) who joined the Hanley firm of Lancaster & Sons, Ltd. Sandland became a partner in 1944, after which the Lancaster firm became Lancaster & Sandland. Sandland was ultimately named managing director of the company. At the time of his death in 1956, he was the last surviving member of the original board of directors (Pugh, 28-30).

Selman, J. and W. – Tunstall; mid-1860s; earthenware toy makers.

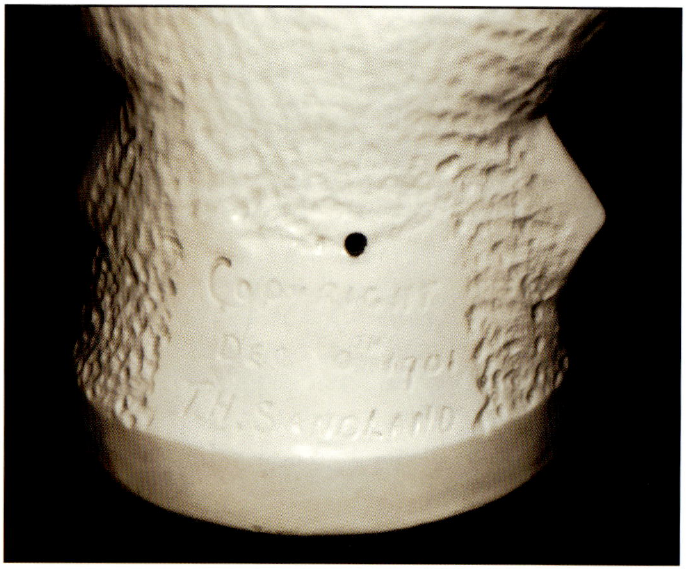

T. H. Sandland mark dated December 10th 1901.
Courtesy of Zane Moss Antiques.

Twentieth century Sandland mark. According to Geoffrey Godden, this mark was used by Lancaster & Sandland Ltd. (Dresden Works, Hanley) from circa 1950 until the firm's closing in 1968.

Sherratt, Obadiah – Obadiah Sherratt was a Burslem potter whose history is obscure. There is no known record of his birth, although various researchers have speculated that he was born sometime around 1775. He married

Anne Davenport in 1797 and they had several children. Anne died in 1810 and Sherratt married Martha Austin only two months later. According to Pat Halfpenny, the 1818 trade directory does not list Sherratt and it is likely that at that time he was working for another potter. Between 1818 and 1823, Sherratt apparently established his own business and is listed in Allbut's (1822-23) as a toy and figure maker at Hot Lane in Burslem. Within the next ten years, he had moved to Waterloo Road, Burslem and in 1846, the business was listed in the name of his son, Hamlet Sherratt, a figure-maker (Halfpenny, 263, 269).

Sherratt is known for large, often complex, figures and groups. These are unmarked but are credited to Sherratt by virtue of a tradition that associates Sherratt with such pieces' distinctive and elaborate style. Many of the figures appear on footed bases (table base models), and some contain bocage. Interestingly, Pat Halfpenny notes that the earliest written attribution of table base figures to Sherratt apparently dates to Reginald Haggar's book, *Staffordshire Chimney Ornaments* (p. 92). An earlier reference to Sherratt's manufacture of bull-baiting groups appears in G. Woolliscroft Rhead's *The Earthenware Collector* (Herbert Jenkins, 1920, p. 295). It would appear that attribution of a particular style of group to Sherratt is based primarily on twentieth century prescriptive right with no documentary or archaeological proof whatsoever.

Misspelled titles are common on Sherratt-attributed groups and have given rise to speculation that Sherratt may have been at least partially illiterate. Sherratt is traditionally said to have produced many figures and groups that are larger than most but somewhat crudely modeled and decorated. He is credited with "showy" pieces and an alternatively farcical and sometimes grisly "chamber of horrors" approach to ceramic representations of actual settings and events. In truth, there is no proof that Sheratt produced any such figures. Obviously, he produced figures of some sort, and it is possible that the tradition has some basis in fact. Unfortunately, there is no documentary confirmation, and as Pat Halfpenny points out, despite numerous attributed figures and groups, the only positive identification of a Sherratt model is a frog mug, two examples of which are impressed "O. SHERRATT" (Halfpenny, 269).

On the lighter side, an amusing Staffordshire legend holds that Sherratt formed the udders on his cow figures from the same mold that he used for Wellington's nose (from G. Woolliscroft Rhead, see Pat Halfpenny, *English Earthenware Figures 1740-1840*, page 269).

Table base group of the New Marriage Act representing the class of figures formerly attributed to Obadiah Sherratt; this group features oak leaf bocage and is set on a table base with pearl beaded feet (see Chapter Five for details on this type of figure). 8". Circa 1825. Value: $3000-$4000. *Courtesy of Jonathan Horne (Antiques) Ltd.*

Smith, Sampson – Sampson Smith potted in Longton and was one of only a few Victorian-era figure makers who used factory marks, however sparingly (Pope, 54). The variety and range of his figures, primarily flatbacks, is comprehensive. He was clearly a prosperous businessman and one of the most prolific figure manufacturers.

As Geoffrey Godden notes, Smith's name is first seen in the records of 1851 and he is listed in Slater's 1853 directory as a toy manufacturer. Rare examples of his figures appear with a mark dated 1851 (see Godden mark #3584), which probably indicates the year his pottery was established and not the year figures so marked were produced (Godden, *Antique Glass and China*, 27-28). Smith marks, when seen, are either "Sampson Smith 1851 Longton" or "S Smith Longton 1851."

Sampson Smith established the Sutherland Works in Barker Street around 1860. The pottery remained in operation long after his death, and did not close until 1963. Figure production ceased around 1918 but was resumed in 1948. At that time, about sixty old press molds were found in an unused section of the Smith factory. The majority of these molds represented animal figures, mainly dogs, which were preserved well enough to be reissued and used for a number of years (Pugh, 17).

Although no source is noted, H.A.B. Turner mentions that Sampson Smith's funeral, on January 1, 1879, was an ostentatious event complete with twenty coaches and a huge number of people in attendance. Turner also notes that, during the funeral, a bull broke loose in Longton High Street and scattered the crowd (Turner, 155). If the solemn occasion was indeed touched by the burlesque Turner describes, it is unfortunate that a surviving potter did not record the moment in earthenware.

Because the Smith factory continued to produce figures into the twentieth century, "Sampy" (as he is affectionately called by collectors) is probably the best-known Victorian-era figure maker. More figures are credited to him, often mistakenly, than to any other potter of his time. It is apparent that contemporary and later potters copied his designs and decorating techniques, and attribution of unmarked figures must be preceded by careful assessment. Some figures made from molds found in 1948, now over fifty years old, may appear at first blush to be nineteenth century figures and must be carefully examined before a date is applied.

Sampson Smith mark.

Sketch of Sampson Smith relief mark, circa 1851-90; Godden mark #3584. *Courtesy of Robert Buczynski.*

Smith, Theophilis – Tunstall, 1789-1801; impressed "T. SMITH" mark on only three known pieces. In 1788, Smith purchased an estate in Tunstall and added a number of cottages, shops, and an inn. He called his small "town" Smithhfield and, in 1789, established a pottery and home called Smithfield Hall. In 1801, he wounded Liverpool merchant Peter Wainwright with a pistol and knife for a dalliance with Mrs. Smith. After hiding in London, he finally surrendered in July 1801. Before his trial, Smith's wife visited him in his prison cell where he managed to shoot her in the shoulder before shooting and killing himself. The Smith factory was sold and its name was changed to Greenfield. (See Pat Halfpenny's *English Earthenware Figures 1740-1840*, pages 155 and 157 for additional details.)

Stephan, Peter – Shelton, circa 1800; a French modeler (Pierre Stephan) who created porcelain figure molds for the Derby Factory.

Stephenson, John – Hanley, circa 1851; toys and ornaments.

Street, John – Shelton, mid-1840s; figure maker.

Stretton, Samuel – Lane Delph figure maker; listed 1828/9.

Stubbs & Bird – Hanley, early 1850s; toy and ornament makers.

Stubbs, William – Shelton, 1862-1897; produced earthenware ornaments and toys.

Till, Edward – Tunstall; the first recorded specialist figure maker, listed in *The Staffordshire Pottery Directory*, 1796 (Halfpenny, 12).

Tittensor, Charles – A number of underglazed figures are marked with the impressed "TITTENSOR" surname. Tittensor was a common family name in North Staffordshire and might relate to any number of potters. However, Charles Tittensor of Hanley is generally associated with a style of marked figures. First recorded as a potter in the *Staffordshire Advertiser* on February 27, 1802, Charles Tittensor worked with Robert Pope. Their partnership terminated in July of 1803, and Charles and John Tittensor continued the business. By 1807, the local rate books listed a firm that operated under the name of Tittensor & Simpson, a partnership that lasted until 1813. *Parson & Bradshaw's Directory* of 1818 lists Charles Tittensor as a potter at Queen Street in Shelton. Pat Halfpenny suggests that his business was a small concern that remained in operation until sometime between 1822 and 1834 when Joseph Jackson took over the Queen Street works (Halfpenny, 108-114).

Tittensor produced many bocage figures and Pat Halfpenny notes that the Tittensor style of bocage is unique and may be significant in attributing unmarked figures to this potter. Tittensor pieces are often large composite groups, some with scoring on the base. Most are decorated with underglaze colors, but a few enamel-painted pieces have also been recorded. As Ms. Halfpenny points out, known Tittensor pieces suggest that he did not specialize in especially high-quality wares but, rather, in wares intended for an inexpensive market (Halfpenny, 114-115).

An earthenware crucifixion group, marked stallion figures, enamel decorated figures, figures with bocage, and figures decorated with semi-translucent glazes are typical of Tittensor's work.

Tittensor Mark (Godden mark #3861). *Courtesy of Robert Buczynski.*

Tunnicliffe, Michael – Tunstall figure maker; listed 1828/9, 1830. Turner notes figures marked in a scroll with a leaf at each end.

Unwin – Longton; several firms of this name are known to have been in operation during the nineteenth century until around 1926; Poole & Unwin worked in partnership beginning around 1871 at the Cornhill Works in Longton; around 1877 Joseph Unwin started his own company called Joseph Unwin & Co.; a few rare figures from the Poole & Unwin partnership are marked P & U (others bear the mark "Unwin"). According to the Hardings a resemblance to figures made by Sampson Smith suggests that P & U figures may have been modeled by the same modeler who worked for Smith (Harding, Book Three, 19).

Voyez, Jean – A modeler who arrived in Staffordshire in 1768 to work for Josiah Wedgwood. By 1769, Voyez was sentenced to be flogged with a cat of nine tails and jailed for three months for running up vast (by eighteenth century standards) debts at his employer's expense, public drunkenness, and using a naked girl as a model, after which he worked at several potteries and as a free-lancer. Figures modeled by Voyez are not known.

Walker, John – Burslem, 1800-1802; chimney ornament maker.

Walley, J. – Cobridge; a museum catalog includes a stag and two hinds, one of which bears the mark "J. Walley's Ware."

Walley, William – Shelton; died 1842; made toys and figures in a small potworks that employed only about eight workers.

Walton, John – John Walton is associated with production of bocage figures and with a school of important figure-makers who produced similarly styled wares. Little, however, is known of his personal life. John Bedford suggests that the potter may have been born to Richard and Sarah Walton in Burslem during 1780 and that he probably worked for other figure-makers during his youth (Bedford, 35), but no documentary confirmation exists. It is likely that Walton began as a potter around 1810; his name first appeared in an 1818 trade directory in which he was listed as a "colour maker and earthenware figure manufacturer, near New Road" (*Commercial Directory*, 1818-20, J. Pigot & R. W. Dean). At that time he had two separate works in Burslem, a color makers in Pleasant Street and an earthenware works at the Hadderage (his house was close by in New Street). By 1822, he occupied a single manufactory in Navigation Road. His last trade entry appeared in the *National Commercial Directory*, 1835 (J. Pigot & Co.) where he was listed as an earthenware manufacturer at Navigation Road and as a toy and ornamental china manufacturer at Waterloo Road, both sites in Burslem (Halfpenny, 220). Records show that Walton was baptized at St. John's Church in Burslem on February 20, 1780 and that he married Ermine Whitmore at Newcastle under Lyme on October 27, 1800. He and

Ermine had several children. On February 6, 1830, their second daughter, Susannah, married George Hood to whom Walton's Navigation Road works passed during the 1830s (Halfpenny, 220-223).

As Mr. Bedford points out, although Walton's figures are not distinctively original in subject and are somewhat crudely modeled, he was most successful in producing versions, not imitations, of Chelsea, Derby, and continental porcelain figures in the Staffordshire earthenware medium, an affordable alternative to more costly ceramics, for a village and small town-house clientele (Bedford, 38-42). The strength of Walton's figures is expressed best by H.A.B. Turner who has written that Walton captured in earthenware "the charms and humor of real life" that were "lost in the cold precision of porcelain" (Turner, 110).

Walton was apparently a prolific potter. Often, marked Walton pieces contain an oval, or similarly shaped, blue-framed panel on the foreground that invites a subject name or description that rarely appears. Walton was partial to bright enamel decoration, often over a pearl glaze. He is noted for two distinctive bocage (leafy, tree-like) forms with painted flowers placed inside the bocage. Leaves in the genuine Walton bocage style are characterized by two separate pieces that were placed back-to-back, and the florets were separately molded and applied rather than molded into the bocage – details often overlooked by reproducers.

Walton's themes included both the sacred and the secular. Figures of Elijah, the Widow of Zarephath, Diana, shepherds, gardeners, and the Irish fighters Spring and Langan were produced among many others. As Pat Halfpenny notes, the large number of marked Walton figures indicates that his figure subject range was broad. A Walton mark, when used, usually consisted of his name in capital letters inside a scroll on the back of figures.

John Walton and Ralph Salt (see entry) best represent the Walton School. Walton School figures are usually small, colorful earthenware groups with simple bocage backgrounds (Bedford, 35). Known potters who produced figures similar to Walton's (with varying degrees of competence) include Charles Tittensor of Shelton, Ralph Salt, John and Ralph Hall of Tunstall and Burslem, John Dale of Burslem, Samuel Grocott of Tunstall, and Daniel and Timothy Edge of Burslem. Bocage was undoubtedly popular, and figures with bocage were also found in the Burslem Old Town Hall cache discussed previously. (See Walton mark illustrated in Chapter Five.)

Walton, Joshua – first listed as a modeler and earthenware figure maker in *Pigot's Directory* of 1830; his last listing appeared in 1841.

Warburton, William, Edward, Jacob, Peter, and Francis – Warburton was a well-known name among Staffordshire potters, although there is no evidence of relationships among some individuals of this name;

Marked John Walton bocage group, impressed mark inside a raised scroll at the back of the figure (Godden mark #4002). 6". Value: $500-$1000.

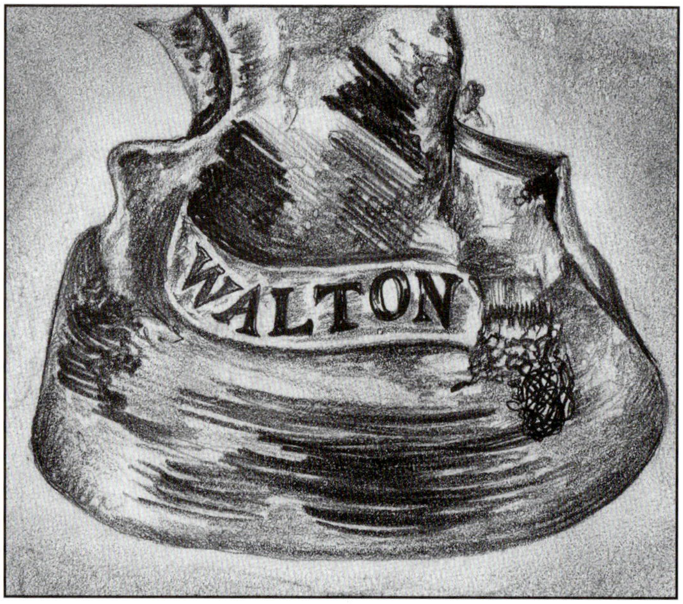

Impressed John Walton mark, circa 1818-35; usually found within a raised scroll at the backs of figure bases (Godden mark #4002). *Courtesy of Robert Buczynski.*

Warburtons operated a potworks in Cobridge for many years; by 1751, the works owned by Thomas Whieldon at Fenton Low were occupied by Warburtons; William Warburton died in 1754 and was succeeded by his son, Edward; Jacob Warburton is listed in the 1796 trade directories; a short time after, Peter and Francis Warburton worked in partnership; after the partnership was dissolved, Peter continued in business alone until the time of his death in 1813, and the site occupied by the Warburtons was then taken over by Ralph and James Clews.

Wedgwood, Josiah – The Wedgwood family name has been traditionally associated with The Potteries for many generations as there have been Wedgwoods potting in Staffordshire since the seventeenth century (Moore, 12). Of all, the most famous and most widely acclaimed is Josiah Wedgwood (1730-1795), the thirteenth child of a potter who died when Josiah was nine years old (Wills, 115). Josiah was a man of vision and a perfectionist by nature, but he was also a kind and warm-hearted individual who suffered illness as a child and the later amputation of a leg. His unqualified genius as a technician and as an artist is synonymous with the Wedgwood name.

Josiah's formal potting career began in 1744 when he was apprenticed to his older brother, Thomas, who had inherited the family pottery at Churchyard Works in Burslem. He worked there first as a "thrower," shaping round objects on a wheel, and then learning various aspects of potting (Theus, 112). After leaving the Churchyard Works (circa 1752), he entered into a brief partnership with two Stoke potters (Wills, 115); in 1754, he formed his famous five-year partnership with Thomas Whieldon at Fenton Vivian (Theus, 112). In 1759 or 1760, Wedgwood leased a Burslem pottery from his cousins and soon after moved to the Brick House Works (Wills, 116) the opening of which occurred in 1764, the year that he married his cousin, Sarah Wedgwood.

Experimentation with colored glazes led to Wedgwood's invention of a green glaze (used on Cauliflower Ware and described in his March 1759 experiment book) and to the development of a yellow glaze recorded in his experiment book of 1760 (Theus, 112-113). Around 1765, Wedgwood presented a number of creamware items to Queen Charlotte (wife of George III) and his own term "Queen's Ware" has been used ever since.

There is no supportive documentation or other evidence to prove that Josiah produced the standard type of earthenware figures, and figures marked "WEDGWOOD" may have been made, as Pat Halfpenny suggests, by another Wedgwood. Ms. Halfpenny further suggests that Ralph Wedgwood may be a strong candidate. Ralph was the eldest son of Thomas Wedgwood, Josiah Wedgwood's cousin and partner in the Burslem factory. Thomas died in 1788 while establishing his own pottery and planning that his younger son Samuel would be master potter. When Samuel died in 1790, Ralph assumed the responsibility (reluctantly, as Pat Halfpenny notes). Ralph Wedgwood worked in Burslem at the Hill Pottery from circa 1790-97 when he went bankrupt. In 1798 or 1799, he worked in partnership with Messrs. Tomlinson & Forster of the Knottingly Pottery in Yorkshire until the end of 1800. While the standard factory mark at Burslem was "Wedgwood & Co.," it is not certain whether or not the word "WEDGWOOD" was used by itself. According to Ms. Halfpenny, Ralph had no reason not to use his own name and it *was* used alone at Ferrybridge (see illustration in Chapter Four) as well as with "Wedgwood & Co." even after Ralph left. Known figures with the impressed "WEDGWOOD" mark seem to be consistent with a 1790s date and because the evidence suggests one firm of short duration with entitlement to mark its wares "WEDGWOOD," Ralph Wedgwood is a likely nominee (Halfpenny, 169-171).

By 1768, Josiah had invented a basalt body and began producing wares in the classical style called "Etruscan" (Theus, 114). On June 13, 1769, he opened a pottery named Etruria where he worked in partnership with Thomas Bentley (Wills, 135) and began working on a jasper body that he perfected around 1775. Jasper Wares appear in shades of blue and green, lilac, pink, yellow, black, and white, usually a single color decorated with classical designs in white relief. Tri-color Jasper Ware is extremely rare and valuable. Wedgwood participated whole-heartedly in the neo-classical revival of the late eighteenth century not as an imitator but, rather, as one who skillfully introduced classical themes and decoration into Staffordshire's expanding inventory (Theus, 116, 117, 119).

Although Wedgwood's early wares, early figures, color-glazed wares produced during his partnership with Whieldon, and certain Creamwares are not marked, "Wedgwood" in capital or lower case letters is impressed on most other pieces. After the McKinley Tariff Act of 1891 required that the country of origin be marked for all items marketed in America, the word "England" was added to the Wedgwood Company's mark.

Three Wedgwood marks. The top mark is impressed in individually stamped lower case letters (Godden mark #4073); the center mark is curved slightly (Godden mark #4074); both circa 1759-69. The bottom mark is a standard impressed mark that appears in various sizes and was used from 1759 onwards (Godden mark #4075). *Courtesy of Robert Buczynski.*

Various marks followed, and copyists have forged all of them at one time or another (Theus, 117-118).

Wedgwood died in 1795 at the age of 65. On a memorial that stands in his honor in St. Peter's Church, Stoke-on-Trent, an inscription states that he "converted a rude and inconsiderable manufacture into an elegant art and an important part of national commerce" (Wills, 142). The business remained in the family's hands until 1967 when it became a public company (Snyder, 66).

Josiah's unchallenged gifts as a potter, his unfailing perfectionism, the benevolent considerations he extended to his workers before such considerations were practiced by most employers, and his business acumen were largely responsible for the perpetuation of his name and the continued production of Wedgwood wares into the current century. Interestingly, there is no documentary or archaeological evidence to suggest that the nineteenth century Wedgwood Company ever produced the standard flatback type of figure.

Superbly modeled and glazed pair of "Whieldon-type" birds set on tree stumps with flowers in relief; decorated in underglaze colors. 7.25". Circa 1755. Value: $30,000-$40,000. *Courtesy of Jonathan Horne (Antiques) Ltd.*

Wedgwood, Ralph – Hill Pottery in Burslem, 1790-1797; produced creamware, jasper ware, and black basaltes, and possibly figures after taking over the business begun by Thomas Wedgwood (died 1788) and continued by Thomas's son, Samuel (died 1790); Ralph was bankrupt in 1797; entered into partnership with Messrs. Tomlinson & Forster of the Knottingly Pottery near Ferrybridge in Yorkshire until the end of 1800.

Whieldon, Thomas – Thomas Whieldon (1719-1795) may well be the most well-known and widely acclaimed potter of the mid-eighteenth century. Whieldon is remembered for his own work and, according to H. A. B. Turner, for the men who trained or apprenticed under him, men who went on to become famous potters, including Josiah Spode, Aaron Wood, Robert Garner, William Greatbatch, and others (Turner, 46, 48).

For some time, based upon Simeon Shaw's writings, it was generally believed that Whieldon began potting at Fenton Low. In actuality, Shaw notes that Whieldon commenced potting at Little Fenton, which early researchers interpreted as Fenton Low (the sites are located about a half mile apart). Pat Halfpenny comments that there is no evidence to support the misunderstanding that Whieldon potted at Fenton Low, although he did own property and a pottery there, which he rented. Accordingly, pottery excavated from the Fenton Low site is most correctly attributed to Whieldon's tenants (one of whom was Edward Warburton). Whieldon *was* in occupancy at Little Fenton, also known as Fenton Vivian, before 1747 and contemporary documents describe his pottery there. Whieldon purchased the Fenton Vivian property in 1748 (Halfpenny, 42).

Whieldon married Anne Shaw in 1744 and his marriage bond records him as a potter. His wife and daughter died within four years and in 1748 he married Alice Parrot. At that time, he was recorded as a "gentleman," suggesting that he was, by then, a successful businessman. His second wife died in 1771 and Whieldon was married again, this time to Sarah Turner of Longton in 1776. By about 1780, he retired from potting (Halfpenny, 42-43).

Pat Halfpenny notes that, in 1968, the Archaeological Society attached to the City Museum & Art Gallery, Stoke-on-Trent, initiated excavations at the Whieldon site and discovered a number of figure models. These include the figure of a small bird on a stump (a two-part molded figure measuring about two inches in height, decorated in sponged manganese oxide, and lead-glazed). Also found were the leg of a buffalo from the figure of a boy and buffalo and various fragments made of cream-colored earthenware fired to biscuit temperature (Halfpenny, 43).

Creamware "Whieldon-type" dog decorated in underglaze oxide colors. 3.50". Circa 1770. Value: $1000+.

As in Astbury's case, little is known of Whieldon's personal life but his name is associated with early cream-colored wares and mottled tortoiseshell glazes. His figures were made from white clays – creamware decorated with oxide colors sponged on the biscuit body before glazing and refiring.

In addition to figures, Whieldon is also known to have produced tea wares, coffee pots, ewers, sugar boxes, mustard pots, salts, and piggins, as listed in a record of goods ordered by one of his customers, a Mr. Green of Aylsham, Norfolk (Wills, 104). He also produced Cauliflower Ware (color-glazed earthenwares in the form of cauliflower, pineapples, and other vegetables and fruits) along with Wedgwood and others beginning around 1750. His most famous partner was Josiah Wedgwood with whom he worked from 1754 until 1759.

Wood Family – Ralph Wood I (1715-1772) married Mary Wedgwood (Aaron Wedgwood's daughter) in August of 1738 and together they had eight children. After Mary died in 1756, Ralph was left with the responsibility of providing for their surviving children. Often in arrears, he was arrested in 1760 for debts owed to Thomas Malkin, but John Wedgwood paid the debt. Ralph I was a modeler in Staffordshire and although earlier research is contradictory, Pat Halfpenny clarifies the fact that there is no documentary evidence to prove that Ralph I was a master potter.

John and Thomas Wedgwood evidently employed him for a number of years and several dated hand-modeled mold blocks bear the initials "RW" or the name "Ralph Wood." John and Thomas Wedgwood's hiring and account books indicate that at times between 1756 and 1772 (possibly during the entire time), Ralph Wood was in their employ at the Big House in Burslem and, therefore, not working in his own manufactory.

His death in 1772 predates the introduction of pearl glazing, which means that he was not responsible for color-glazed figures in that class of ware (Halfpenny, 48-49, 70).

Josiah Wood was Ralph I's eldest surviving son and was married to Thomas Wedgwood's daughter, Mary.

Rare Wood family elephant decorated in enamel colors. 10.50". Circa 1785. Value: $6000-$8000. *Courtesy of Jonathan Horne (Antiques) Ltd.*

Josiah Wood's name appears in a 1784 directory as a Burslem potter. He died in 1789, aged forty-nine, and nothing else is known about him (Halfpenny, 70).

Ralph I's younger sons, John and Ralph II, are somewhat easier to discuss. Ralph II received early training at the Wedgwood's Big House, and his older brother, John, was trained in Josiah Wedgwood's London warehouse and salerooms (Halfpenny, 70).

John Wedgwood's account book notes that between August 1772 and March 1773, John and Ralph II were given money by their great-uncles in the sum of £65 to help establish a pottery. The business was unsuccessful as mentioned in a letter from Josiah Wedgwood to his partner Thomas Bentley that was dated April 3, 1773 (Halfpenny 71). Pat Halfpenny notes that Ralph left Burslem and went to Bristol where he married Sophia Lambert in 1774. Baptismal records exist in Bristol for three children. Another failed business venture followed and Ralph returned to Burslem by 1783. Ralph and Sophia's last child, Josiah, was baptized there in 1783 but died within a few months. In 1784, Ralph is listed in *Bailey's Directory* with his cousin Enoch Wood as a manufacturer of various wares. Accounts of the time suggest that Ralph was a rather insignificant member of the partnership that dissolved within five years. Identification of figures from the Ralph and Enoch Wood partnership is not possible as there are no marked samples and the model variations recorded cannot be identified. An 1802 map, probably compiled in 1800 or 1801, shows the cousins operating separate potworks. It is plausible to assume that after Enoch left, Ralph II remained at the cousins' site and continued to operate the works, incorporating the same wares, expanding the stock, and marking pieces with his own name. Ms. Halfpenny suggests further that Ralph II began as a master potter somewhere around 1789. He died in 1795. Ralph II's son, Ralph III, kept the firm in operation until his own death, only six years after his father's (Halfpenny, 71-77-82).

Some figures made by the Ralph Woods were marked "R. WOOD," "R. Wood," and "Ra. Wood, Burslem" during a brief production period of only twelve years. There is no conclusive proof to warrant attribution of these marks to a particular time during those twelve years. Many marked pieces are of superb quality and recorded models are decorated in both colored glazes and overglaze enamels (Halfpenny, 83).

The John Wood branch of the family was more successful in business than the Ralphs but tragedy touched their lives as it had their relatives. After the partnership between John and Ralph II failed in 1773, John apparently spent time in Bristol with his brother. While in Bristol, he married Mary Price on June 30, 1775. It may be that John and Ralph II worked together for a short time, but John returned to Burslem by the end of 1775. In March of 1776, he potted in partnership with John Wedgwood and when John Wedgwood passed away in 1780, John Wood continued potting on his own. He is listed in Bailey's 1781 *Northern Directory* as a Burslem potter. His business was successful and included, among other wares, a range of figures (Halfpenny, 86-88).

John and Mary Wood had five children. John Jr. survived along with three girls. In 1797, a Dr. Thomas Oliver asked permission of John Sr. to "pay his addresses" to the eldest daughter, Ann Marie. When he was refused permission, Oliver shot John Sr. and the potter died three days later. John Jr. kept his father's pottery, Brownhills, in operation and married Mary Baddeley in 1807. Vari-

Ralph Wood mark. *Courtesy of Robert Buczynski.*

A standard 20th century Woods Ware blue printed mark; Godden mark #4288; used by Wood & Sons Ltd. from circa 1917 onwards. This mark is commonly found on the firm's "old traditional patterns" like Blue Willow.

Left: Rare color glazed Wood family figure of a young girl holding a marmot in a box. Jonathan Horne notes that this unique figure was modeled after an original by Paul Louis Cyfflé. 7.25". Circa 1785. Value: \$1500-\$2000. *Right:* Wood school lion decorated in colored glazes with the underside of the base dry. 7". Circa 1770. Value: \$1500-\$2000. *Courtesy of Jonathan Horne (Antiques) Ltd.*

ous business interests (including banking) and a wealthy wife appear to have kept the family more than solvent (Halfpenny, 92-93). Pat Halfpenny suggests that John Wood may have been a more important potter than Ralph II or Ralph III and that his unmarked wares have not received the credit they deserve because of the large number of marked R. and Ra. Wood pieces. Ms. Halfpenny notes that it is possible, judging from sales ledger entries, that John may also have made a number of the figures attributed to Ralph Wood.

Mold numbers associated with Ralph Wood figures appeared in an incomplete list complied by Frank Faulkner early in the twentieth century and comprise an interesting area of further study for serious Wood family students. Another area of study, and certainly one recognized by many collectors, is that of Toby jugs (typically styled after the few marked Ralph Wood models), which became a popular and widely imitated production item among contemporary and later potters. (Toby Jugs are named for Toby Fillpot, a character in the song "The Brown Jug." According to the lyrics, "fat" Toby Fillpot died, was buried, and became clay; a potter dug Toby's clay and used it to make a brown jug – an interesting characterization of the old saying attributed to Staffordshire's potters: "We make our pots of what we potters are.")

The early Ralph Wood genealogy may be summarized as follows: Ralph Wood I (1715-1772), John Wood (1746-1797), Ralph Wood II (1748-1795), Ralph Wood III (1775-1801), John Wood II (1778-1848), Aaron Wood (brother of Ralph I, 1717-1785), and Enoch Wood (son of Aaron Wood, 1759-1840, of whom additional biographical data will follow).

Wood & Caldwell, 1789-1818, (see entry for Enoch Wood).

Wood, Ephraim – Burslem; specialist figure maker listed at Nile Street in 1822 and at Wood's Bank in 1828-29; related to the Ralph Wood family.

Wood, Enoch – Enoch Wood (1759-1840), of the illustrious Wood family, was the son of Aaron Wood, the nephew of Ralph Wood I, and the cousin of Ralph Wood II. He established an incredible home and manufactory called Fountain Place in Burslem, fathered twelve children, lived over eighty years, and was, most likely, a major figure maker throughout this life.

Enoch Wood is believed to have worked for Josiah Wedgwood and was, at one time, apprenticed to Humphrey Palmer. In 1784, when Enoch was about twenty-five years old, he went into business with his cousin Ralph II. Around 1790, he established a partnership with James Caldwell, buying Caldwell out in 1818 and changing the Wood & Caldwell firm to Enoch Wood & Sons (Wills, 163).

The Wood factories closed in 1840, the year of Enoch Wood's death (Halfpenny, 251). Enoch was not only a potter but a master sculptor as well. He is especially noted for his bust of the preacher John Wesley (signed "E. Wood, Sculp., Burslem") but is most famed for his blue-printed wares. He also modeled various figures and groups decorated with overglaze enamels. These pieces achieved a porcelain-look but lost the effective quality of earlier processes in which he incorporated color into the glaze (Theus, 137-138 and Wills, 163-165).

Like other potters of his time, Wood produced chimney ornaments in conjunction with manufacture of various other wares. Today, more of his blue-printed wares enter the market than his figures and figure groups. It has been recorded that Enoch Wood was one of the largest exporters of earthenwares to America; he was also a ceramics collector and a surviving portion of his collection is currently housed in the Dresden Museum.

Pat Halfpenny notes that, despite the small number of marked figures, caches left by the potter in recovered time capsules have supported attribution of a greater range of figure models to Enoch Wood. The most well-known time capsule site is St. Paul's Church in Burslem. There, a large number of marked wares intended for the American market, along with several figures, were found inside a sealed chamber in the buttress foundations of the church. Wasters and factory seconds were major among the finds that also included animals in the forms of a small reclining deer and an undecorated peacock. In 1938, other figure fragments were discovered under the pavement near Burslem Old Town Hall.

Impressed Wood & Caldwell mark, circa 1790-1818; Godden mark #4256. *Courtesy of Robert Buczynski.*

Some of the figures appeared to have colored glazes and were initially attributed to Ralph Wood, but what appeared to be colored glazes was actually the result of misfired color. Figures with bocage (four different forms) and enameled figures were also found along with fragments that are very like marked examples from Enoch Wood's factory and some that are the same as pieces found in the St. Paul's time capsule. A Toby jug of the sailor, which matches a marked "WOOD & CALDWELL" Toby in the Victoria & Albert Museum, was found as well. As Ms. Halfpenny concludes, the evidence suggests that these pieces are from Enoch Wood's factory, which was located nearby (Halfpenny, 187-188 and 246-249). Wood was a philanthropist and introduced some notable reforms in an attempt to ameliorate the conditions of factory workers and for this is known as "Father of the Potteries."

Wood, George – Hanley, circa 1851; toy maker.

Chapter Three
Modeling, Molding, Decorating, and Sources of Inspiration

Staffordshire figures and groups appear in dazzling assortment. During the eighteenth and nineteenth centuries, the growth of Britain's merchant, trading, and working classes heralded an increasing amount of "spending money" and, with it, consumer demand for ornamental wares that could rival expensive porcelains with cheaper prices. The potters responded with a prodigious output of decorative figures. Modeled, molded, and decorated through various methods, these figures reflected the advancements in technology and contemporary decorative art styles of their time. Figures and groups numbering in the hundreds of thousands were produced as portraits of actual people, mythological and literary characters, quill holders or inkwells, spill vases, inanimate "dummy" clocks for those unable to afford the real thing, watch holders, pastille burners, holy water stoups, and a vast array of other figures with no other function than to serve as decorative accessories. Production was so vast that at one period, to help with their drainage, roads in Staffordshire were built on ground up "wasters" (pottery spoiled or flawed in manufacture). Staffordshire was, literally, built on pottery!

Andromache weeping over the ashes of Hector. Although the subject of the figure was a popular one during the late 18th and early 19th centuries, this figure is very unusual in that the body used is terracotta. 9.25". Circa 1800. Value: $1000+.

To refer to the vast body of Staffordshire figures as "Staffordshire pottery" is simplistic as many of them were, in fact, not pottery, but other ceramics like bone china or porcelain, and made up of numerous different clay bodies that did not originate in the region: while North Staffordshire was rich in native clays that ranged in color from buff/gray to reddish brown, most figures were actually made from white clays that were imported from Devon and Dorset. Clays are readily identifiable by their malleability. Once quarried and transported, they were prepared at the potteries where they were mixed with water, sieved, supplemented with other ingredients like ground flint, and dried. The clays could then be mixed with water to form slip or kneaded to remove air bubbles (a process called wedging) and readied for press molding.

Any discussion of the technical aspects of pottery figure production is open to conjecture as each pottery held dear its own proprietary formulas and techniques for figure making. The basics, however, were relatively standard. Eighteenth century figures were made of earthenware and various different types of stoneware but, by the Victorian Era, the potters had at their disposal a far wider range of bodies from which to pot their figures, making identification of specific components and proportions and specific production techniques difficult to analyze.

In response to the growing market demand for figures, nineteenth century production methods moved away from the slower process of hand modeling to a range of techniques: first to using a combination of molds and hand construction, then, as cost became an overriding consideration, to the production of completely mold-formed figures. To think of the potbanks as efficient modern establishments of their time would, however, be in error as revealed in the observations a pottery worker of the 1840s who wrote of the "toy manufactory" at which he was employed: *"...a curiosity in structure and management. It was rusty and grim. As for form it might have been brought in cartloads from the broken-down cottages on the opposite side of the street. The workshops were neither square, nor round, nor oblong. They were a jumble of the oddest imaginable kind, and if there had been an ordinary number of workshops on an average size potworks, placed as these were placed, it would have been impossible to find the way in and the way out."*

In the Round and Flatbacks

During the eighteenth century, all Staffordshire figures were made in the round: three-dimensional with fully modeled and decorated fronts and backs but, by the time of Queen Victoria's reign, a new phenomenon known as the "flat back" figure was introduced.

Figures with flat, undecorated backs first began to emerge during the late 1830s and by the time Victoria acceded to the throne in 1837, interest in the "here and now" as inspiration for figures affected the direction of figure making's future.

To answer the urgency of "here and now" production, modeling was simplified and the "flatback," with few details on its reverse, came into being to be placed on mantelpieces flush against chimneys (hence the name "Chimney Ornaments"). They were only intended to be viewed from the front and, therefore, did not require in the round modeling or decorating. Increased consumer demand and a need to cut production costs and time were undoubtedly the driving factors in the development of this type of figure, which became the style of choice by the mid-nineteenth century. Simplistic modeling made it possible to create some flatbacks from a minimal number of molds, and one-sided coloring cut decorating time in half. Flatbacks were quick, easy, and cheap to produce, and they were more affordable for consumers than earlier figures.

Hand Modeling

Hand modeling is the simplest production technique and essentially involves working wet clay by hand to model a figure. Completely hand modeled pieces with limbs formed by rolled "snakes" of clay, facial features formed either by impressing their simple clay ball heads with pointed tools, or by applying tiny clay lumps are rare and are not seen in figures other than early "pew groups" (men and women posed sedately on a pew-like settles), and "bell women" (with their voluminous skirts); however, hand modeled details were sometimes added to molded figures and groups. In a commercial sense, time-intensive hand modeling is impractical and completely unsuited to mass production, and by the peak production period of the nineteenth century, hand modeling was all but replaced by press molding.

Molding

The use of molds to give ceramic items a desired form is more involved than hand modeling but is better suited to large-scale production because it is more labor and cost efficient. After plaster of Paris was introduced in The Potteries, the use of molds was widely accepted, initially in the production of tea and tablewares and, later, for figures, figure groups, and other items.

Interior of a press-molded figure of Diana Vernon showing very clearly the gouge marks made by the fingers of the potter while pressing the clay into the mold. Interestingly, from the angle of the finger marks it appears that the potter was right-handed, as it is very difficult to replicate the marks left-handed. Further join marks where separately molded components of the figure were connected can be seen at the top of the picture indicating where the top of the figure was joined to the lower sections. Close examination of the interior of this figure reveals the tell-tale brushing of liquid clay over the seams where the separately molded pieces were joined – a white path of slip is clearly evident.

Techniques for mold production used by the Staffordshire potters were relatively straightforward but involved a number of very time consuming steps and a level of expertise from the mold maker. It is hardly surprising that the services of a master mold maker were highly valued by potbank proprietors. Mold making started with the original model made by the design maker in oily clay that was then encased in plaster of Paris. The parts were removed, usually breaking the original in the process, to become the master-mold or "block-mold" forming a sort of "negative" of the original piece. The mold's parts were reassembled, leaving a hollow interior into which more plaster of Paris could be poured to make additional, or working, molds. Master molds were usually preserved by the potteries, and some have survived to the present. The master-mold was further encased in plaster and additional "working-molds" were struck. If only a very small run of figures was required, a working-mold was unlikely to be made, but for popular pieces a large number were created. The working life of a mold was usually up to two hundred figures, at a rate of two or three a day depending on drying times. The first figures from the molds were the best and exhibit sharp details because as the mold became worn, molded details lost crispness, and the mold had to be replaced. Simple figures needed only three-part molds that provided a front, a back, and a bottom; however, many figures and groups required supplementary molds to provide the realistic details seen in more complex figures and groups. Records exist of figures that required not only up to twelve individual molds, but hand modeled and applied parts as well. Numerous molds and additional time added to the costs incurred by both the potting firms and the consumers, consequently, such figures did not have large production runs and are now very rare.

The Spaniel pair illustrated here shows the kind of crisp molding and sharp details that indicate production from a fresh mold. 10.50". Mid-to late Victorian. Value: $500-$1000.

Back view of the previously illustrated Spaniel pair exhibiting crisp molding.

Press Molding

One of the most popular techniques for figure production during the mid-nineteenth century was "press molding" in which flat, damp sheets of clay were pressed by hand or with a sponge into the sides of the mold parts, following the contours of the sculpted design and leaving the center area open and hollow. The edges were trimmed with a knife and then painted with liquid clay (with the consistency of cream and known as "slip") to ensure adhesion. Then the halves of the mold were pressed together and secured with string. The inside seams were either brushed with more liquid clay or sealed with thin rolls of clay ap-

Press molded figures of a water buffalo (center) and two leverets or hares at the left and right; all decorated in underglaze colors. Buffalo: 9". Circa 1755. Value: $5000-$6000. Leverets: 3.50". Circa 1755. Value: $1500-$2000. *Courtesy of Jonathan Horne (Antiques) Ltd.*

plied through the open bottom, which, by Victorian times, was nearly always covered with another sheet of clay to "close" the figure.

The still "in-mold" figure was then placed on a shelf where it remained until the clay was dry to the touch. While drying, water was drawn off by the porous plaster mold and the figure shrunk adequately to allow the removal of the mold. When the clay was sufficiently dry, the mold was separated and the figure removed. Release holes, normally smaller than the diameter of a pencil, were opened in the base and/or back of the figure, unless it contained a spill or other opening, to allow expanding air and gasses produced during firing a means of escape. Were these vents not added, the figure would explode during firing, something that occasionally occurred despite the potters' best efforts, and whole kiln loads of pottery were destroyed. Less dramatic consequences of inadequate venting can been seen on some figures that display fissure-like lines along their joins.

It was at this stage that additional molded parts were added and the seams were trimmed and smoothed. Various edible analogies, such as "spaghetti," "parsley," or "crumbs" have been applied to the decorative clay finishes added to some figures in order to simulate fur, foliage, or ermine on robes. These finishes were added at this stage through the application of extruded clay forced through a sieve, or with granulated clay to achieve a "pebbled" effect. The name given to the worker who undertook these tasks was misleading: "the repairer." After these steps in the process had been completed, the figure was fired at about 1100 degrees Celsius to form a brittle, matte and white product known as the "biscuit."

Example of a Poodle with the typical rough coat achieved through use of granulated clay or by application of extruded clay through a sieve. 7". Mid-Victorian. Value: $500-$1000. *Courtesy of Anita L. Grashof, Gallerie Ani'tiques.*

Hand painted underglaze color was applied and the figure was fired again to protect the colors during glazing. At this point, the figure was dipped into a liquid lead glaze and fired again. Heating and cooling freshly glazed figures required great care as the glaze needed to cool at the same rate as the body of the figure to prevent shrinking and crazing (small cracks in the glaze) from occurring. Once cooled, overglaze colors could be applied, and the figure was fired for the last time, unless gilded details were required which would necessitate an additional firing. All in all, a figure could be fired up to five times!

Despite the "technologies" of mass production methods, each figure changed hands several times during production and is therefore unique because it carries each worker's personal touch. Sometimes, when the bottom of a figure is removed, the fingerprints of a pottery worker are found inside – reminders that although production line techniques were used, the process was not mechanized and relied on the by-hand work of individuals.

Today's collectors seek figures in which the molding is sharp and crisp. Each figure that was made caused deterioration of the mold and each figure was less sharply detailed than those that had come before. In collectors' terms, the first figures taken from a mold are superior to those that were produced toward the end of a mold's usefulness. Well-used molds produced figures that are less well defined and less attractive.

Slip Molding/Casting

Another type of molding called "slip molding" was borrowed from the techniques used for other ceramics like Parian wares, but was infrequently used in Victorian Era figure production. Strictly speaking, very few slip-cast figures date to the crest of figure production (circa 1835-1875), but slip-molded figures and groups *are* seen in various reproductions.

A slip mold was created in the same manner as a press-mold, but once the working mold was produced, its parts were bound together and slip was poured into the mold until it was full and left for about thirty minutes. The porosity of the plaster mold caused the water from the slip to be absorbed and to form a layer of clay against the walls of the mold, creating a hollow shell. The remaining mixture was poured out of the mold and discarded, and the figure was left to dry. When the slip "shell" that had formed was thoroughly dry, the mold was opened and the figure removed. The processes for decorating, glazing, and firing were completed in the same manner as they were in press molding.

Figures and groups made by the slip casting method often have open bottoms or large base holes (most often, one or two through which the slip was poured in and out), and the finished products are usually lighter in weight than those that were press molded. Slip molding results in a smooth interior, which reflects the contours of the exterior, a condition achieved because an even coating of clay built up on the walls of the mold. The disadvantage of this method for the potters was that the working-molds quickly deteriorated because they absorbed large amounts of moisture. As a result, these molds could not be used for the production of more than twenty figures, and popular models required a large number of working molds.

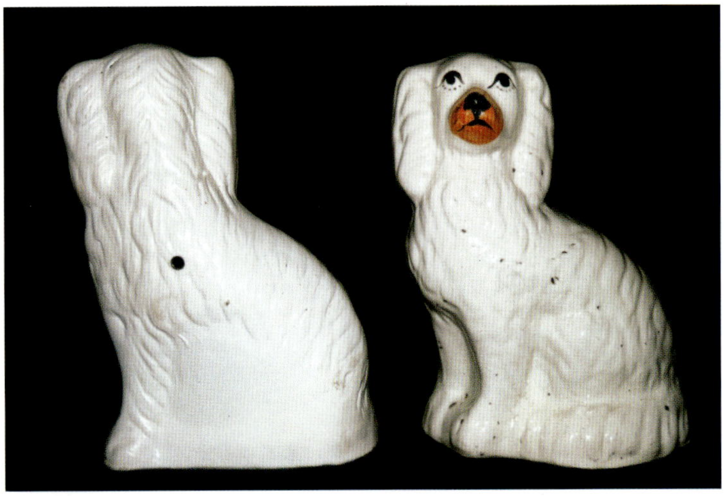

Illustration of a small release hole indicating 19th century production.

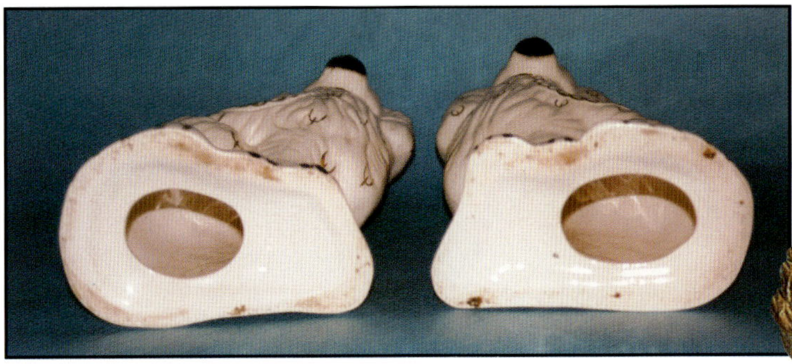

Large release holes commonly used in slip molding.

Salt Glazing

Salt glazing was popular in stoneware production during the eighteenth century and was so widely used at one period that the Elers brothers faced a deputation from the residents surrounding their factory who protested the vast and noxious clouds of smoke forced into the air. During firing at temperatures up to 1300 degrees Celsius, salt was added by flinging it into the kiln at the pottery through ports designed specifically to accommodate the salt glazing method. The sodium chloride, and moisture, turned into sodium oxide and hydrochloric acid. The sodium oxide reacted chemically with the surface alumina and silica to create a glassy glaze with a slightly rough texture similar to that of an orange skin (Turner, 224). Salt glazed figures are rare.

Saltglazed figures are extremely rare; shown here is a very good pair of King Charles Spaniels, seated on high plinths, and made of saltglazed stoneware in Brampton, Derbyshire. 14 3/16". Circa 1830. Value: $8000-$10,000. *Courtesy of Jonathan Horne (Antiques) Ltd.*

Lead Glazing

Lead glazing has been used since the medieval period, and while lead ore powders were still being used during the seventeenth century, liquid glaze had been introduced. In lead glazing, lead ore was ground, or calcined, to a fine particle size – the finer the particle the better. When dusting with lead powder it was difficult to achieve an even coating, but lead ore, ground and mixed with slip, held the lead in even suspension and figures could be dipped for a successful glaze. When ground lead was mixed with water alone, the lead ore sank to the bottom of the mix: a good slip was viscous enough and necessary to hold the lead ore in even suspension (Halfpenny, personal communications).

During the eighteenth century, a small amount of cobalt oxide was added to the glaze used in many figures in an attempt to counteract the yellow staining common in glazes of the period, to imitate the fine glazes on Chinese porcelains, and called, rather unimaginatively, "china glaze." The glaze is now called "Pearlware" and can be identified by traces of transparent blue, especially in crevices (Halfpenny, 307), and by its wonderful translucency.

Overglaze Colors

While most Staffordshire figures were lead glazed, this Spaniel left the factory in the unglazed biscuit state. 10.25". Mid-Victorian. Value: $500-$1000

Overglaze colors (enamels) were added over the glaze before refiring at a low temperature, usually about 800 degrees Celsius. Overglaze colors tended to fade under the heat of the glost oven and required mixing with a vitreous flux (glassy glaze) to form a mixture that could be painted on by hand, with transfers, or with rubber stamps and fired again (Pugh, 88).

Stronger and darker colors required less flux in order to avoid color dilution. Therefore, darker colors did not adhere as strongly to the figure surface and were more likely to wear after firing. Black enamels, for example, are very subject to flaking, but most other colors, unless subject to an error in firing temperature, only wear away as a result of cleaning or scrubbing.

Certain figures remained in vogue for prolonged periods and saw interpretation in different styles and different types of ceramics. Illustrated on the left is a Victorian version of a much earlier creamware rendering of "Winter," itself a copy of a porcelain original. Right-hand figure 10", late 18th / early 19th century. Value Right-hand figure: $100-$500. Left-hand figure 8.50", circa 1860. Value: Left-hand figure $500-$1000.

Colored Glazes

Glazes tinted with color were popular during the eighteenth century and provided an alternative to underglaze painting. However, the process was more expensive than china glaze or underglaze painting and had a number of drawbacks. Not only did these glazes cost more than others, they required additional time and care in application, their color range was very limited, the methods required for their firing were more exacting, and the glazes themselves were less robust in the firing process. Hardly surprisingly, some color-glazed figures indicate hasty or less than careful decoration where the bare earthenware body is not completely covered with color (Halfpenny, 308).

Underglaze Colors

Simply explained, underglaze colors are, as their name suggests, colors applied under the glaze. Figures made during the last half of the eighteenth century were often decorated in underglaze oxide colors in typical earth-tone shades.

For the most part, Victorian-era figures and groups were decorated with underglaze colors that were bright, varied, and natural looking. Most underglaze painted decoration was applied by hand and today's collectors look for fine brush strokes, feathered details, a comprehensive and realistic color palette, and application of color that suggests a sense of energy or movement.

A pearlware version of "Winter" decorated using enamels and displaying the square base typical of many figures of this period. 7.5". Circa 1800. Value: $500-$1000

Spraying is achieved, as the term suggests, by literally spraying color onto a figure; the technique is quick and easy but produces inferior products that lack the fine details of hand painting. The result is a relatively even coating of color that is unexciting, uninspiring, and monotonous. Although spraying *was* infrequently used during the late Victorian Era, most sprayed figures are post-Victorian.

One of the more noteworthy underglaze colors was a rich cobalt blue, one of only two underglaze colors to make it through to the Victorian period. This blue was often used in the decoration of coats, bodices, dresses, and other garment details. Sometimes referred to as "Thenard's Blue," it has been noted that this blue was invented in or around 1802 and, because it was made of thirty per cent cobalt and seventy per cent alumina, it was much cheaper to use than even reduced quality cobalt oxide. Importantly, the dilution with alumina did not cause a significant lessening in the quality of the color (Turner, 228). Despite its popularity, the use of underglaze cobalt blue was discontinued after 1863. Curiously, there seems to have been an abrupt halt to the color's use rather than a gradual discontinuation or tapering off. There is no documented reason for cobalt blue's termination, but it is possible that its chemical properties were discovered to be harmful. The only other underglaze color that managed the transition into the Victorian era, underglaze black, never achieved any real measure of popularity.

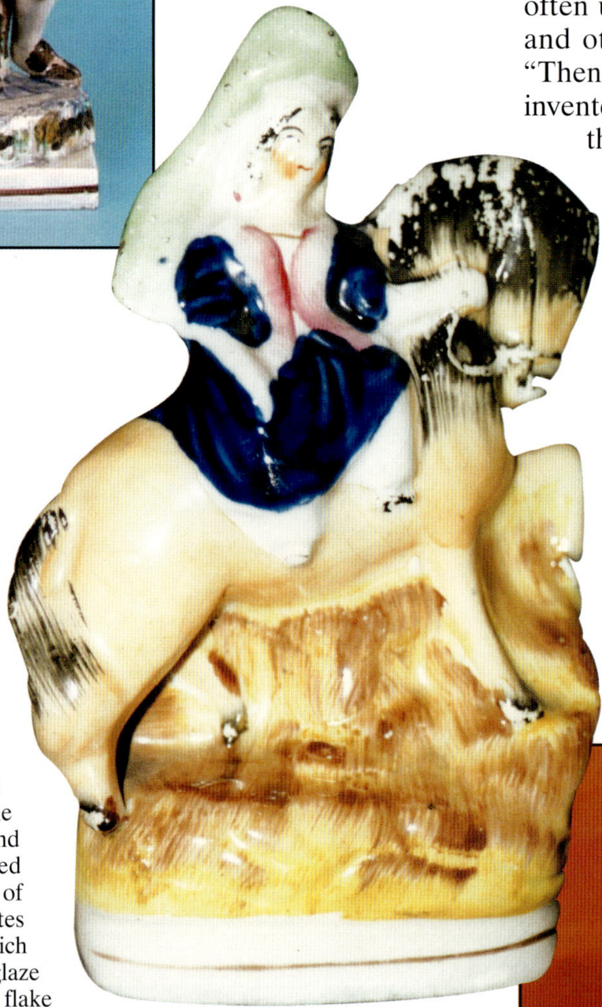

This group of a young girl (presumably the Princess Royal and originally paired with the Prince of Wales) illustrates the manner in which black overglaze painting tends to flake as particularly evident in the horse's mane and the girl's hair. 6.50". Early Victorian. Value: (for the single)$100-$500. *Courtesy of Anita L. Grashof, Gallerie Ani'tiques.*

Large and small dogs that have been decorated with sponged color. 8" and 4.75". Late Victorian. Value large dog: $100-$500. Value small dog: $100-$500. *Courtesy of Anita L. Grashof, Gallerie Ani'tiques.*

Sponged color was also used to decorate some eighteenth and nineteenth century figures. In addition, various later vintage animal pieces were sprayed with color. Sponging is achieved when a sponge has been dipped into paint and pressed against the body of a ware. Faster and less laborious than hand painting, its effect might be light and lacy, or might resemble the horizontal extensions of stratus clouds.

All-Black Figures

During the eighteenth and nineteenth centuries, a number of animal figures were decorated in striking black and accented with gold highlights. These figures are popularly called "Jackfield," taking their colloquial name from a class of earthenware in which a black glaze was applied over a red earthenware body.

It is believed that wares of this type originated from the Jackfield Pottery in the Shropshire town of Jackfield from about 1750-1775 (Theus, 227). Jackfield was a long-standing ceramics center as there were potters working there as early as 1560. In general, Staffordshire "Jackfield" figures are most accurately described simply as *black glazed wares*. Apart from the famous cats, dogs, and cockerels depicted in this type of pottery, other black glazed figures, including the occasional milkmaid and cow creamers (which form their own category of collecting), may be discovered.

All-White Figures

Although all-white figures were produced concurrently with well-colored versions, in general, most figures produced after 1875-80 were not modeled or decorated with the same degree of care and attention to detail as earlier examples. They characterized the declining years of Victorian figure production and were inferior in all ways to figures produced earlier. The precise reason for less coloration is unknown, but it was very likely a result of economics, waning consumer interest, competition from Continental imports, or a combination of all three. These figures were glazed (painted white under the glaze and not to be confused with the finer and marble-like Parian wares) and were often produced with little more than gold overglaze highlighting, overglaze enameled flesh tones, enameled hair and shoes for persons, and enamel-painted paws and facial features for animals. The Parr Factory, which maintained a higher quality later into the century, produced notable exceptions. However, even these figures were not up to the standard set by earlier Parr pieces (Harding, Book Three, 22).

An all-black Spaniel of the "Jackfield-type," one of a pair. 11". Mid-Victorian. Value for the pair: $1000+. *Courtesy of Anita L. Grashof, Gallerie Ani'tiques.*

Patriotic figures of children mounted on stags demonstrating the different levels of decoration available on figures. The figure on the right would have been a more expensive version than the white and gilt figure. Left-hand figure (damaged) 10.25"; right-hand figure 10.75". Circa 1850. Value left-hand figure: $100-$500 (undamaged condition). Value right-hand figure $500-$1000.

Gilding

Gilding was widely used in nineteenth century Staffordshire figure decoration, and two types of gilding were popular during the Victorian era. Gilding was used sparingly over enameled colors to avoid the additional firing needed to fix the color (Pugh, 88), but it was used extensively over underglaze colors.

Bases were often highlighted with gold, and gold collars, padlocks, and chains were a characteristic of many Spaniel and Poodle models. Gold was also used in the body decoration of all-white figures, especially during the late nineteenth century when varied colors were applied more judiciously.

A selection of eight all-white Spaniels produced during the latter years of the 19th century when the degree of care and attention to detail had begun to deteriorate.

The first type of gilding was achieved through use of a powdered mercuric gold called "best gold," which required mixing with mercury in order to create a "mercuric flux" to fix the gold to the figure. After firing, it was so dull that it required burnishing with an abrasive, either an agate stone or special sand. This type of gilding produced a warm, light, natural effect, but was discontinued because of the horrendous effects it had on the health of those working with it. The expression "Mad as a Hatter" arose from hat makers' exposure to mercury during the felt-making process and which led them to develop epilepsy-like symptoms as a result of heavy-metal poisoning. The potters suffered the same chemical contamination, and the practice of using mercury as a flux was discontinued. An alternative method of gilding used "aqua regia" (a mixture of nitric and hydrochloric acids) in which gold filings were dissolved. Once the mixture was dried it was ground to a fine powder and then applied with a borax flux and fired.

By the 1880s, the gilding used on Staffordshire figures was a product called "bright gold," a liquid gilding that was brushed on to produce a highly reflective effect. This type of gilding fixed to the body more securely than best gold without the toxic results and did not require burnishing. It is easily identified by its brassy, mirror-like shine, and it appears on many late model and reproduction figures. Despite the fact that best gold is preferred over bright gold among collectors, it tends to rub off, especially from raised areas, giving a worn appearance. But best gold, in any condition, is far more appealing and much more realistic than bright gold.

Titling

While most Staffordshire figures were not titled, a substantial number were, making identification of the subject remarkably easy. With the advent of the portrait figure, naming pieces became more common and a wide variety of styles emerged for adding titles to figures. Whether each pottery adopted a single style of titling or employed several is not known, and some of the same figures and groups appear with and without titles. Titling styles included raised capitals that were either gilded or painted black or another color. This type of lettering was applied to the body of the figure by either engraving the mold, the title being formed in a separate mold and pressed on later while the figure was still "green" (unfired), or by being forced with an engraved roller into the surface of the figure to achieve an "indented" title, a technique used by a few potteries including the Parr Factory and the so-called "Alpha" Factory. Gilt script lettering was usually applied with a transfer, while the much more rare gilt capitals were hand-

A late 19th century titled figure of "Dog Tray" that was produced earlier in well-colored versions. In one recorded example the title was hand painted in black capitals (see Staffordshire Animals p. 63). Various titling styles were used through the Victorian Era. 13". Circa 1870. Value: $500-$1000.

painted. Black or maroon capitals were also hand-painted and are even less frequently found than gilt examples. Black transfer titles, sometimes containing a verse or Biblical quote, are rare and were used almost exclusively by the Parr factory.

Sources of Inspiration

Potteries either hired independent artists or secured the talents of family members and in-house artisans to design their figure molds. While some were professionally trained, it is unlikely that the smaller potteries would have had the resources to secure the services of skilled modelers. Many Victorian figures and groups were inspired by Pre-Victorian pieces, for which the figure makers had drawn upon classical and mythological characters, Biblical personalities, events and persons in the news, and everyday life. Improved printing and lithography techniques brought a wider distribution of printed copies of famous artworks to the general public than ever before, and an increasing public fascination with art encouraged the figure makers to use these and other printed materials as sources for their figures. Along with newspapers and periodicals like *The Illustrated London News*, *Punch*, *Cassell's Illustrated Family Paper*, and ephemeral publications like broadsides and broadsheets, the modelers and potters made "muses" of music-fronts, Penny Plain or Tuppence Coloured Prints, and Baxter and Le Blond Prints.

Figures and groups drew inspiration from a range of sources. In this example, a quotation from Shakespeare appears at the base of the group of Romeo and Juliet shown in Chapter Fourteen. Here is a good example of the type of transfer printing used on mid 19th century Staffordshire figures. Best gold may be seen at the top and base of this transfer displaying its characteristic mellow sheen.

A very noteworthy example of printed materials as a source of inspiration for the potters is seen in the series of figures derived by Thomas Parr from the Tallis Shakespeare Gallery prints (1852-53). Parr's figures are remarkably accurate pottery facsimiles of the prints and serve not only as a tribute to his modeling instincts, but also make the collector very grateful that copyright restrictions in the nineteenth century did not preclude the creation of such small masterpieces. Playbills featuring characters from popular plays (and the actors and actresses who played them onstage) also provided a wealth of material for the potters.

Numerous artworks and printed materials have been matched to corresponding figures and groups. Famous statues and famous or notorious buildings were also fair game for the figure makers' craft, and it is this notoriety that assists many collectors in identifying the sources of figures. For some, identification becomes something like the quest for the Holy Grail, but such obsessions detract from the ingenuity and inventiveness of the modelers and potters.

The greatest source of inspiration for the potters was not so much printed materials as the Victorian public. It must be remembered that, despite appreciable improvements in education, illiteracy was still widespread during the Victorian era and for those illiterate Victorians who wanted to know about wars, crime, or who was making headlines, and for those who longed for heroes, nostalgia, and romance, Staffordshire figures brought them a sense of the news and popular literature. They brought royalty to the mantelpiece, and undreamed of animals to the hearth. They even brought the theater and the opera to those who could not afford to attend, or had minimal leisure time. For the people who purchased and lived with them, Staffordshire figures were more than quaint pieces of folk art – they were, above all, an account of life as it was lived in their time, an earthenware history book that anyone could "read" and enjoy.

Porridge Figures

A mysterious group of figures exists that very little has been written about and with which many collectors are unfamiliar. The "Porridge School," as termed by P. D. Gordon Pugh (Pugh, 25), refers to a small group of figures with yellowish clay bodies flecked with brown impurities and clear glazes stained with occasional blue or grey speckles. The glaze texture of these figures is "gritty" and gives them a salt-glazed appearance. There are, however, differences in salt and Porridge glazes. Salt glaze may be distinguished by an "orange-peel" surface of tiny craters while "Porridge" figures have pinhead sized "pimples" that cover their surface. Although most "Porridge" figures are completely uncolored, a few were decorated with dark brown or black accents on features like boots or horses' manes.

There are few recorded subjects made in "Porridge" form, including the King and Queen of Prussia, Sir R. Tichborne, and, most commonly, the temperance group depicting the Independent Order of Good Templars; the latter two figures also exist in fully colored versions. Recent Staffordshire scholarship holds that these figures were all produced during the period between approximately 1863 and 1873 and attribution has been assigned to Sampson Smith due to similarities in the modeling of some of the "Porridge School" figures and recognized examples of Smith's pottery. Such a theory suggests that the two types of figures were made concurrently using the same molds and would indicate that Porridge figures were not mistakes that were left undecorated to be sold off as "seconds."

The "seconds" theory of the "Porridge School" of figures remains, however, the most credible. Several factors support this assertion: the distinguishing glaze "pimples" of "Porridge" figures is indicative of an incomplete knowledge of glaze compositions as are the flecks of color in what should be a clear glaze. Likewise, the staining of the body of the figures is indicative of a similar lack of knowledge of clay, or even the use of inferior and cheap clay. That a pottery of Sampson Smith's longstanding and financial success would make such mistakes is unthinkable. The potters never persisted with economically unviable figures and for Smith to have done so do with an entire line of products is not likely. Smith's business acumen and the track record of potteries to on-sell molds they no longer required provide the best clues to the creation of this group of figures. Because the recorded group of "Porridge" figures has a very definite "best by" nature (celebrating specific current events such as royal weddings, battles, and trials), it is very likely that Smith sold his no longer current molds to another pottery, possibly one that was newly established and cash-strapped. This pottery, lacking a sound working knowledge of ceramics, used the Smith molds (decades after the figures were originally created) to make their own figures. A flawed or incomplete knowledge of the glazing process, coupled with the possible use of cheap and inferior clays, gave rise to a small group of figures with pimpled and flecked glaze: the "Porridge School."

An average kiln of the late nineteenth century (when most Porridge figures were very likely made) could hold three to four hundred figures and, given the extreme rarity of the Porridge figures, they could represent the outcome of a single flawed firing rather than the sustained output of a specific school of potters. The potters could have rectified their mistakes and proceeded to produce a less distinctive and more commercially viable type of figure, or they simply went broke – either way, Porridge figures were to remain a "one off." The glaze imperfections evident in these figures are very distinctive and would most likely have resulted from one flawed batch of glaze. Common problems with glazing included running, streaking, straining, and failing to adhere to the surface of pottery, but the problems with Porridge glaze are unique and are almost impossible to replicate without a sound knowledge of chemistry, further supporting the "single kiln" theory.

Assigning a late date to these figures would support the Smith sell-off premise, and the figures themselves suggest late nineteenth century production. Their paucity of decoration is not only due to presumed "seconds" status, but is indicative of the reduced decoration typical on all figures produced during the late 1880s and 1890s. The lightness of these relatively large figures is surprising and might indicate slip casting. Like reduction in decorative detail, slip casting indicates a later date than the 1863-73 previously assigned to these unusual figures.

Group of a Scotsman and dog in the curious "Porridge School" style. As in this example, better "Porridge "figures have whiter bodies and fewer flecks and stains. The surface of this group is consistent with the Porridge glaze. 14.50". Circa 1865-1875. Value: $500-$1000. *Courtesy of Anita L. Grashof, Gallerie Ani'tiques.*

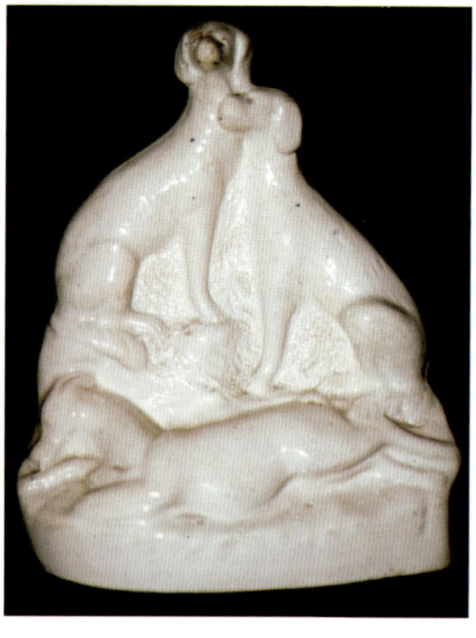

"Porridge" type group of hunting dogs with kill; although smaller in size than most Porridge figures, the gritty glaze and blue speckles characteristic of this type of ware are present. 6.75". Circa 1865-1875. Value: $100-$500. *Courtesy of Anita L. Grashof, Gallerie Ani'tiques.*

Chapter Four
Pre-Victorian Figures

The North Staffordshire region of England has produced ceramics since Roman times, with production increasing in the eighteenth century: tablewares, utilitarian articles, and decorative pieces including figures. The figures most commonly collected – Spaniels, portrait figures, and flatbacks – represent only a fraction of the potteries' output. These figures are from the nineteenth century, by which time Staffordshire had become a thriving industrial hub and answered not only local needs, but exported worldwide. Victorian Staffordshire figures cannot be considered in isolation, as they are the product of much trial, experimentation, artistry, and tradition; they must be seen as part of a long tradition of ceramics production. They represent cultural continuity as much as they represent the massive social fracturing that was a consequence of the Industrial Revolution. All art has a context and this is the context of the Victorian Staffordshire figure.

Until the mid-eighteenth century, the district remained an agrarian backwoods where families produced utilitarian ceramics in farmstead potworks – where kilns dotted country lanes and farmers milked cows beside their potting sheds – until the Industrial Revolution took effect and enterprising potters turned their talents toward commerce. The eighteenth century was a time of tremendous economic change in England that heralded increased merchandising and trade. Beginning around 1740, Staffordshire's figure-making industry began to emerge, and the potters' launched a long-standing practice of providing less affluent buyers with an affordable alternative to expensive porcelain.

The history of Staffordshire figures is complex, but there are a number of styles that characterize production periods and can provide a crude but useful overview of their development. Figures may be divided into four major periods: hand modeled figures of the middle part of the eighteenth century, mold produced underglaze and enamel painted figures of the late eighteenth and early nineteenth centuries, bocage and table-base figures of the 1820–30 period and, finally, Victorian figures.

Figures of the first category, now remarkably rare, expensive, and unlikely to be found outside museums, were salt glazed earthenware, creamware decorated with underglaze oxide colors or colored glazes, pearl glazed (with underglaze painted decoration), and overglaze painted. Among the figures produced from about 1740 are salt-glazed stoneware models of small animals, people, and intriguing *Bell Women* (figures of women designed in the shape of hand bells with spherical heads crudely decorated with clay eyes, noses, and ears). Salt-glazed *Pew Groups* of the same period are groupings of two or more persons seated on high-backed benches or settles. Although these were naïvely rendered, some variety was achieved and the potters cleverly provided insights into human nature by suggesting relationships among the persons presented. A devout nineteenth century collector may have coined the term *pew group* and, although the potters probably envisioned their characters seated in public ale or meeting houses, the "ecclesiastical" name has survived. *Arbor Groups* form another important sub-category of eighteenth century figures and take their name from characteristic arbor-like settings that frame fashionably dressed lovers or gossiping women. By the third quarter of the eighteenth century, arbor groups were slightly more sophisticated (Halfpenny, 30). Modeling and decorating evolved from primitive forms, and some of the more ornate arbor groups were encrusted with floral sprays and rosettes like those on ornamental tea wares, circa 1750-75 (Halfpenny, 30). An important fact to keep in mind is that every figure of this period was produced by hand-construction techniques and each is completely unique, unlike later figures that were produced by mold technology.

Artist's sketch of a bell woman that was produced in salt glazed stoneware during the mid-18th century. *Courtesy of Robert Buczynski.*

Artist's sketch of a mid-18th century pew group depicting two men and a woman holding a dog on her lap. *Courtesy of Robert Buczynski.*

Artist's sketch of a circa 1750-1770 arbor group. Set in arbor or garden pavilion-like settings, arbor groups were inclined toward the romantic and often depicted fashionably dressed lovers in various stages of courtship. *Courtesy of Robert Buczynski.*

Artist's sketch of an unusual mid-18th century pew group in which a Negro serves tea to a well-dressed lady who holds a dog in her lap while, beside her, a gentleman plays a violin. *Courtesy of Robert Buczynski.*

The salt glazes of these figures, readily identifiable by a slightly pitted surface texture, was widely used in Staffordshire's potteries from at least the late 1600s and is exhibited in works made by John Dwight during the 1690s. Although the development of the salt-glazing technique has been attributed to Dwight, folk tradition held that a farm laborer boiling pork for his supper was actually responsible for the discovery of the method. According to the tale, while boiling pork in strong brine the laborer let the liquid overflow down the sides of the earthenware vessel in which it was cooking. Once cooled the earthenware was discovered to have a hard bright glaze. Whether true or not, the story accurately describes a simplified version and outcome of the salt-glazing process!

As figure making was more widely embraced by the potters, innovative coloring and glazing techniques were introduced, quality increased, and subject matter widened. The introduction of cream-colored earthenwares and colored oxide decoration led to a new class of figures, the earliest of which were substantially less sophisticated than those that followed. Some salt-glaze subjects were repeated in creamware, and a range of huntsmen, gamekeepers, animals, lovers embracing, seated women with dogs in their laps, and women with panniered skirts joined ranks with high-based equestrians and uniformed military personnel.

Little is known about the early potters as most did not mark their wares and remain anonymous, but a few luminaries are recognized through marked figures, pottery site excavations, surviving documents, and tradition.

Two, John Astbury and Thomas Whieldon, are synonymous with eighteenth century figures. John Astbury was said to have gleaned his technical knowledge from the Elers brothers, seventeenth century pioneers of commercial pottery who came to England from Holland, presumably with the court of William of Orange. So jealous were the Elers of their trade secrets that they only took on employees who were said to be "idiots." According to popular legend (and supported by Shaw's 1829 *A History of the Staffordshire Potteries*), at the age of about twelve, Astbury posed as simple-minded, gained access to the brothers' secrets, and set up his own pottery. Such cunning and subterfuge at such an early age seems improbable, it is more likely that Astbury was taken on as a bonded apprentice and that he set up his own pottery only after the Elers went bankrupt and closed.

Small figures attributed to Astbury were crudely modeled, but they showed originality and imagination and included a range of animal and human subjects. Production combined press molding and hand modeling accentuated by slip-crafted details like eyes and buttons. Colored decoration was achieved through use of metal oxides that were applied in brown (manganese), green (copper), yellow (iron), and blue (cobalt) streaks. Color application was followed by liquid lead glazing and refiring. Because Astbury never used a signature or potter's mark no single piece can be categorically attributed to him, and "*Astbury-type*" serves as the generic term used to identify a class of mid-century figures. It is likely that some wares called *Astbury* were made by later family members and that several potters were involved in a twenty-year production period (Halfpenny, 19-20). Recorded "*Astbury*" figures include a modest subject range that reflects aspects of mid-eighteenth century life and were produced in several sub-groups, the best known (and reproduced) includes figures of tradesmen and musicians that were made from white Devon and Dorset clays mixed with flint and often set on red Staffordshire clay bases.

A "Dog of Fo," made in Staffordshire of saltglazed stoneware and picked out with brown slip, copied from a Chinese Blanc de Chine original with additional clay pieces to increase the dog's ferocious demeanor. 8". Circa 1730-35. Value: $8000-$10,000. *Courtesy of*

Thomas Whieldon (1719-95) is perhaps the most celebrated potter of his time, exercising decisive influences on the tastes and styles of his era. Whieldon started his career, after completing an apprenticeship to Astbury, in a comparatively humble manner. From his cottage in Fenton, he produced agate knife handles and snuffboxes that he hawked among the cutlers and silversmiths of Sheffield. Like Astbury, Whieldon followed the technology of his time and used press molds to make his figures. His contemporaries occasionally criticized him for being conservative, but he was at all times the consummate businessman and, during times of financial duress, he managed to run his pottery by paying employees in a form of barter. One record indicates that he gave an old coat to Josiah Spode as part-payment for his work. Of all Whieldon's work it would be fair to say that his "agate ware" pieces are the most striking. The solid "agate" was made by thinly rolling different colored clays, placing the slices on top of each other, and doubling them over and rolling them until the veined marbled effect desired by the potter was achieved. Whieldon's most famous agate ware figures are cats. His name is also associated with early cream-colored wares, black ware with gilt decoration similar to Jackfield pottery, colored oxide decoration, and mottled tortoiseshell glazes. Whieldon's most famous partner (1754-59) was the great, but at the time very young, Josiah Wedgwood. Other future ceramic luminaries including members of the Spode family and Aaron Wood were, at some time, in his employ. Undoubtedly, one of Whieldon's gifts was the ability to spot potential talent! On his death, Whieldon left a sizeable fortune, making him not only one of the most significant of the "peasant potters" of Staffordshire, but also one of the most wealthy. Excavations at his Fenton Vivian pottery site have revealed various figures and fragments that include soldiers, musicians, gamekeepers and other rural subjects. Other unmarked wares of similar style are classified as *Whieldon-type*.

With the second main phase of figure production, styles begin to change, and a move to exclusively mold produced figures took place. Importantly, the source of much of the potters' inspiration was also transformed: no longer did it draw exclusively from the potters' everyday world and society. Increasingly, themes were prompted by a wider range of sources including imported oriental ceramics (immensely popular among wealthier purchasers) and classically inspired sources (made popular in English and Continental porcelains). By the mid- to later eighteenth century, figures of Nikes, heroes of antiquity and Classical literature, portrait busts of English and Continental notables, Chinese gods, and peasant boys perched atop buffalos joined the previously exclusivist English population of Staffordshire figures. As the potters expanded their ranges, the practice of specializing in any one type of figure came to an end.

An exceptionally fine mounted officer with two holsters impressed "GR" and decorated in underglaze colors. 9.75". Circa 1760-70. *Courtesy of Jonathan Horne (Antiques) Ltd.*

The Wedgwood name has been associated with Staffordshire's potteries for many generations. Josiah (1730-95) is the most famous of the family and is universally lauded for his unqualified genius as an artist-technician. When Josiah was nine years old, his father died, and Josiah was apprenticed to his brother Thomas. The apprenticeship was cut short when the young boy contracted smallpox. This illness was to leave Josiah handicapped with a weak leg that eventually had to be amputated. After leaving his partnership with Whieldon, Josiah hired his cousin Thomas ("Useful") Wedgwood in 1764 and commenced production of a large range of domestic wares. Josiah's contributions to the development of the Staffordshire figure are not so much those of a "figural" nature, but are more in the area of technical innovation. As well as perfecting a number of beautiful glazes that were to become very influential in the development of future ceramic finishes, Josiah also perfected creamware bodies using a combination of pipe clay and flint, which he complemented with a silky lead glaze that led creamware production for many years in England and in Continental Europe. Josiah also improved the transfer process, then in its infancy, for decorating pottery. In 1765, he was appointed "Potter to the Queen" after making a creamware tea-service for Queen Charlotte – coining the title "Queens Ware" that is still in use today for cream-colored earthenware. After perfecting creamware, Josiah turned his attention to "Egyptian Black," or "Black Basalt Ware," made from Staffordshire clays, ground ironstone, and ochre of manganese that resulted in fine stoneware so hard that it could be finished on a lapidary wheel. Wedgwood's ultimate step into pottery immortality was, however, his creation of Jasperware. As well as being remarkably creative himself, Wedgwood employed a number of artists, including the talented but unruly John Voyez who, having crossed the strict moral and ethical bounds held dear by Josiah, ended up unemployed and imprisoned for three months. In addition to his technical and stylistic legacies, Josiah was also instrumental in introducing steam power to the Potteries and in the improvement of roads and canals. In short, Josiah Wedgwood was responsible for transforming the Staffordshire region from a rural, semi-homecraft pottery-making concern into what was to become a mass-production industry with export accounts throughout the world. While there is no documentary or other evidence to prove that Josiah produced the standard type of earthenware figure, marked Wedgwood figures were produced by other family members, very possibly by Ralph, eldest son of Josiah's cousin Thomas (Halfpenny, 169-171).

As previously mentioned, figures produced at the end of the eighteenth century marked a radical departure from those of the earlier period in style and subject matter. Among the superstars of the time were several Wood family potters: Ralph I (1715-72), John (1746-97), Ralph II (1748-95), Ralph III (1775-1801), John II (1778-1848),

Aaron (brother of Ralph I, 1717-85), and Enoch (Aaron's son, 1759-1840). This family established the pottery industry as it was to function for the next century and set new standards of excellence in figures; the naturalism of figures produced by Enoch having never been surpassed.

The Woods are renowned for superb modeling and for use of colored glazes and overglaze enamels, exemplified in *The Vicar and Moses*, *St. George and the Dragon*, shepherds, shepherdesses, classical representations, and various animal pieces. Figures marked "R. WOOD," "R. Wood," and "Ra. Wood," and some with impressed numbers or a rebus of a group of trees to signify the name "Wood," cover a production period beginning in 1789 and continuing for a brief, but glorious, twelve years.

The elder Ralph Wood, after finishing his apprenticeship with John Astbury, worked at Thomas Whieldon's pottery where he produced a range of stoneglazed and tortoise-shell glazed pottery, including figures. For a period, Ralph and his two sons, John and Ralph II, worked at the Wedgwood family's Big House Pottery as block mold cutters before starting their own pottery. By 1777, ledgers reveal that the Woods were already producing a substantial range of immensely successful Toby jugs and pottery figures including Faith, Hope, Charity, Apollo, Venus, shepherds, sailors, gardeners, lost sheep, stags, and a remarkable range of others. These figures were decorated in colored glazes similar to those used by Whieldon and are easily recognized by their large hands and the strange and almost goiterous appearance of their eyes.

In 1784, Enoch Wood joined the pottery, and figures became available in both colored glaze and enameled options. The enameled figure was a remarkable and expensive innovation that imitated its finely colored porcelain competitors and represented a major breakthrough in pottery technology. These figures are collectively described as "Pearlware" due to the satiny surface of their glazes in which the liquid glaze was enhanced by a small amount of cobalt to achieve a pearly, bluish finish. Pearlware figures were made from white clays, fired to biscuit stage, then painted or sponged with a limited range of colors (yellow, green, brown, purple, blue, and black), glazed, and refired.

Enoch, referred to as "The Father of the Potteries," is acknowledged as the most talented modeler of all times. Enoch started his lengthy career in The Potteries as an apprentice to Humphrey Palmer before commencing work with his cousins and distinguishing himself with his very attractive, well modeled, and well colored figures. He later set up a short-term partnership with James Caldwell with whom he produced some remarkably monumental and handsome figures. In time, he opened a pottery with his sons. As well as a skilled artist and humanitarian attempting to improve the working conditions of the employees of the potteries, Enoch was also a historian. He established a remarkable collection of works that recorded the history of the Staffordshire region and its pottery. He also left time capsules of his own factory's work under numerous sites in Staffordshire.

Pre-Victorian colored glaze king and queen. These figures would have originally been part of a much larger figure and flanked a "faux" clock. Left-hand figure 5.50", right-hand figure 5.75". Circa 1780. Value pair as shown: $100-$500; undamaged complete figures $500-$1000.

Colored glaze money box in the form of a house. Originally the house would have been flanked by figures of a man and a woman. 5.25." Circa 1780. Value as shown: $100-$500; undamaged $500-$1000.

Other firms copied Enoch Wood's figure making style, notably Lakin and Poole, and James Neale and Co. Other important potters of the era included Edward Warburton (noted for using a green glaze on a creamware body), William Greatbatch (figures similar to the Wood family, circa 1775 to 1780), and Samuel Bourne. Along with various Staffordshire potters, the Leeds Pottery in Yorkshire produced noteworthy pearlware figures with a distinctive style of modeling and emphasis on classical and allegorical subjects.

Simultaneous with Enoch Wood's enameled figures were those that are broadly known as *Pratt Wares* today. This convenient label, a collectors' term, is not supported by documentary or archaeological evidence that the Pratt family produced any figures, and it encompasses a wide body of underglaze decorated earthenwares, made by various potters, between 1780 and 1840. Although production of this class of pottery was concentrated on plaques, jugs and other utilitarian wares, some figures were produced including soldiers, sailors, politicians, and royalty, as well as allegorical pieces, watch-stands, moneyboxes, and purely decorative subjects. The body of these figures is usually white or pale cream, with decoration in a limited range of blue, green, yellow, orange, brown, and black oxide colors, restricted by their ability to fuse with the glaze. The quality of the figures varies from tiny (and decidedly haphazard) to well executed figures reminiscent of those made by the Woods.

The remarkable and innovative early Staffordshire figures are most frequently encountered in museums and specialty shops or at up-market antiques shows, but they *do* appear from time to time in the general marketplace and occasionally turn up on Internet auctions. While values are high, these pieces are more than a sound monetary investment – they possess a unique aesthetic and represent an era of British ceramics history that set the stage for a figure-making industry that reached the pinnacle of commercial success during the Victorian Era and has yet to be surpassed.

Pair of pearlware figures of seated children with cornucopias. Left-hand figure 4", right-hand figure 3.75". Circa 1790. Value: $1000+.

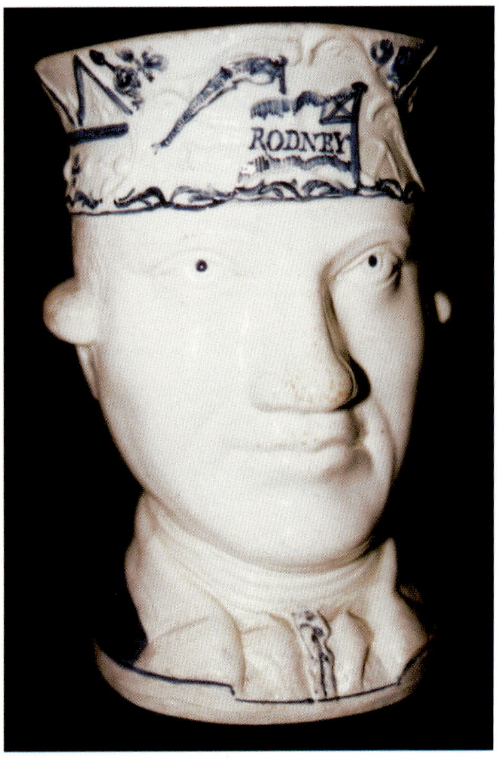

Front and aide views of a creamware character jug portraying George Brydges Rodney, 1st Baron (1719-92); English naval officer. 8.50". Late 18th century. Value: $500-$1000. Courtesy of *Jane McClafferty Antiques.*

Pearlware figures of Juno with a peacock and Jupiter with thunderbolts and an eagle. Juno 6", Jupiter 6.5". Circa 1800. Value: Pair $1000+.

Bust of the Duke of York on a waisted socle displaying the initials "GR" (George III) and a royal crest. 6". Circa 1805. Value: $1000+.

Bust of Lord Nelson on a waisted socle displaying the initials "GR" (for the reigning monarch of the time, George III) and a royal crest. 6". Circa 1805. Value: $1000+.

Reverse of the bust of Nelson showing the impressed title "NELSON."

Reverse of the York bust showing the impressed title "DUKE OF YORK."

Pearlware figure of Dianna the Huntress by Enoch Wood. 12". Circa 1800. Value: $1000+.

Pearlware Cupid and Psyche by Enoch Wood. 4.50". Circa 1800. Value: $500-$1000.

"Widow & Orphans," titled pearlware figure of widow and children gathering wood. 10.75". Circa 1800. Value: $1000+.

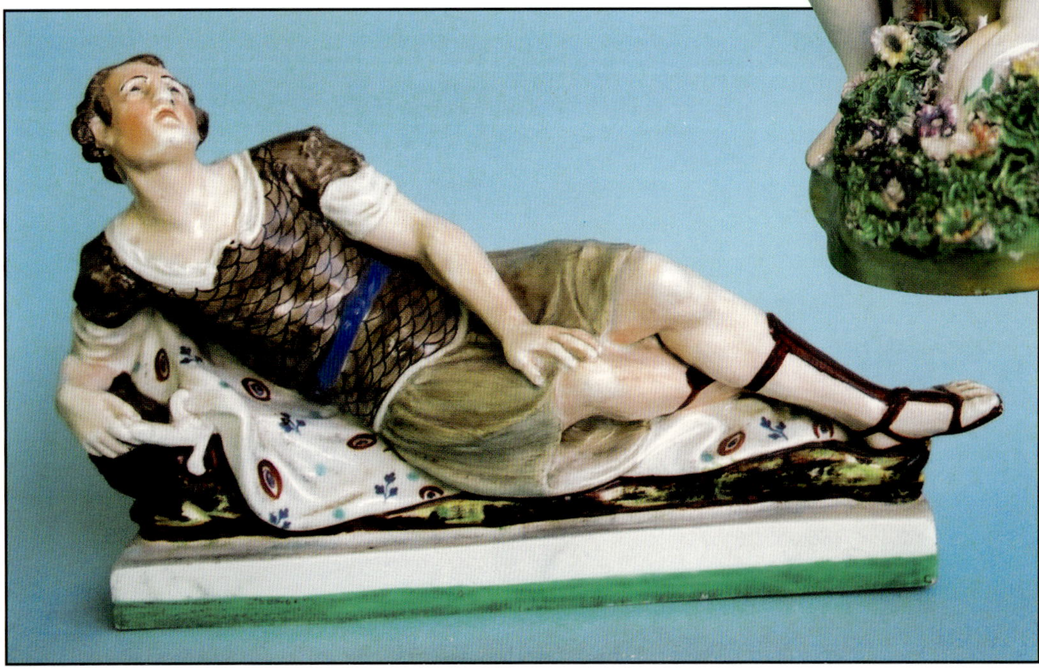

Rare Wood and Caldwell pearlware figure of Marc Anthony on square base. This figure displays the fine modeling characteristic of Enoch Wood's work. 12.50" (length), 7" (height). Circa 1800. Value: $1000+.

Rare marked example by Ralph Wedgwood depicting Apollo and displaying the characteristic muted colored enamels used by the potter. 7.75". Circa 1790. Value: $500-$1000.

Reverse of the figure of Apollo displaying Ralph Wedgwood's mark.

Underglaze figure of a child in a crib. These figures were popular as gifts for newborns and in earlier examples sometime bore the name and date of birth of the recipient. 4.75" (length), 2" (height). Circa 1800. Value: $100-$500 (as shown), $500-$1000 (undamaged).

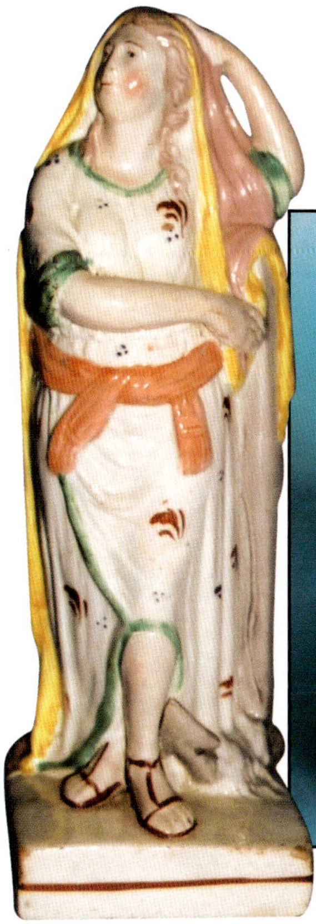

Pearlware square based figure of Hope with symbolic anchor. 8.75". Circa 1800. Value: $500-$1000.

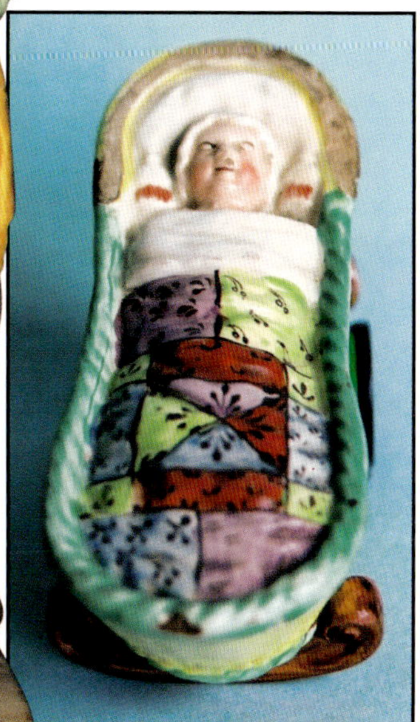

Underglaze figure of a baby in a rocking cradle. Originally this figure would have had a roof on the cradle. 5" length, 2" height. Circa 1800. Value: $100-$500 (as shown), $500-$1000 (undamaged)

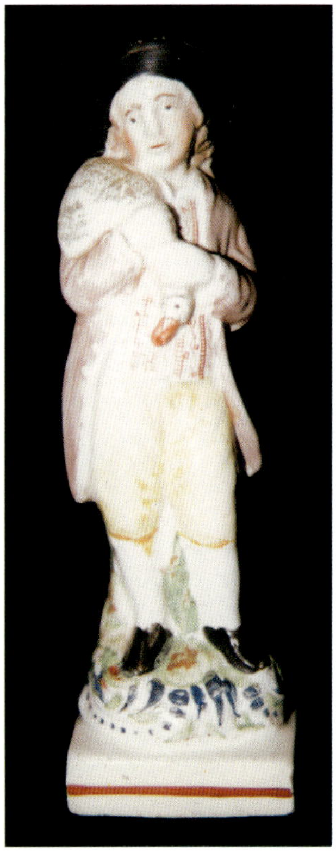

Young man holding a goose and set on a square, red-lined base. 5.50". Early 19th century. Value: $500-$1000. *Courtesy of Jane McClafferty Antiques.*

Fish and Fowl. A very fine Staffordshire bird model decorated in underglaze colors at the left; 3.75", circa 1770. Value: $2500-$3000. A Staffordshire toy basket containing a large fish decorated in underglaze colors at the right; 2.75", circa 1770. Value: $3800-$4000. *Courtesy of Jonathan Horne (Antiques) Ltd.*

Recumbent creamware sheep, sponge-decorated under the glaze. 5.50". Late 18th century. Value: $1000+. *Courtesy of Zane Moss Antiques.*

Small creamware dog made around 1770-1780. 2.75" (height). Value: $1000+. *Courtesy of Jane McClafferty Antiques.*

Pearlware figure of a performing lion decorated in underglaze colors intended, as Jonathan Horne notes, to let the lion seem friendly. Possibly made in Staffordshire and possibly inspired by "The Menagerie of Mr. Clark" (advertised in 1788 at the Exeter Exchange with emphasis on a lion and lioness, secured in dens so that ladies and gentlemen might view them in safety). 7". Circa 1800. Value: $5000-$6000. *Courtesy of Jonathan Horne (Antiques) Ltd.*

This early pearlware group of a jockey mounted on a stallion is decorated in Pratt-type colors. The group is marked with the initials "HE" on the base. The rider is somewhat unconventional as he wears a jockey's costume but has the saddle and hunting horn of a hunt-servant. Later jockey figures were abundant, some of which were portraits of jockey Fred Archer (see Chapter Eighteen). The jockey illustrated here: circa 1820-40. Value: $1000+. *Courtesy of Jonathan Horne (Antiques) Ltd.*

Miniature group of a child seated in a chair and holding a cat. 3". Late 18th or early 19th century. Value: $500-$1000. *Courtesy of Jane McClafferty Antiques.*

Triple spill vase pastoral group with overglaze enamel decoration. 11". 1810-1820. Value: $1000+. *Courtesy of Jane McClafferty Antiques.*

Early Red Riding Hood group in which the wolf is portrayed with a decidedly benign appearance. Red Riding hood was a popular subject in fairy tale form and on the Victorian stage, and a wide range of later, variant, models were produced. This group was press molded and decorated in overglaze enamels; the open bottom reveals a smooth interior that does not conform to the contours of the exterior. 8". Early 19th century. Value: $500-$1000.

Cow creamers, some with milkmaids, were popular through the late 18th and 19th centuries and form their own category of collecting. This example (one of a pair) was decorated with sponged "Pratt-type" underglaze colors. 5.50". Late 18th or early 19th century. Value for the pair: $1000+. *Courtesy of Zane Moss Antiques.*

Pearlware figure on a square base from a set representing the seasons. This young man represents "Autumn." 6.75". Circa 1810. Value: $500-$1000.

Pearlware figure of a young woman representing "Winter" set on square base. 6.75". Circa 1810. Value: $500-$1000.

Beautifully decorated in "Pratt-type" underglaze colors, this performing lion was most likely made in Staffordshire during the early 19th century. 7.50". Value: $3000-$4000. *Courtesy of Jonathan Horne (Antiques) Ltd.*

A previously unrecorded, to the authors' knowledge, bust of a gentleman; possibly the Duke of Wellington, serving the purpose of a window stop. Window stops are now very rare as they were the luxury items of their time. Window glazing was not commonplace during the early 19th century, and large sheets of glass were both difficult to make and very expensive. The imposition of the "Window Tax" in 1696 by the British government (not repealed until 1851) exacerbated the situation by further increasing the cost of window glass and, as a result, few homes could afford to have all their windows glazed. The tax was calculated by the number of windows that tax collectors saw on the outside of a home and was so prohibitive that it forced many families to either brick-up or board-over their windows. To possess an article like this window stop (originally one of a pair) was indeed an indication of prosperity. 3.75" (height), 2.75" x 2.25" (base). Circa 1825. Value: $100-$500. *Courtesy of Golden Age Antiques.*

Rare and extraordinary group of the ancient Greek goddess Athena; rich with symbolism including an owl to represent wisdom. This group is not previously recorded to the authors' knowledge. Approximately 12". Circa 1790-1800. Value: $1000+. *Reproduction with permission of the W. R. Johnston Trust.*

Chapter Five
Bocage and Table Base Figures

A vigorous expression of a genuine folk art saw its genesis during the early years of the nineteenth century when Staffordshire's potters drew away from the Classicism, gentilities, and foreign influences of the late eighteenth century and began to focus on their immediate world for inspiration. Their figures became more uniquely English, bridged the gap between eighteenth and nineteenth century figures, and served as models for the Victorian figures that would follow. In the past, there has been a tendency among some collectors and critics of Staffordshire pottery to dismiss the figures of this period as naïve and inferior. Their modeling, however, reflects a remarkable ability to manipulate the medium of pottery to achieve complex results hitherto unattained and duly represents the third major stylistic period of the Staffordshire figure. These figures not only display the technical mastery of the potter over his medium, but also demonstrate a startling creativity in the composition and modeling of individual figures and groups – something not present in the brilliant, but static figures of the previous century. The archetypically English subject matter of early nineteenth century figures and groups made them new and anarchic in their own subtle manner. In addition, their composition made them a dramatic departure from earlier groups. No longer isolated figures, or simple groups of figures, these figures were contained in their own microenvironments: trees, animals, even buildings in an attempt to render in clay the world of the viewer. There was a new camaraderie between the figure and its early nineteenth century audience – we know you; we are the stuff from which you are made. If modern viewers try, and they will not have to try very hard, they will find themselves identifying with the warmth, humor, and integrity of these figures.

The "bocage" type of Staffordshire figure drew its initial inspiration from eighteenth century British and Continental porcelain makers who incorporated leafy tree forms encrusted with small florets into their figure designs. These "tree" forms, known as bocage (from the French meaning *woodland*), were not purely ornamental. They also served the functional purpose of providing a measure of movement against warping or melting in the kiln as well as support against collapse during the firing process (Halfpenny, 215). Important factories like Chelsea, Bow, and Derby made extensive use of bocage in their delicate porcelain figures, but these figures were expensive and were intended for an up-market clientele. England's working and middle classes aspired to the ornamental embellishments of the upper classes and sought to achieve a sense of relative prosperity and luxury in their homes. Staffordshire's potters, keen businessmen that they were, began imitating costly porcelain styles in the less expensive medium of earthenware during the last half of the eighteenth century. With an eye on upper class interest in bocage figures and middle class yearnings, the potters turned their skills toward manufacture of figures that did not merely mimic porcelain bocages but, rather, translated them into a new medium that was admittedly less refined but no less exceptional.

Earthenware figures of this class required numerous mold parts and complicated assemblies. They were more expensive and time-intensive to produce and, therefore, more costly to purchase than other figure types; but production time and expense notwithstanding, earthenware bocage figures were infinitely more affordable than porcelain figures of similar design. Interestingly, the earthenware medium was more stable than porcelain, and earthenware bocage, not needed to protect or support the central figures, was purely aesthetic.

Typically, a tree-like form set behind a central figural motif distinguishes bocage figures. The "tree" was enhanced by abundant foliage that was inset with multicolored florets. Occasionally, bocage was applied at the sides of figures, without the central tree form, to create an alternative effect. While most bocage figures lack the refined elegance of their porcelain counterparts, they are nevertheless a cut above the average chimney ornament and possess a naïve charm and colorful brightness. The variety of leaf styles suggests that different potters produced variations on the bocage theme: palm frond, oak leaf, small and large leaf, pine cone, curly leaf, multileaf, and others (Halfpenny, 246, 252, 253-256). As a decorative style, bocage was introduced to earthenware between 1810 and 1820 (Halfpenny, 219). The modelers drew upon established subjects for their bocage figures: religious personalities and classical characters, shepherds, gardeners, sportsmen, archers, musicians, and country themes (Halfpenny, 215). Small animals, especially dogs, sheep, and charming recumbent deer, were all time-honored subjects that were given new interest and form with the addition of bocage.

Like other figure types, bocage groups reflected the potters' astuteness in satisfying middle market interests and consumer demand. The popularity of traveling menageries gave rise to bocage figures in which monkeys and bears danced to hurdy-gurdies, and clever anecdotal pieces with political and satirical intent poked fun at the New Marriage Act of 1823 and the practice of tithing. Along with classically inspired figures, nattily dressed "Dandies," quaint bird nesting pairs, and hunters shared the leafy spotlight with more serious figures of Christ, the Apostles, the Holy Family in flight to and from Egypt, Elijah, and the Widow of Zarephath.

One particularly striking religious bocage group is a crucifixion scene with crescent-shaped bocage above and to the sides of the *patibulum* or horizontal bar of the cross. The slumped position of Christ's head suggests the moment of death immediately following his last words, "Father, into your hands I commend my spirit." In this wonderfully balanced and expressive group, a standing man and a kneeling woman (possibly St. John and the Virgin Mary) are placed at each side of the cross with their arms upraised to the crucified Christ. In keeping with local focus on Bible reading, both the Old and New Testaments were well represented in bocage figures, some of which were based on the newly available printed illustrations that cottage dwellers hung on the walls of their homes.

Of the numerous potters working in Staffordshire during the pre-Victorian nineteenth century, the name most closely associated with the production of bocage figures is John Walton. Details about Walton's life are sketchy. He was possibly born in 1780 to Richard and Sarah Walton. The date at which he commenced his career as a potter is also uncertain; it is known, however, that he had an earthenware factory at Hadderage and a color works at Burslem. While many of his contemporaries went bankrupt in the period 1815-1835, Walton apparently prospered: a tribute no doubt to the range of tastes to which he catered with the subject matter of his figures. Listed in contemporary trade directories from 1818, Walton "signed" many of his bocage figures on the back with his name in indented capitals inside a raised scroll. Some signed Walton figures have curious empty panels in the base fronts that look as if they were prepared for titles that were never included. The number and variety of signed Walton figures, produced over a period of about twenty-five years, resulted in use of the potter's name in identifying other bocage figures and makers as "Walton School."

One Walton contemporary and fellow bocage figure maker was Ralph Salt, who also "signed" some of his figures with his name in indented capitals. Ralph Salt began his career as a lusterer and enameller, before he turned to figure making and the Walton style. Salt's figures were not as sophisticated as Walton's and many of his titles were misspelled (for example, "Archar," "Shepherdiss," and "Gardners"). Noteworthy among his bocage figures and groups are a set of the elements (earth, air, fire, and water), and his introduction of luster decoration to bocage groups. Because most Staffordshire figures were unmarked by their makers, it is impossible to know how many potters produced bocage pieces. However, a few signed figures, along with documentary and archaeological evidence, identify Samuel Hall (a neighbor of Ralph Salt), Charles Tittensor (noteworthy for his use of very strong and vibrant colors and a characteristic swirling "scored" texture on the surfaces of his figures' bases), John Dale, Edge & Grocott, and the great Enoch Wood. When excavations beneath the pavement at Burslem Old Town Hall began in 1938, figures and fragments from Wood's potworks revealed four distinct bocage forms, including the acorn and oak leaf of which only one other example is known in a figure titled "Jesus Praying" (Halfpenny, 246). Another unique bocage style found at the Burslem site is a palm or fern frond, which matches paired figures of Andromache and Hygeia that have been attributed to Enoch Wood (Halfpenny, 249).

Excavations at a site in Tunstall, where figure makers George Hood, Samuel Grocott, and Michael Tunnicliff worked, have also revealed bocage fragments. Some are similar to Walton's and may have been the work of his son-in-law and successor, George Hood (Halfpenny, 222). Other excavated material suggests that Thomas Dudson may have produced bocage figures, but bocage fragments found, unique in form and color, have not yet been linked to any complete figures (Halfpenny, 252).

Bocage figures produced from 1810-30 were made of pearl glazed earthenware with overglaze enamel decoration. The leafy bocage elements were always produced in separate front and back pieces that were separately molded and applied, as were the florets. Typical bocage bases were generally ornate and well colored. Many early figures in this class were decorated with a "grained" paint effect (achieved through the application of heavy opaque enamels with a stiff brush). Many bocage bases were oval in form and some were decorated with bits of slip-crafted shrubbery. The more ornate were set on footed table bases or on scalloped bases that contain "C" and "S" scrolls (sometimes colored in blue). Others bases were produced with a "cinctured waist" shape.

Because bocage figures were not produced in the enormous quantities that later Victorian Era flatbacks were, they are relatively rare and are often more highly valued. Prices start at around $400 and can rise into the thousands (depending on rarity, condition, and popularity). When bocage figures began to generate increased collector interest during the last half of the twentieth century, reproductions began to enter the marketplace. Collectors should be aware that Walton's figures have been widely reproduced. Red flags include pale coloration, florets molded into the bocage (not individually molded and applied), and white earthenware bodies (that do not correspond to the bluish pearl glaze used on authentic bocage figures). Newer bocage figures are decorated under the glaze rather than with overglaze enamels. In addition, many authentic bocage figures have open bottoms that reveal how clay was pressed into the mold and smoothed resulting in relatively smooth interiors that do not reflect exterior contours (a sign of the press molding process used by the bocage figure potters). Prospective buyers should also know that new bocage figures are often titled or signed in sans serif lettering, unlike figures made during the canonical production period when serifs were used. Heavy artificially-induced crazing and, sometimes, color-enhanced glazes are used in some bocage figure reproductions – clear signs of something "not right."

The William Kent Company made many bocage figures and groups during the twentieth century. These were made from old molds and have some degree of credibility, but they were not created with the same attention to detail as the originals. Fortunately for collectors, the Kent Company issued catalogs that illustrate its bocage figures and provide an excellent source for comparison and identification. For example, *Tenderness* appears as number 506 in the catalogs of 1955 and 1960, and *Girl with Lamb* is illustrated as number 456. Unfortunately, the Kent Company ceased operation in 1962 and Kent molds have been subsequently leased and sold to other firms that continue to produce "modern Staffordshire." These include "Walton" bocage figures, along with models produced with an earlier Enoch Wood mark.

More "muscular" in subject matter and style, and more crudely modeled are table base figures and groups mounted on flat platforms that resemble tables with four or six squat legs and bracket-type feet; hence their name. While most Staffordshire figures are set on bases of one sort or another, table bases are unique. They are literally square, rectangular, oval, or round pottery "platforms" on which the drama of the piece is "enacted." In short, there is nothing quite like them in Staffordshire's entire figure making history. Their presence is uncompromising and earthy, at times bold and imposing, and their subject matter ranges from the spectacularly grisly to the humorous and to the devout. There are few pleasantly bucolic pastoral themes among the table base groups (other than groups like *The Reading Maid* and *Court Ship*). In most table base figures, the realities of early nineteenth century life are superbly represented with a bravado that is rarely found in other figure classes.

Like other figures and groups of their time, table base pieces were made of pearl glazed earthenware and were decorated with overglaze enamels. Their construction required multiple molds and intricate assemblies; some included bocage. While single figures are recorded (usually paired), most table base figures are groups of two or more persons and often include buildings or animals. Many are vignettes, like "slices of life," that give the impression of a stage on which the action has been momentarily stopped. Several table base groups are titled. Some titles appear in scalloped "tabs" that project below the bottom of a base and are centered between two front legs. More often, titles were set within elliptical panels or cartouches above relief-molded swags. Often the title is divided between two panels as in the case of the *Grecian . Daughter*, *Bull Baiting . Now Captin Lad*, and the Abraham and Isaac group titled *Abraham . Stop*.

Dating approximately to the late 1820s and early 1830s, table base subjects recorded the issues and events of their time in an unprecedented style. The well-known bull-baiting group titled *Bull Beating. Now . Captin Lad* adopted the theme of earlier groups but with a raw sensory approach that was much less vigorous in its predecessors and, indeed, renders earlier groups tame, if not facile, by comparison. In the table base group, a large bull has tossed a dog up onto its back and lowers its head as it prepares to gore another. A man stands to the left with arms uplifted and shouts to the onlookers, perhaps with the words inscribed in the title: "Now Captin Lad." This group was produced at a time when public outcry against the savagery of bull baiting had begun to be heard. An article in the November 23, 1833 edition of *The Staffordshire Advertiser* recorded a particularly brutal bull-baiting at Rowley Regis Wake in which a two year old bull was *"...worried for hours, the whole of his head and face being too mangled and covered with blood, in a manner too shocking to describe"* (Turner 130-131). Similarly horrific and recorded in a table base group was the death of Lieutenant Hector Monroe who was savagely killed by a tiger on December 2, 1792 near Calcutta.

Table base "Bull Beating" [sic] group in the manner traditionally attributed to Obadiah Sherratt. 7" (length), 6" (height). Circa 1820. Value: $1000+.

Monroe was attacked and dragged by the head as reported in the *Gentleman's Magazine*. Amazingly, Monroe survived despite severe injuries to his head and body and crawled back to camp where he died of his wounds (Turner, 131). A table base group of the incident depicts the doomed Lieutenant lying beneath a huge tiger whose blazing eyes and savage jaws loom just above Monroe's head. The horror of the moment is cleverly reconstructed in Monroe's helpless position, underscored by his left leg hanging over the front of the base. This group, and groups representing, albeit less luridly, the Corder/Marten murder at the Red Barn (illustrated in Introduction and discussed in Chapter Fifteen) take on a sensational Madame Tussaud's Chamber of Horrors aspect. Like the famous waxworks, they provide visual documentation of historical events.

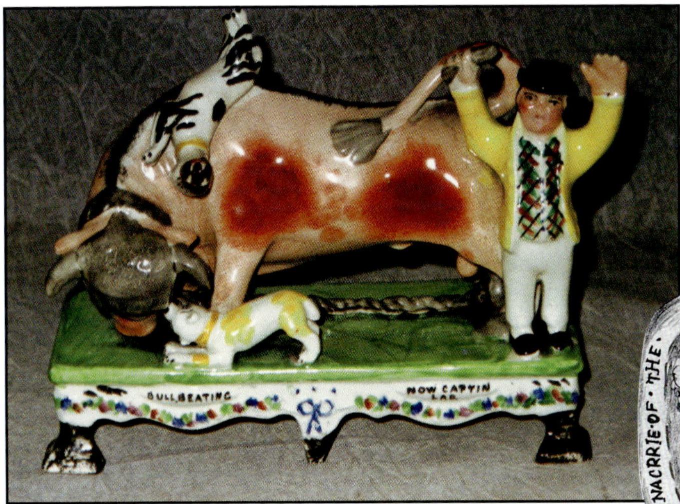

Another version of the table base bull baiting group with the title, "BULLBEATING . NOW CAPTIN LAD" [sic] in capitals within elliptical panels above relief molded swags on each side of the table base. This is a larger and later rendering of the group of the same title that was produced around 1820 (see previous illustration and note the differences in painted decoration). 9.75". Value: $1000+. *Courtesy of Madelena Antiques.*

Two of the most extraordinary table base groups represent the entrances to Polito and Wombwell's menageries (the former of which served as the model for the latter). Produced in several variants (the most noteworthy being a little over a foot tall), these represent two of the nineteenth century's most popular traveling menageries. The vibrant overglaze colors highlight elaborate depictions of circus animals and performers, and, as flamboyant as the group itself, the Polito group is titled: *"Politos Menagerie of the Wonderfull Birds and Beasts from Most Parts of the World, Lion and Giraffe"* [sic]. The group stands on a six-footed table base and contains several people (who might be barkers and sideshow performers), monkeys, a lion and a tiger, and an elephant (complete with a howdah on its back) that crowns the group in the upper center. There is an exciting busy-ness about the group that suggests the raucous delights of the traveling show. Historically, Mr. S. Polito toured a menagerie through England for several years before purchasing the Exeter Exchange Menagerie around 1810. Polito died in 1814, but his menagerie continued to tour until it was lost with its transport ship while crossing the Irish Sea in 1836. George Wombwell's menagerie began touring around 1807; when Wombwell died in 1850, three menageries belonging to family members toured until 1884. These elaborate table base groups were produced in a range of models and sizes and have been widely reproduced. Today, current market guides suggest values of more than $30,000 for choice authentic pieces.

Artist's sketch of a Polito's Menagerie group. Various Polito's and Wombwell's Menagerie groups were produced throughout the 19th century. These groups have been widely reproduced in recent years; originals are rarely seen outside museums and private collections and are valued in the area of $35,000. *Courtesy of Robert Buczynski.*

In other table base groups, domestic life was lampooned in a hearty, humorous style. In a group titled *Ale Bench*, a man and woman are set on the floor between two empty chairs and with crenellated castle towers behind (a curious inclusion in several table base groups). The man, on his knees, suffers his wife's anger as her fingers hold his nose in a viselike grip. A companion piece, *Tee Total* (with the same background and base), offers a scene of household harmony in which husband and wife share a pot of tea. The husband, however, is depicted with one hand to his head in a gesture that suggests the after effects of his alehouse experience. The humor in each is obvious and, no doubt, the underlying issue of male drunkenness and female attempts to curtail it was not lost upon the buying public. Interestingly, the subject in general and the "Tee Total" phrase in particular may have been a response to Fr. Theobald Mathew's abstinence campaign during which the "Tee Total" term was coined. The potters' newly assumed responsibility as social commentators is again seen in their "investigation" of the issue of a woman's role in the home and in the workplace, which was much debated during the nineteenth century as more women secured employment outside of their homes and women's rights activists began to emerge. A related and amusing table base group titled *Who Shall Wear the Breeches . Conquer and Die* depicts a man and his wife standing in front of their fireplace and tugging at a pair of trousers.

Putto, or cherub, with bocage by John Walton. 5.25". Circa 1820. Value: $500-$1000.

Reverse of the Walton putto showing the potter's characteristic impressed "WALTON" mark surrounded by a scroll.

Grotesque footed table base figure of a gesticulating putto and cornucopia. 10". Circa 1820. Value: $500-$1000.

Detail of a grotesque footed table base figure displaying a distinctly lion-like paw.

Unlike our predominantly secular society, religion was not only a topic of interest in nineteenth century Staffordshire, but a fact of life and, along with other religious figures, a christening group (sometimes titled *Baptism of Mary*), Abraham about to Sacrifice his son Isaac, Samuel anointing David, and St. Peter healing the lame man were produced with table bases. *Christ's Agony* (also titled *Father Let This Cup Pass*) is a moving depiction of Christ in Gethsemane kneeling in prayer on a coffin-like structure as an angel with a cup in its hand rests on a brick pillar. Set in almost jarring juxtaposition to the "Chamber of Horrors" and witty groups, these verify the mixed preoccupations of early nineteenth century British citizens.

Other table base groups include *The Roran Lion* and a rather graphic *Grecian and Daughter*. There is also a bust of Maria Foot (very close in modeling to one attributed to Enoch Wood but with the addition of a four-footed table base) and some classical figures, which fail in their lack of delicacy and gracefulness (Turner 132-133). These figures were beckoning to a new age of progress and, indeed ruthlessness, and managed to personify the transition to Victoria's empire. They began with a table base figure produced on the death of the French opera singer Maria Malibran in 1836 that was miraculously renamed and reissued as a portrait of the young queen when Victoria acceded to the throne in 1837. The unknown potter was ahead of his time, not in his use of colors, or the table base, but in his choice of subject matter: the here and now, and how Staffordshire's potters learned to adapt their art in answer the immediacy of historical events.

Bocage figure of titled "GIRL . AND . A . LAMB" "Girl and Lamb" by John Hall. 5.5". Circa 1820. Value: $500-$1000.

"GARDNERS" [sic] bocage figure by Ralph Salt. 5.50". Circa 1820. Value: $500-$1000.

Reverse of the Hall figure "GIRL . AND . A . LAMB" "Girl and Lamb" showing the impressed mark "HALL."

Reverse of the Salt "GARDNERS" showing the impressed mark "SALT."

The question of who created the table base figures and groups is one that has generated much debate in recent years. Table base models were produced in relatively small numbers, and among those examples that still exist, the same subjects are treated in similar forms. One means of differentiating among the various bases is the style of the legs or feet. Some are pearl beaded, some are grotesque footed (like a deformed claw), and others are ridge footed. Similarities in other molded details are equally difficult to analyze (Halfpenny, 273) and have led to conjecture as to whether these stylistic differences suggest a single table base maker who varied his models or several makers who adopted the table base style and added their own touches. There is little refinement in the table base figures and groups, and many of their titles are misspelled, suggesting at least partial illiteracy on the part of the potter or decorator. For some time, attribution to Obadiah Sherratt was generally accepted as fact. However, attribution based on a presumably long-standing tradition has not been traced further back than 1920 when G. Wooliscroft Rhead, in his book *The Earthenware Collector*, credited Sherratt with producing a bull-baiting group. In his 1929 *Staffordshire Pottery Figures*, Herbert Read noted similar attribution to Sherratt with reference to Rhead's earlier book. More specifically, Reginald Haggar states, in his 1955 book (*Staffordshire Chimney Ornaments*), that he believes the table base groups may have been the work of one potter, who, Haggar suggests, was Obadiah Sherratt (Haggar, 92). These figures and their creators are, essentially, enigmas. They are part of a pottery sub-culture produced in the back streets of Staffordshire by small potbanks, and Sherratt's history remains no less shadowy than the table base figures themselves.

Little is known about Sherratt's early life, and the only positively attributable items are two pearl glazed earthenware frog mugs that bear his impressed first initial and surname (Halfpenny 269). There are no records of his birth or baptism in extant parish records. It *is* known that he married Ann Davenport in 1797 and that they had several children before Ann's death in 1810. Within a few months, Sherratt remarried, this time to a widow named Martha Austin who worked with him in his pottery. Together they had four children. One, a son named Hamlet, died in infancy. A later son, who was christened in 1814, was given the same name. The second Hamlet died in 1863 (Turner, 129).

Sherratt may have entered the pottery trade as a worker in one of Staffordshire's potteries. He is not listed in any of the trade directories before 1822-23 when Allbut's *Newcastle and Pottery General and Commercial Directory* lists him as a toy and figure maker in Hot Lane (Halfpenny, 263, 269). Within ten years, Sherratt had moved his potworks to Waterloo Road, which was listed in 1856 as occupied by Hamlet Sheratt and advertised for sale in 1859 (Halfpenny, 269). Exactly what Sherratt produced and how much of it remains unknown, but legends abound. One, recorded by Wooliscroft Rhead, is that Sherratt produced cow creamers and formed the udders from the same mold he used for the nose on a depiction of Wellington (Halfpenny, 269).

A rare pearlware group satirizing the once controversial "New Marriage Act" of 1823 that reads "THE . NEW . MARRIAGE . ACT ." "JOHN FRILL . AND ANN BOKE . AGED 21 THAT . IS . RIGHT . SAYS . THE . PARSON . AMEN . SAYS . THE. CLERK." In an attempt to reduce elopements and secret marriages, the act found any clergyman who performed a marriage for which the banns had not been read to be guilty of a felony, although the marriage was considered legally valid. 7". Circa 1825. Value: $1000+.

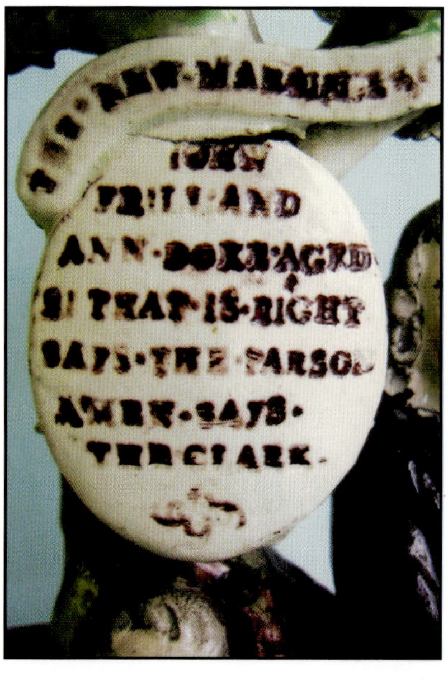

Detail of the text of "The New Marriage Act".

Rare pair of pearlware figures of the "Traveling Hairdresser" and the "Traveling Shoe Seller" taken from 18th century Derby originals. Both of these figures originally had bocages, but due to the particularly brittle nature of the body of the pottery all that now remains are stumps of the original trees. Hairdresser 6.50", Shoe Seller 6.75". Circa 1820. Value for each (as shown or undamaged): $1000+.

Pearlware musicians and squirrel with a circular bocage and square base. 8.50". Circa 1820. Value: $1000+.

"Elijah and the Ravens" featuring an unusual circular bocage and multi-tiered square base – repairs to the figure's hands. This figure was very popular during the late 18th and early 19th centuries and was paired with a figure of the Widow of Zarephath (see Chapter Thirteen). 10". Circa 1820. Value: $1000+.

Turner notes that when Sherratt married Ann Davenport, both he and his new wife signed their names with a cross, suggesting that they were illiterate. The same was true of his marriage to Martha Austin. It is odd that someone who could not write would establish his own business, but if Sherratt was indeed illiterate, or even partially so, the numerous misspelled titles on table base figures might well be explained. It has also been recorded that in addition to pottery making, Sherratt and his second wife operated an alehouse in Burslem (Turner, 129). Again, a connection between an alehouse publican and some of the table base figures may be established. This would certainly be true of the *Ale Bench* and *Tee Total* groups. As Turner points out, the owner of an alehouse would have heard the quips and jibes concerning "local men and their overbearing wives," and, while the connection is admittedly a stretch, it may add to the case of Sherratt as the creator of "spoof" groups like *Who Shall Wear the Breeches . Conquer or Die* (Turner, 130).

Often, tradition begins in truth, and despite recent disclaimers and cautions against incorrect attribution, there is much in the Sherratt tradition, and something in the table base groups as well, that urges collectors to *want* to believe a single potter – Obadiah Sherratt – was responsible for these incredible and unrivaled figures and groups. If Sherratt *was* responsible for them, it is easy to believe that his was a personality as colorful and as forceful as the earthenwares he produced. Whoever he was, the potter who created the table base figures and groups was a revolutionary. When he looked at his nineteenth century world he saw around him poverty, brutality, and drunkenness, not Olympus. When he looked at a bull he did not see Zeus seducing Io, he saw a great, dangerous brute animal that provided meat and entertainment for the workers of Staffordshire, and he potted it that way. Walton and the Walton School potters may have brought the graces of rural England to a new respectability and desirability among the pottery-buying public, however, the table base potter (or potters) brought the public down to earth with cruder and more robust figures that served as "reality checks" that established a new role for the earthenware figure – the role of social barometer and recorder, which helped set expectations and tastes for the coming age of Victorian Staffordshire figures.

Another example of the potters' sense of humor: the Tithe Pig. A shocked minister rejects the latest offspring of a farming couple, who taking the law to its letter, give unto the church one tenth of everything they have produced – the notorious "Tithe." Children included! 6". Circa 1825. Value: $500-$1000.

An allegorical figure of a woman representing "Air" from a set of the four elements. 7.25". Circa 1820. Value: $500-$1000.

One of a pair of figures representing sailors and their sweethearts: in this group the sailor (complete with packed trunk) departs to seek his fortune. The companion figure represents the sailor carrying a sack marked "$" returning to his beloved. Given the prevalence of maritime war and exploration during the 19th century, the popularity of this and similar groups was not surprising, and variations on the subject were depicted throughout Victoria's reign. 9.25" (damage to bocage). Circa 1820. Value: (as shown or undamaged) $1000+.

"WATER," an allegorical pearlware figure of a woman representing one of the four elements. Examples of this figure have been found with the mark "I DALE BURSLEM." This figure, however, is unmarked. The absence of a mark may be explained by one of two possibilities: (1) even if factories were in the habit of marking their figures, not all figures received a stamp and (2) molds were frequently sold to other potteries. 8". Circa 1820. Value: $500-$1000.

A figure frequently attributed to John Walton, but unmarked, of the Holy family's "Flight into Egypt." The pair to this figure represents "Return from Egypt" in which the Christ-child is depicted as a toddler. There were many versions made of this popular subject throughout the 19th century. 6.75". Circa 1820. Value: $1000+.

Bocage group titled "CHRISTS AGONY" [sic] with the title centered in an oval panel (bocage restored in the example shown). In this group Christ kneels on a high, ornate plinth that resembles a coffin-like structure as an angel with a cup in its hand rests on a brick pillar at the left. Additional script, "FATHER LET THIS CUP PASS," appears beneath the angel. 11.50". Early 19th century. Value: (as shown and undamaged) $1000+. *Courtesy of John and Barbara Gair, Castle Antiques.*

The Widow of Zarephath was another well-liked subject of the potters of the late 18th and early 19th centuries, popularizing as it did wifely devotion, suffering, and thrift; numerous versions, paired with Elijah and the Ravens, were available. 10.50". Circa 1820. Value: $500-$1000.

Extraordinary sheep with exaggerated bocage set on an ornate scalloped base featuring "C" scrolls. Early 19th century. Value: $1000+. *Courtesy of Madelena Antiques.*

Figure of Christ praying in the Garden of Gethsemane and titled with the quotation from Scripture: "FATHER IF THOU BE WILLING REMOVE THIS CUP." A variant of several Christ in Gethsemane figures and groups, this example is missing the bocage that originally rose from the back of the figure, a fact that decreases the figure's value but does not detract from the dramatic presence of the piece. 9". Early 19th century. Value: $500-$1000. *Courtesy of John and Barbara Gair, Castle Antiques.*

Hart and hind pair with bocage, decorated in overglaze enamels. 6". Early 19th century. Value: $1000+. *Courtesy of Zane Moss Antiques.*

Back view of the figure titled, "FATHER IF THOU BE WILLING REMOVE THIS CUP." *Courtesy of John and Barbara Gair, Castle Antiques.*

Black and white hind recumbent on a green mound base; bocage in background; originally paired with a matching hart. 5". Early 19th century. Value for the pair: $1000+. *Courtesy of Zane Moss Antiques.*

Vibrantly colored pearlware bocage figure of the Old Testament prophet Jeremiah. 10.75". Circa 1820. Value: $1000+. *Courtesy of John and Barbara Gair, Castle Antiques.*

Group titled "GRECIAN & DAUGHTER," based on the legend of Cimon and Pera – variously credited to Greek or Roman origins. A later Victorian group (see illustration in Chapter Sixteen) eliminated much of the detail present in this earlier depiction, but has been somewhat more faithful to proportion. The over-sized portrayal of Cimon seen here suggests that he was something of a giant and probably quite capable of escaping his captors without the assistance of his loyal daughter. 9.25". Circa1830. $1000+. *Courtesy of John and Barbara Gair, Castle Antiques.*

A figure on a rectangular table base with beaded bracket feet depicting the founders of ancient Rome, the twin brothers Romulus and Remus, being suckled by a she-wolf. 8". Circa 1820. Value: $1000+. *Courtesy of John and Barbara Gair, Castle Antiques.*

Chapter Six
Victorian Era Figures

Beginning with figures of Queen Victoria, at the time of her accession to the British throne in 1837, a new and distinctive category of Staffordshire figure began to emerge. The figures of this production period were unlike any ever made before in form, style, subject matter, and even the body of the clay from which they were made. This new type of figure, that subsequently came to be snared under the generic title of "Portrait," was built on the "here and now" premise of the early nineteenth century figures and groups that preceded them and heralded a "new age" of figure making that was synchronized with Britain's most dazzling era. The potters entered into a new period of confidence where they no longer saw the need to create their figures in imitation of their more expensive and less dynamic counterparts. It seems appropriate that a new style of Staffordshire figure accompanied a new age, and even more appropriate that the first figures of the era were portraits of the new young queen. Victoria's six-decade reign saw the evolution, ascendancy, and decline of the portrait figure from, at their best, immediately recognizable likenesses of the notable and notorious to, at their worst, cursory attempts that did little more than vaguely reflect the subject's gender and age.

Improved communication technology, increased literacy within the working classes, and the newfound need to possess (or at least infer through display) some measure of affluence and progressive spirit, were entrenched in Victorian consciousness. As Britain became the foremost nation in the world for Christianity, confidence, commerce, conquest, culture, crime, and science, Staffordshire's potters rose unflinchingly to meet the challenges of consumer demand. People wanted to *see* their heroes and foes; they wanted to express support for the good and condemnation for the bad and the ugly; and they wanted tangible expressions of their actual or pretended learnedness. The potters answered *these* desires with a tidal wave of distinctive figures.

Portrait figures and groups brought high interest persons into "everyman's" home with the immediacy and familiarity of family members. In the middle class world, unleavened by opportunities for personal glamour and glory, these figures provided their purchasers with a facility for make-believe. They could make-believe they were well-read and aware of current events, they could make-believe they were cultured patrons of the arts or theatre-goers, they could make-believe they were philanthropists and reformers who espoused and supported "enlightened" modern thought, they could make-believe they were pious and god-fearing. They could pretend to be part of the "pomp and circumstance" of Britain's gilded age, and they could add their personal passions to those of their royal family and, indeed, of their entire nation. All they required was a sympathetic assortment of pottery portraits atop their mantelshelves.

Victoria, Queen of the United Kingdom of Great Britain and Ireland and Empress of India (1819-1901) who succeeded to the throne in 1837 on the death of her uncle, William IV. Victoria married her first cousin Prince Albert of Saxe-Coburg-Gotha. When Albert, the Prince Consort, died in 1861 Victoria entered a deep state of mourning from which she never recovered. Undoubtedly she was the most powerful and influential woman of the modern era under whom technology, science, medicine, art, and even the geographical boundaries of the world saw change unequalled to that of any other era.

When Victoria's first portrait figure was issued, photography was still two years away from Louis Daguerre's public announcement on August 19, 1839; but even the advent of the Daguerreian Era would not provide the average consumer with readily accessible photographs of historical persons and all the people who were currently in the news. Consumers were accustomed to "pictures" of mythological characters, personalities from scripture, and the rich and famous, but painted and printed portraits lacked the vitality of three-dimensional figures, and the production of portrait figures that followed Victoria's accession was completely unprecedented in Staffordshire's history – in any history – and it offered consumers more than contemporary printed materials ever could.

While a few examples of portrait figures were produced prior to the Victorian period, Victorian portrait figure production was, in part, a response to avid interest in the newly emerging cult of the celebrity. No type of figure is more evocative of its age than the portrait figure, and none presents a more fascinating "living history" of royalty, politicians, foreigners, criminals, war heroes and heroines, preachers, saints, actors and actresses, singers and dancers, writers, sideshow and circus performers, and even popular animals. The "cast" included hundreds of personalities, most of which are incorporated into the various content areas treated in subsequent chapters of this book.

Partial set of the seasons modeled after 18th century originals. The Victorians were not so far removed from their agrarian roots that they failed to appreciate the importance of the role played by the ever-capriciousness Nature in their everyday lives. All figures 8.25". Circa 1860. Value set: $1000+; individual figures $500-$1000.

High quality early Victorian figure of a fiddler modeled in the "round" in great detail. 6.25". Circa 1840. Value: $1000+.

Reverse of the figure of the fiddler indicating the careful modeling required to create the figure. The chair rungs, amongst many other details, would have required individual molds and some hand construction and have had to be separately added to the main part of figure once it was removed from its mold. *Alice M Richards Bequest 1941. Collection: Ballarat Fine Art Gallery (Acc. No. 1941-13).*

Although the potting of figures was directly related to contemporary events, different categories of subjects gained ascendancy during specific periods of Victoria's reign. At the start of the era and into the 1840s, portrait figures of Victoria, her prince consort Albert, and their royal continental relatives and counterparts were immensely popular (see Chapter Nine). In the 1840s came the very plentiful royal progeny riding ponies, playing with pets, or perched on their parents' laps. But one can only have *so* many royal offspring before they become passé; and passé they became, to be replaced by figures representing politics and the Crimean War. Soldiers, sailors, British and allied leaders, personalities like Florence Nightingale, and even sites of major engagements like the fort of Sebastopol, became the primary focus of the potters and public during the 1850s. The 1860s drew from domestic politics, the Indian Mutiny and, once again, the British royalty, whose children obligingly generated headlines with engagements and marriages. The Franco-Prussian and Russo-Turkish Wars provided a new fount from which the Staffordshire potters drew subject matter during the 1870s. During the same decade, a proliferation of traveling evangelists (see Chapter Thirteen) offered a wellspring of new inspiration ironically set in juxtaposition to the increasing respectability and popularity of theaters and music halls with their various performers (see Chapter Eighteen). The 1880s saw the beginning of the decline of the portrait figure and the production of the last portrait of Queen Victoria: a monumental figure commemorating her Golden Jubilee in 1887. With a few exceptions, the art of the figure and the subject matter that inspired it had become moribund by this time and saw eventual expiration with the First World War.

Unusual vase with a woman and oversized grape leaves. 8". Circa 1860. Value: $100-$500.

Rare clown and cherub figure modeled "in the round" originally the lid of a tobacco jar. 8". Circa 1850. Value: $1000+.

Combination candlesticks and inkwells with children and birds. Scrolled bases and hand-painted floral decoration make these interesting and unusual pieces. 12". Circa 1860. Value for each: $500-$1000.

Unusual Staffordshire interpretation, in the form of a watch holder, indicative of the "Chinioserie" craze that was endemic in Victorian Britain. Undoubtedly theatrical in inspiration, this figure has so far defied identification. 11.50". Circa 1860. Value: $1000+.

Watch holder depicting the "Three Graces." 10". Circa 1860. Value: $500-$1000.

Very fine porcelaneous watch holder depicting two cherubs and featuring applied floral decoration. 8.50". Circa 1850. Value: $1000+.

Watch holder depicting a child in classical attire and posed with a dog. 8". Circa 1860. Value: $500-$1000.

Throughout the long and varied period of portrait figure production, the potters relied heavily on the popular media of the time as subject matter sources. Newspapers, broadsheets, magazines, books, music sheet covers, and theatre programs also provided the necessary "evidence" of physical likeness that was appreciated but not essential in creating a ceramic portrait of the celebrity. The ingenuity evidenced in the potters' adaptation of images from two-dimensional sources is sometimes remarkable. Although extreme accuracy and fidelity to the details of original sources was the aim of some potters, many others were not so conscientious in their adherence to reality and, when actual portraits of their subjects were unavailable, they relied on a far greater asset than print media: their imaginations. Many exotic and historical identities may be found sporting not only inaccurate, but totally improbable costumes and, where it appeared likely that artistic license stood in the way of ready identification, the potter was able to resort to the failsafe of the portrait figure: a title. As previously discussed, figures could be titled through a variety of methods: impressed with a stamp, an applied plaque, gilt script or capitals, colored enamel capitals, or through the application of a transfer. Interestingly the potters even managed to befuddle themselves in their production of portrait figures, and there were a few mix-ups even when titles were used; for example, titled George Washington figures appeared several times with Benjamin Franklin's features.

Watch holder in the form of a dancing couple, damage to the couple's arms.12". Circa 1870. Value: as shown or undamaged $100-$500.

As more subject matter was drawn from popular culture, and as more consumers began to purchase figures, speed and economy became crucial to figure production. Perhaps the record for a figure's production was set with a portrait of James Braidwood, superintendent of the London Fire Brigade. After Braidwood's death in 1861, the potters only took a week to model, produce, and market figures commemorating the fire fighter that were sold at his funeral as souvenirs of the occasion. Many potters made portrait alterations to suit themselves and to make potting easier. While some potters, like Thomas Parr, produced remarkably accurate and immediately recognizable likenesses of celebrities in their portrait figures, others rejected accuracy as too time-consuming and expensive. Complete faithfulness to an original source might require up to six or more molds. To overcome this and other production issues, the potters invented a new minimalist and almost abstract figural style in their endeavors to create identifiable and economically viable likenesses. During this period, truncations, foreshortenings, warping of perspectives, and odd proportions of the human form were not the product of lackluster modelers, but part of the pottery "shorthand" developed by the potter. Allied to this "shorthand" in figural representation came the introduction by the potter of a type of ceramic symbolism in which the public's cooperation was tacit. Esoteric to the modern viewer, and sometimes serving to render the significance or meaning of a figure impenetrable, this ceramic "sign-language" included a vast array of objects and gestures that were immediately familiar and accessible to the Victorian viewer. These symbols were not used as mere decorative devices. They were important keys to help enrich the viewer's understanding and appreciation of the subject and content of Staffordshire pottery figures. Anchors, flames, doves, flowers, lambs, swords, cannons, feathers, and coronets were among the vast lexicon of symbols available to the potters.

Two lovers embracing under a watch holder flanked by cherubs. 12". Circa 1860. Value: $500-$1000.

These were part of the "cultural literacy" of every Victorian, that helped add meaning and identifiably to their portrait figures. For example, Prince of Wales feathers gave the viewer an immediate clue to the figure's identity: royalty. Such clues narrowed down the possibilities and decreased the time required by the potters to achieve unerringly accurate likenesses of their subjects in "tribute" figures.

The Princess Royal and the future Edward VII sleeping under the protection of a guardian angel. Figures and groups depicting the Royal Children were immensely popular during the mid-19th century. See Chapter Nine for an illustration of the engraving on which this figure is based. 9". Circa 1845. Value: $1000+.

Part of the Victorian fascination with all things oriental: a small porcelaneous figure depicting an Eastern musician. The figure is modeled in the manner of John and Rebecca Lloyd of Shelton. 4". Circa 1840. Value: $100-$500.

Victorians were often very amused (and the potters shared their sense of humor) as indicated by this tiny inkwell that features the figure of a young girl wearing a night shirt and squatting on a chamber pot. 3.25". Circa 1860. Value: $100-$500.

The reverse of "potty girl" showing the opening through which ink could be accessed.

A small porcelaneous figure depicting an Eastern opium smoker. The figure is modeled in the manner of John and Rebecca Lloyd of Shelton. 4.25". Circa 1840. Value: $100-$500.

A female musician resting next to a stylized tree, bird, and nest. 7". Circa 1860. Value: $100-$500.

To further answer the urgency of remaining in sync with current events, modeling was simplified and the "flatback" with few details on its reverse and intended for placement on mantelpieces was invented (see Chapter Three). The name "Chimney Ornaments" refers specifically to this figure style. Flatbacks, many of which were portraits, were a departure from the previous figures that had been modeled "in the round" to be viewed from all sides. This simplistic, but sometimes ingenious, modeling made it possible to create some figures from a minimum number of molds. They were quick, easy, and inexpensive to produce and were more affordable than earlier figures. They were cheaper and lighter due to the reduced amounts of clay and time required for their production, and they were produced in the tens of thousands, factors that brought decorative art within the reach of most Victorian households. There were, however, consequences of speed and economy. Quality deteriorated, and late Victorian figures were poorly modeled and molded. Most were sparsely decorated (predominantly in white with touches of flesh-tone, black, and gilt) and represent the pallid generation in Staffordshire figure making's otherwise colorful genealogy. Despite their eventual decline, the figures and groups produced from about 1840 until 1900 comprise a remarkable panorama that remains one of the most significant and enduring outpourings of "commercial folk art" ever created.

Simultaneous with portrait figures, animals became increasingly popular subjects for the potters. These were not merely animals with useful agrarian applications like the farmyard animals depicted in pre-Victorian figures. Victorian animal figures included domestic pets with little relevance other than the diversion they offered their masters or mistresses. As always, the potters proved themselves to be unerring recorders of the times with an almost seismographic precision. Deprived of traditional settings in which animals played an integral role in their lives, England's recently urbanized populace was eager to introduce animals into their homes not just for pest-control, but for companionship, something Queen Victorian helped cement through her very public love of her dogs. Soon a veritable pottery kennel that included Pugs, Dalmatians, Lurchers, Mastiffs, Greyhounds, Whippets, Poodles, and, most popularly, Spaniels, became available to figure buyers along with figures of cats, rabbits, birds, and even the odd squirrel and rat (see Chapters Seven and Eight). Architectural figures in the forms of castles, cottages, churches, and crime scenes joined figures cleverly adapted to more utilitarian purposes, including watch-holders, candlesticks, moneyboxes, and pastille burners (see Chapter Nineteen).

Victorian Staffordshire figures of every kind infused their purchasers' hearts, hearths, and homes with the same sense of teeming life that characterized Victoria's great Empire. For the people who made them and for the people who bought them, they were both a way and an expression of life; their meaning and relevance is distanced from today's collectors only by time. These figures are peerless in their ability to record an era – its motivations, its morals, its aspirations, and its aesthetics. In no other period have technology and innovation, "trademarks" of the Victorian age, been so skillfully and authentically applied to a "folk art" that reflects the "personality" of the society that gave rise to the art.

Spill holder depicting children and their pets sheltering under an umbrella. 8". Circa 1850. Value: $100-$500.

A spill holder representing two children and celebrating the availability of fresh water. Hardly a reason for celebration in modern cities but, until the establishment of the Board of Health in 1848 that enforced laws relating to sanitation, drinkable water was not something the Victorians could take for granted, as frequent cholera outbreaks indicated. Numerous Victorian Era figures were made to commemorate initiatives undertaken by reformers like Lord Shaftesbury who was among the first to introduce health and social reform. 10". Circa 1870. Value: $100-$500.

King Charles Spaniels – a breed of royal choice, popular mantelpiece ornaments, synonymous with Staffordshire figures, and quintessentially Victorian. 12". Mid-Victorian. Value: $500-$1000.

The Victorians' "love affair" with dogs, inspired by their Queen's affection for her pets, resulted in a huge range of dog-breed models other than Spaniels. Among the many dog figures produced in Staffordshire, puppies and puppy groups are among the most appealing. This English Water Spaniel pup, originally one of a pair, sits on a tri-colored cushion base, was modeled in the round, and has two separately molded front legs. 5". Pope dates this figure at circa 1850. Value for the pair: $500-$1000. *Courtesy of Marla Chaikin, William Charles Antiques.*

Along with an enormous range of domestic animals, thousands of other animal figures and groups were produced during the Victorian Era. Most were flatbacks, produced in facing pairs and designed for placement on mantles. Religion was deeply felt in Staffordshire, and this charming lion and lamb group is perhaps a modeler's interpretation of the scripture verse (Isaiah 11:6) in which the prophet tells of a king to come who will bring peace among animals that are natural enemies. 4.25". Mid-Victorian. Value: $100-$500. *Courtesy of Zane Moss Antiques.*

Rare figure of a standing fox. 6.75". Circa 1860. Value: $500-$1000. *Bequest of Colin Hicks Caldwell, 1990. Collection: Ballarat Fine Art Gallery (Acc. No. 1990.90).*

Bird Nesting group of a boy and girl on each side of a spill holder and with a bird and nest of eggs at their feet. The Victorian concept of "childhood" was often mixed with idealized, rural imagery, and the potters complied with a wide range of variations on the theme. 6". Mid-Victorian. Value: $100-$500. *Courtesy of Anita L. Grashof, Gallerie Ani'tiques.*

Bucolic spill holder group depicting two young girls with lambs at their feet and a bird near the top of the spill holder. 7.75". Mid-Victorian. Value: \$100-\$500. *Courtesy of Marla Chaikin, William Charles Antiques.*

The Victorians' love of adventure and the unusual was strongly reflected in many figures and groups that seem, at first blush, to be rather incongruous. In this group of a woman, parrot, and cage, the woman wears a curious headpiece, cobalt-colored bodice, short skirt, and Turkish-style trousers. Searching for a historical context is part of Staffordshire figures' intrigue. This may be an untitled portrait of Lady Hester Stanhope who crossed the Middle Eastern desert, camped with Bedouins, and adopted Middle Eastern dress (see Chapter Sixteen). 9.25". Mid-Victorian. Value: \$100-\$500. *Courtesy of Anita L. Grashof, Gallerie Ani'tiques.*

The Victorian potters' range of subject matter included persons representing Royalty, the internationally and locally applauded, the famous and infamous, and common folk from various areas of Britain. This group, originally one of a pair entitled "Welsh Hunters" depicts a mounted huntsman (with game) in traditional Welsh costume. 11". Circa 1850. Value (for either single or the pair): \$1000+.

Chapter Seven
Spaniels: Staffordshire's Pet Project

Although a few late eighteenth and early nineteenth century Spaniel figures were produced, the typical Spaniel "look" was uniquely Victorian. More than any other animals, Spaniels became a "pet project" of the Staffordshire potteries from around 1840 through the 1890s. These Spaniels were produced in such abundance and are currently so well known that they are virtually synonymous with Staffordshire figures in general. Originally modeled after the King Charles Spaniel, a breed of royal choice, the traditional "Staffordshire Spaniel" still exists today and is currently known as the Cavalier King Charles Spaniel.

It seems only right that the Staffordshire potters focused so much of their attention on Spaniels as the breed was immensely popular among the aristocracy in Britain and in Europe for many centuries and was even enthusiastically portrayed on canvases and on tapestries. In 1570, Doctor Johannes Caius, physician to Elizabeth I, wrote a treatise on dogs entitled *"De Canibus Britannicus."* Interestingly, a third of the work was devoted to the *"spaniell gentle or comforter – a delicate, neat and pretty kind of dog."* The terms *Comforter* or *Comforter Dog* are sometimes used interchangeably with *King Charles Spaniel,* and some sources suggest the term derives from a centuries-ago practice of women keeping small Spaniels beneath their wide skirts for added warmth or comfort during the cold winter months. Spaniels have enjoyed a long history as companions to their masters and mistresses. One especially poignant Spaniel tale dates to the execution of Mary Queen of Scots in 1587. After Mary was beheaded, a little black and white spaniel was found hiding beneath her petticoats. According to a witness the faithful dog had to be pulled by force from her clothes, and even then would not leave its dead mistress. In 1648, the fugitive King Charles I was accompanied in his exile by his spaniel "Rogue" who, after the King's execution, was taken by a Roundhead and paraded round the city. King Charles II (for whom the breed was named) and James II were also great Spaniel fans, and a popular dog "tale" tells how the latter monarch's first command was *"Save the dogs!"* during a storm at sea when orders were given to abandon ship.

Queen Victoria herself owned a King Charles Spaniel, named "Dash," who came to the throne with the young queen and who probably inspired the wave of Spaniel figures produced during the time she ruled. If contemporary tales are to be believed, Victoria, immediately after her coronation, "dashed" home to change her robes and give her Spaniel his afternoon bath. Victoria's Spaniel became so popular with the public that portraits of Dash sitting royally on a tasseled cushion became a set piece for Victorian needlewomen to stitch, and many of these stitched pieces can still be found today. As well as being the de facto "Pet By Appointment to Her Majesty," Spaniels are often seen in Staffordshire pottery as the companions of children (often the Royal Children) and adults, either at play, resting, or literally in the lap of luxury on

Group of five red and white Spaniels. Spaniels like these were produced in pairs and are found in red and white, black and white, and white and gold, often with numbers on their bases that range from one to six, indicating sizes (one being the tallest at approximately 12.50", two at 10", three at 9", four at 7.75", five at 6.50", and six at 5.50"). Considered "classic" Spaniels or Comforter Dogs and produced throughout Victoria's reign, the best examples feature painted decoration with fine feathering and good detail in the eye and muzzle areas.

their master's or mistress's knees. A number of portrait figures featuring Spaniels exist, including one of the poet Elizabeth Barrett Browning, who at the age of fifteen sustained an injury and was forced to lie on her back for years to recuperate. The poet was portrayed with her faithful Spaniel "Flush," making the group a "double" portrait of the poet and her pet.

Often described as naïve or primitive, Staffordshire Spaniels exhibit the hearty, rustic character and the cottage-industry quaintness typical of nearly all Staffordshire figures. Most Spaniels were produced in facing pairs and were modeled with a basic breed resemblance, which makes them all uniquely similar. They all possess the well-known Spaniel "personality" and are characterized by an inverted "smile," wide painted eyes, and usually a collar, padlock, and chain. Most Spaniels were produced from simple two part molds and with blocked-in legs. Spaniels with one or more separately molded legs, which required additional molds, cost more to make and purchase in their own day and are generally more highly valued today.

A number of Spaniels were set on bases or plinths, usually in smooth oval forms decorated with simple gold lines. However, more elaborate bases (including scalloped, footed, and Rococo styles) are sometimes seen, and some Spaniel groups made before circa 1863 appear on cobalt-colored bases.

Pair of #1, red and white seated Spaniels. 12". Mid-Victorian. Value: $1000+. *Courtesy of Jane McClafferty Antiques.*

Spaniels produced from about 1840 until 1880 usually exhibit finer modeling and decorating than those produced toward the end of the century. Detailed modeling (features molded into the body) and fine brushwork and feathering in painted decoration set the standards for quality and value. Painted muzzles, usually orange or pink, with clearly delineated noses and whiskers, along with dotted eyelashes, are more desirable than plain black muzzles and lack of detail around the eyes.

Significantly, like other Staffordshire figures, factory marks were rarely used on Spaniels, a fact that makes dating difficult and attribution to specific makers impossible for most examples. Nor was Spaniel production connected to specific events, which would make precise dating possible. Spaniels were mass-produced in huge numbers and many potteries were small, operating with limited work forces. Potworks opened and closed with some regularity and frequent changes in ownership were common. When firms went out of business, molds were often sold. New owners used the previously owned molds in their own manufactories and, hypothetically, a mold issued in 1850 might be used by the original owner for several years, sold, and then used by another pottery for an additional period of time. Dating Spaniels from such molds at circa 1850 (plus or minus three to five years) would, therefore, be inaccurate as the figures produced might not date to 1850, but to a decade or more after. To compound the problem, potters often copied other potters' designs and decorating styles. With all of this in mind, it should be understood that despite the fact that dealers and collectors like to date Spaniels as early as possible, variables come into play that often make precise dating problematic at best.

Seated Spaniels are seen most commonly, but several sub-categories provide charming and interesting variations on the seated Spaniel theme. Spaniel groups were produced in some quantity along with recumbent or lying Spaniels, Spaniels with bright flower baskets in their mouths, and pipe-smoking Spaniels. Disraeli Spaniels with a distinctive row of curls on their foreheads were produced in limited numbers and have been familiarly named for Victoria's Prime Minister, Benjamin Disraeli, who wore a center forehead curl. Glass-eyed Spaniels were produced, for the most part, during the latter years of the nineteenth century probably in an effort to boost market potentials at a time when consumer interest had waned. All-black Spaniels, known generically today as "Jackfield Spaniels," appear to have been most popular during the decade that followed Prince Albert's death in 1861. Quill and watch holder models, spill holder models (also called "spill vases," designed to hold slim rolls of paper used by less-than-affluent families in place of expensive matches), and inanimate or faux clock groups (figures with painted clocks) sometimes incorporated Spaniels. Novelty Spaniels in the form of jugs, tobacco humidors, bookends, window stops (designed to keep windows open through placement between the sashes and window sills), and other *un*Spaniel-like items were also popular among the Victorians. Many of the variant styles are rarer and more highly valued than seated Spaniels.

It has been noted that Spaniel pairs often include one partner that is slightly larger than the other. A commonly held theory suggests that the mold sculptors deliberately designed a larger male and slightly smaller female to create "Mr. and Mrs." pairs. There is, however, no contemporary documentation to support this theory and, most likely, size differences were the result of mold changes, mismatching at the factories, or later "marriages" of similar singles.

Pair of red and white Spaniels exhibiting fine modeling, crisp molding, and good feathered decoration. 10". Mid-Victorian. Value: $500-$1000. *Courtesy of Jane McClafferty Antiques.*

Pair of black and white Spaniels. Number "2" on bases. 10". Mid-Victorian. Value: $500-$1000. *Courtesy of Jane McClafferty Antiques.*

There also exist a few interesting, amusing, and even naughty "Spaniel tales." It has been noted that during the nineteenth century, pairs of white Spaniels were popular wedding gifts and that presenting a bride and groom with a pair of "wedding white, Mr. and Mrs." Spaniels was a wish for marital bliss. It has also been suggested that black or Jackfield-type Spaniels were given to the bereaved as tokens of condolence.

Large and very well modeled red and white spaniel with finely "feathered" decoration, separate front legs, and "best gold" collar and padlock. 13". Circa 1850. Value: $500-$1000.

Another "Spaniel tale" tells how the wives of sailors and men in the seafaring trade would place a pair of Spaniels in a window, facing outward when their men were at sea, and facing inward when the men returned home. On the naughty side, one story relates that in a Scottish seaport town a sailor who was frequently away at sea decided to buy his young wife a present – a pair of Spaniels. The sailor was experiencing a bit of guilt because he was in the practice of consorting with women in his various ports of call. The wife was delighted with what she believed was a thoughtful gift and placed the Spaniels in a window of their cottage. However, the plot thickened: the wife soon leaned of her hubby's philandering and decided to get even by using the Spaniels in a plan for revenge. When her husband was home, she placed the two Spaniels in the window facing each other. When her errant husband was at sea, she set the Spaniels back to back, indicating to any interested lads sailing into port that hubby was away and that she was alone and "free." The husband, having assuaged his guilt, was so pleased by his wife's reaction to the Spaniels (little did he know why) that he told his equally wayward shipmates to get

Spaniels for their wives and all would be sweet. In short order, all the other wrongly-done-by dames of the town put Spaniels in their windows and used the same signaling system to summon up a bit of extra-marital entertainment. Thus, the naughty sailors provided their good wives with exactly what the ladies required to exact payback. In a similar risqué vein, Spaniels are sometimes called "Wally Dogs," an expression derived from women's practice of placing two Spaniels in their windows to indicate that their husbands were home, and one to show that they were away. As a result, much trysting took place, and the cuckolded husband in each case became known as a "Wally," from which the colloquial term "Wally Dogs" is derived.

These "tales" may or may not be factual, but they are good fun to tell. It *is* a fact that that most Spaniels were purchased by families of modest means and that they were generally not treated as prospective heirlooms in the manner that their fine china, porcelain contemporaries, or earthenware portrait figures were. Most Spaniels "lived" humble lives in humble homes and many were lost, broken, or consigned to dustbins long before twentieth century collectors took notice of them.

Today, although Staffordshire Spaniels remain plentiful, the best examples are becoming increasingly difficult to find in mint or near-mint condition, and their values are appreciating dramatically and rapidly. Spaniels that sold for a few pennies in their own time currently realize prices in the hundreds of dollars. Fascination with Staffordshire Spaniels still exerts its power on the twenty-first century collector; no Victorian interior, and no Staffordshire figure collection is complete without at least one pair.

Unusual mid-Victorian white and gilt Spaniel pair with separately molded front legs. 9". Value: $500-$1000.

Variation of the standard large spill vase Spaniel. 13". Mid-Victorian. Value: $500-$1000.

Paired black and white Spaniels with separately molded front legs. 9". Mid-Victorian. Value: $500-$1000.

Standard model for large spill vase Spaniel pairs on bases. 12.50". Mid-Victorian. Value: $1000+.

Paired white and gilt glass-eyed Spaniels. 11.50" Slip cast and probably made toward the end of the 19th century or during the early 20th century. Value: $500-$1000.

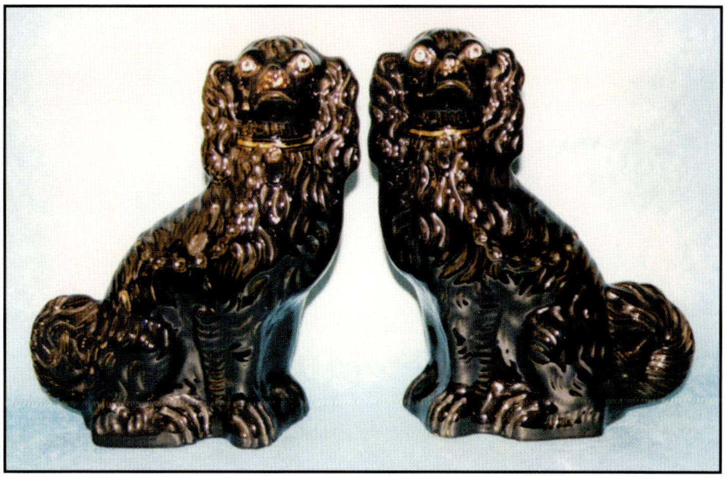

Paired Jackfield-type Spaniels with white eyes and highlighted in best gold. 12". Mid-Victorian. Value: $500-$1000. *Courtesy of Anita L. Grashof, Gallerie Ani'tiques.*

Jackfield-type Spaniel, one of a pair. 9.75". Mid-Victorian. Value for the pair: $500-$1000.

Very rare white and gold flower basket Spaniel (one of a pair) with an unusual coiffure that is similar to that of the "Little Lion Dog" recorded by Clive Mason Pope (see Pope, figure 2, page 117). 10". Mid-Victorian. Value for the pair: $1000+. *Courtesy of Jane McClafferty Antiques.*

One of a pair of Spaniels decorated in white and copper luster. This type of decoration is seen most frequently in Spaniels and is actually made from gold, which sometimes resulted in a light purple halo around the decoration when applied to a white body. Copper luster Spaniels were produced in a wide range of body styles and sizes during the latter part of the 19th century. Other luster colors (including a pearly variety) were created when metallic compounds became iridescent during firing. 13". Late Victorian. Value for the pair: $500-$1000.

Superb red and white flower basket Spaniel; one of a pair. 6.50". Mid-Victorian. Value for the pair: $1000+. *Courtesy of Jane McClafferty Antiques.*

Left and right: Paired chunky-bodied black and white Spaniels with red painted collars and padlocks rather than the more frequently seen gold. 7.50". Mid to late Victorian. Value: $500-$1000. Center: Black and white flower basket Spaniel; one of a pair. 5.50". Mid-Victorian. Value for the pair: $1000+.

Miniature red and white flower basket Spaniel; one of a pair. Mini flower basket Poodles were also potted and are usually seen decorated in white and gilt with orange flower baskets. 4.50". Mid-Victorian. Value for the pair: $1000+. *Courtesy of Jane McClafferty Antiques.*

Centerpiece clock group including a Poodle at the top and differently colored Spaniels at each side. Variations of this group feature three Spaniels and three Poodles. 9". Mid-Victorian. Value: $500-$1000. *Courtesy of Marla Chaikin, William Charles Antiques.*

Exceptional paired red and white Spaniels set on gilt-lined bases. 7.75". Mid-Victorian. Value: $1000+. *Courtesy of Jane McClafferty Antiques.*

"Roll out the Barrel!" This barrel group has been produced in smaller, less detailed versions, and has been widely reproduced (most reproductions are substantially inferior to this original and are easily identified as new). 8.50". Mid-Victorian. Value: $100-$500.

Paired parent and pup groups on cobalt blue bases and colored in reverse. Although such groups were very likely sold in pairs, the differences in these suggest that they are not a true pair and may have been mismatched at the pottery or "married" some time after their manufacture. 6". Mid-Victorian. Value for each: $100-$500. *Courtesy of Marla Chaikin, William Charles Antiques.*

Paired figures of cupids on the backs of Spaniels. While groups of children on seated or recumbent Spaniels' backs are seen with some frequency, this group is extremely rare. 6". Mid-Victorian. Value: $1000+. *Courtesy of Marla Chaikin, William Charles Antiques.*

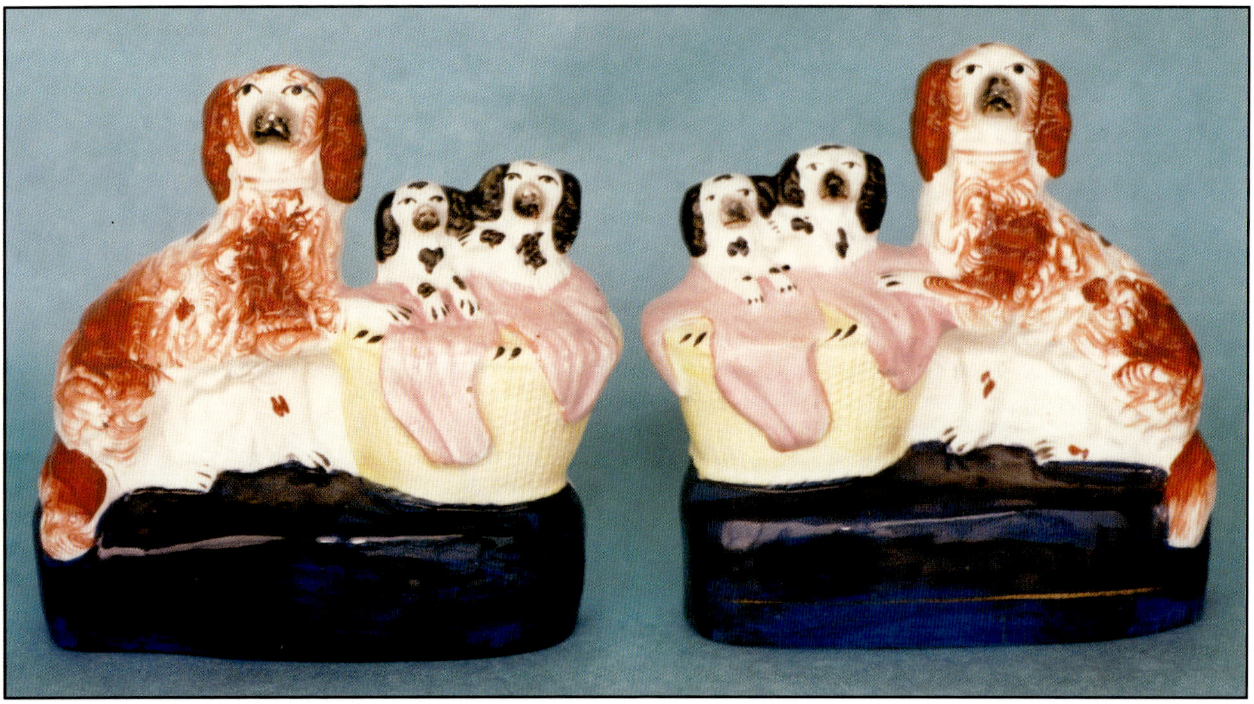

Rare paired "wash basket" Spaniels set on oval cobalt blue bases. 5.75". Mid-Victorian. Value: $1000+. *Courtesy of Marla Chaikin, William Charles Antiques.*

While the mold design for this rare trio of miniature parent and pup Spaniels is similar, no two figures make a correct pair. 3". Mid-Victorian. Value for each $100-$500. *Courtesy of Marla Chaikin, William Charles Antiques.*

Rare parent and pup Spaniels set on an orange cushion base with tassels and swag and modeled in the round. 6". Mid-Victorian. Value for a single: $100-$500; for a pair: $500-$1000. *Courtesy of Marla Chaikin, William Charles Antiques.*

Spaniels and people appear together in a large number of Staffordshire figure groups. Often the Spaniel appears incidental; however, in this group the oversized Spaniel is very much the "center of attention." 10". Mid-Victorian. Value: $100-$500. *Courtesy of Marla Chaikin, William Charles Antiques.*

Pastoral life, birding, and bird-nesting groups found favor among Victorian consumers and often included the ever-popular Spaniel. In many cases, while not central to most of these groups, the Spaniel's inclusion attests to the breed's popularity during the Victorian Era. Value for each of the groups: $100-$500. *Courtesy of Marla Chaikin, William Charles Antiques.*

Hunting and fowling were popular Victorian activities, and Spaniels were incorporated into many related Staffordshire groups represented by those shown here. Mid-Victorian: Value for each: $100-$500. *Courtesy of Marla Chaikin, William Charles Antiques.*

Watch holder group featuring a shepherd and shepherdess (holding a lamb) with a black and white Spaniel in the lower center. Watch holders or watch stands (in a wide range of models and sizes) were designed to hold portable timepieces. 12.50". Mid-Victorian. Value: $100-$500.

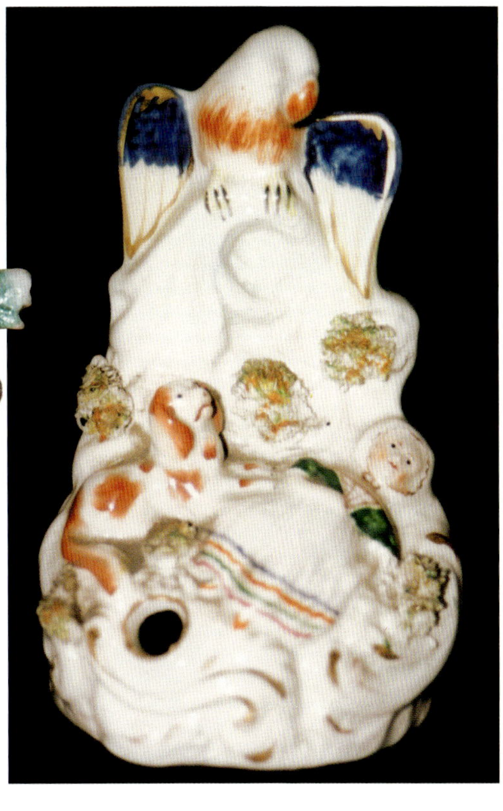

Quill holder group (designed to hold quills used for writing) in which a Spaniel is cast in the role of protector as it guards a child from an eagle. Similar "animal guardian" groups were popular among purchasers. 10". Mid-Victorian. Value: $500-$1000. *Courtesy of Marla Chaikin, William Charles Antiques.*

Disraeli Spaniels, with characteristic forehead curls, were often produced in the typical seated Spaniel style with blocked-in front legs. This unusual example, originally one of a pair, has separately molded front legs. 6.50". Early to mid-Victorian. Value for the single: $500-$1000.

Spaniels were included in groups of every size and style and were frequently depicted with royalty. During the 1840s, when the Crown Prince and Princess Royal were very young, they were often portrayed with Spaniels (possibly modeled to represent Queen Victoria's beloved Spaniel Dash). In this titled portrait of the Prince of Wales, issued around the time his engagement was announced in 1862, the Prince's hand rests on a large Spaniel's head. 14.50". Value: $500-$1000. *Courtesy of Marla Chaikin, William Charles Antiques.*

Exceptionally well-made pair of Disraeli Spaniels with separately molded front legs. 11". Early to mid-Victorian. Value: $1000+.

Pipe-smoking dogs were undoubtedly modeled after a painting by Sir Edwin Landseer entitled "A Quiet Pipe" (circa 1829) in which a dog is painted with a pipe in its mouth. Queen Victoria commissioned Landseer to paint several of the Royal Family's pets, and his works included an 1836 portrait of Dash (see Pope, page 73). The extremely rare pipe-smoking dog illustrated here may not be correctly identified as a Spaniel but is included as a companion to the previously illustrated pipe-smoking Spaniel. Most pipe-smoking dogs were issued in pairs and all are rare and collectible. This figure and smaller versions were also produced in red and white and white and gold (see Pope, pp. 132-133, figures 2-5) 10.75". Mid-Victorian. Value for the single: \$1000+. *Courtesy of Zane Moss Antiques.*

Begging Spaniels were produced in several styles and sizes and usually in the form of pitchers or jugs. This rare Jackfield-type begging Spaniel holds a pipe in its mouth and was not modeled as a jug. 13.75". Mid-Victorian. Value: \$1000+. *Courtesy of Jane McClafferty Antiques.*

Spaniels were so popular that the potters created various novelty Spaniel figures including bookends, window stops, tobacco humidors, and money banks like the one shown in this illustration. 5.50". Mid-Victorian. Value: \$100-\$500. *Courtesy of Jane McClafferty Antiques.*

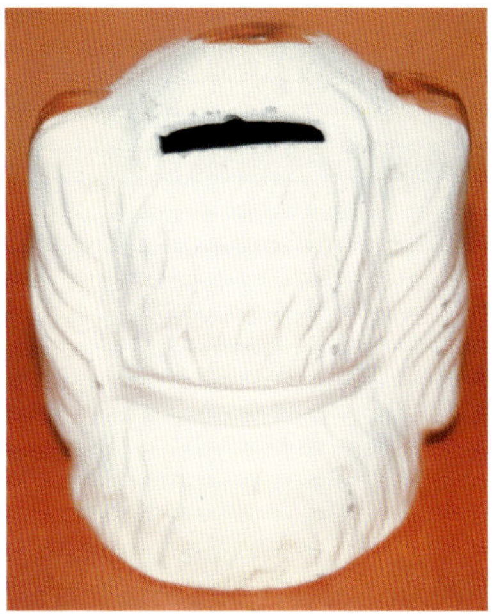

Back of the Spaniel money bank, showing the coin slot.

Chapter Eight
Staffordshire Animals: A Noah's Ark

"All things bright and beautiful, / All creatures great and small, / All things wise and wonderful: / The Lord God made them all." These words from an early nineteenth century hymn by Cecil Frances Alexander and based on Genesis 1:31 have never failed to evoke joy and delight in creation. That appreciation was felt particularly strongly by eighteenth and nineteenth century Britons, and Staffordshire's potters responded with a remarkable array of domestic, wild, and exotic animals. Like other Staffordshire figures, earthenware animals were characterized by their vigorous character, rustic charm, and colorful, cottage personality. While animals were among the earliest figure subjects produced by Staffordshire's potters, it was the infamously sentimental Victorian period that saw production of more animal figures than all other pottery production periods combined. Such figures were remarkably popular with the Victorians and, for many of today's collectors, animal figures out-rank all others. Most were produced in pairs (in every size, color, and category), and they comprise a unique Noah's Ark. Through these pieces, Staffordshire's potters exhibited a provincial charisma and a strongly felt affinity for the earth and its creatures.

With the advent of the Victorian Era's scientific and humanistic developments there also came a burgeoning interest in nature and all it entailed: principally animals. Initially, the potters and modelers drew upon the fields and forests of North Staffordshire to create familiar forest, farm, and domestic animal figures. From as early as the mid-eighteenth century, harts and hinds, foxes, squirrels, bears, lions, dogs, cattle, and even water buffalo were popular figure subjects. In time, however, these animals no longer satisfied consumers whose knowledge of the animal kingdom had expanded exponentially with the availability of books and periodicals that offered a wealth of travel and natural history subjects. These printed materials resulted in a Victorian preoccupation with flora and fauna, with botany and zoology. In addition, traveling menageries and circuses brought about direct contact with exotic animals, and these curiosities generated increased interest in wildlife as well as in earthenware animal figures and groups.

The Victorians were an eclectic mix of mawkish sentimentality and scientific resolve: characteristics that shaped their world view and their empire. They may not have invented the concept of "companion animals," but they took it up with an enthusiasm unparalleled by any period hitherto and since, perhaps with the exception of our own. The output of earthenware animals from Staffordshire's potteries resulted in a remarkable expansion of furred, finned, and feathered figural subject matter. Most Victorian-era animal figures were press-molded and decorated with underglaze colors. Some examples feature overglaze enamels over the entire surface of the figure or in details like muzzle areas and paws or hooves.

Lions were modeled in a wide range of styles. Performing lions, lion and unicorn groups, lions with lambs, lion "toys," and other variations on the theme are recorded. This large performing lion is one of several similar models.14.25". Early19th century. Value: $4800-$5800. *Courtesy of Zane Moss Antiques.*

Domestic and rural animals are seen most frequently, especially sheep, cows, goats, and dogs. Cat figures are rare and it has been recorded that dog models outnumber feline figures by a ratio of one hundred to one. The parade of domestic animals continued with horse figures. These were produced during both the eighteenth and early nineteenth centuries, but few are seen without riders. During the Victorian era equestrian models of the royal family were especially popular, followed by a long line of kings, queens, lords, ladies, and military celebrities. Mounted jockeys and polo players are seen from time to time along with criminals like Turpin and King. Victorian-era groups of mares and foals are particularly charming. Herding, hunting, and sporting animal models were produced in some quantity during the nineteenth century along with pastoral figure groups of shepherds, shepherdesses, lambs, and dogs. Models of huntsmen and dogs (with and without their prey) were popular along with gamekeepers, dogs chasing deer, and Greyhound and hare models. Some researchers of Staffordshire pottery have posited the theory that the large number of Whippet figures produced during the period was the direct result of the land enclosure acts of the nineteenth century. Whippets were a favorite with the working classes because of their hunting instincts. Their ability to catch rabbits on private land while evading farmers and landowners (along with willingness to be raced) would have endeared them to their owners. A rabbit for the pot without running the risk of imprisonment gave Whippet owners every reason to celebrate their well-trained dogs by placing pottery likenesses on the mantle-shelf.

Rare lion and tiger by Thomas Parr. This figure is missing the stand of palm trees originally modeled as background, but still displays the fine quality workmanship present in Parr's work. 6" as illustrated. Circa 1860. Value: (as shown) $500-$1000, (undamaged) $1000+.

Animals featured in other more rare "entertainment" or "spectator sport" figures with brutal subjects such as bull- and bear-baiting groups and rat catcher groups were also potted. Glimpses of animals at their less ordinary were provided for the potters and their public by traveling menageries (see Chapter Eighteen). These were immensely popular, and figures of circus and exotic animals were produced in some quantity. Several striking lion models were produced during the eighteenth and nineteenth centuries and, in the nineteenth century, elephants, zebras, giraffes, leopards, and monkeys were also well represented. Queen Victoria was known to appreciate performing animals and her royal patronage helped cement the popularity of traveling fairs and menageries like those of Polito, Wombwell, Ballard, and Manders and Sangers with the public. Giraffes, elephants, camels, tigers, leopards, monkeys, and zebras were confined and dragged around the British Isles in cramped cages and provided both diversion and excitement through their frequent escapes and attacks on their keepers. Fairs were transformed into itinerant zoos and so was the product of the Staffordshire potters. In 1826, accompanied by its exotically attired Arabian keepers, the "Nubian Giraffe" was the first giraffe ever to be exhibited in England. Known originally by the hybrid name of the "cameleopard," because it was regarded as the misbegotten offspring of a leopard and a camel, the giraffe became a sensation with royalty, the public, and the potters alike. By 1836, the original giraffe was followed by four of its number "in the flesh" and thousands "in the pottery."

Rare, large spill holder of lioness, cubs, and snake. 11.75". Circa 1870. Value: $1000+.

Staffordshire pottery figures of fish are rare, although dolphins were featured from time to time, and several fish seller figures and groups are recorded. Ornithological subjects were produced during the eighteenth and nineteenth centuries: many would give ornithologists nightmares because of the "flights of fancy" that seized the potters in their production! Such artistic license was not blanketing, as some of the eighteenth century bird figures were particularly well executed, recognizable, and are currently highly valued. Parrots, hawks, roosters, hens, peacocks, and a profusion of exotic birds are recorded. Pigeon racing was an immensely popular sport during the nineteenth century, and the bird-fancying potters did not stint in their depictions of proud and pouty-chested champions. During the nineteenth century, birds were most frequently incorporated into figure groups.

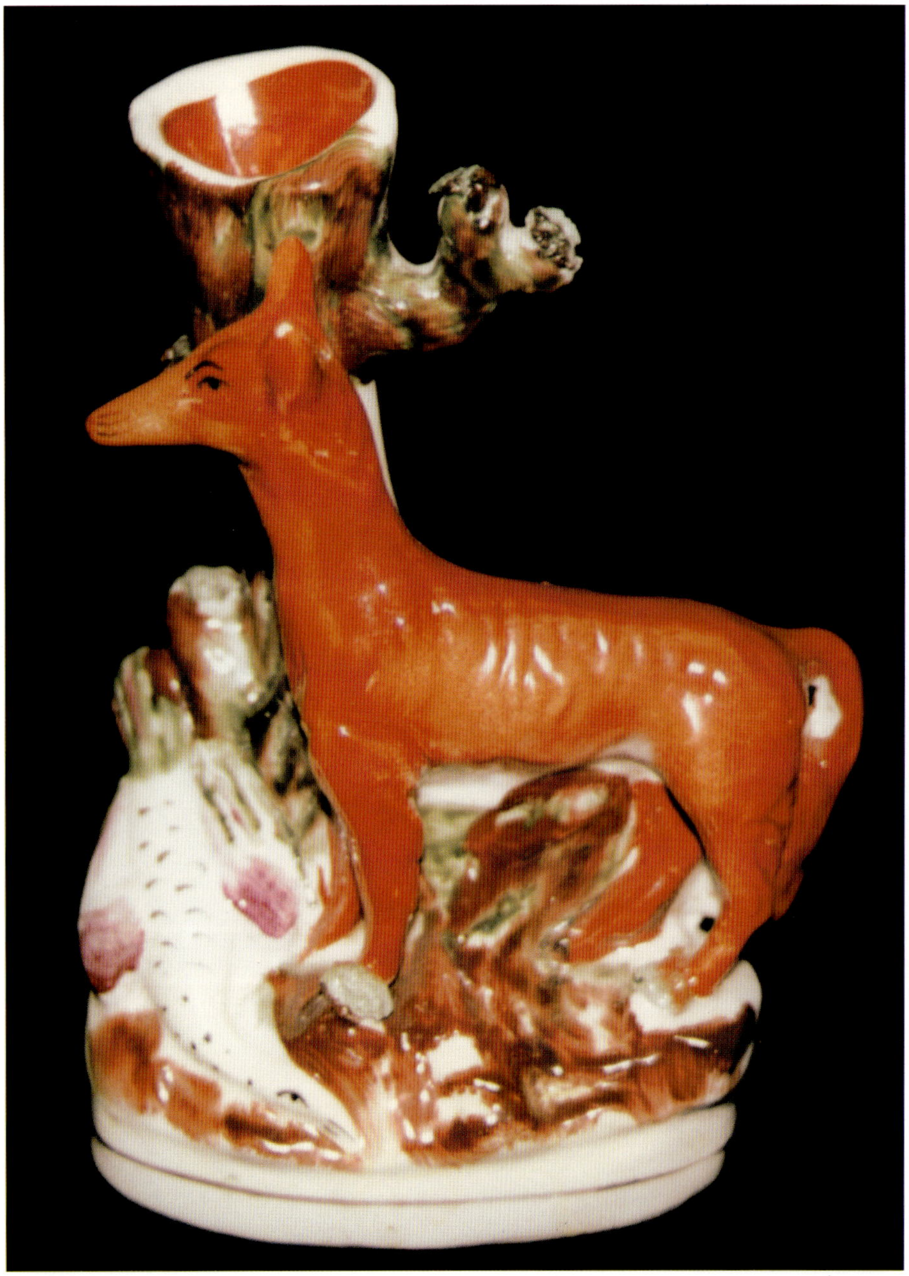

Fox and pheasant quill holder. 7.75". Mid-Victorian. Value: $100-$500. *Courtesy of Zane Moss Antiques.*

Victorian Romanticism was never more evident than in the range of "rescue" animals. Animals were "cast" in heroic roles during Victoria's reign when animals in general were highly regarded. Typically, the rescue animal was a dog modeled in the act of saving a child from an eagle, snake, or other threat of danger. "Guardian Angel" animals, again usually dogs, were modeled as faithful guardians of children and, like rescue animals, are rare and sought after today. One of the most famous of these canine crusaders was "Gelert," protector of Prince Llewelyn of North Wales in the thirteenth century. On returning home, the young prince's father, King John, found his child missing and Gelert covered in blood. Thinking his son was slain by the gore-soaked hound, King John ran the dog through with his sword. John then discovered his son safe under his cradle and realized that the faithful hound had, in fact, saved the child from certain death by killing a wolf. The pathos, drama, and historical context of the tale managed to cement Gelert into the canine hall-of-fame as an all-time favorite and inspiration for a series of best-selling Staffordshire animal groups (see illustration of Gelert in Chapter Sixteen).

Animals and children were a natural, and winning, combination, and the potters produced thousands of figures and groups that included children charmingly posed beside, astride, and otherwise "involved" with a huge range of animals. The Royal Children, in particular, were frequently depicted with favorite pets.

Today all animal figures are popular. Animals appear in a huge number of quill holder or ink well models or as part of spill holder, inanimate clock, and watch holder groups. Their values depend on subject matter as well as on the techniques used by the potters in design and production. Animal figures are often seen on molded bases, the most ornate of which are also the most costly. Animals with separately molded legs (rather than blocked-in) are desirable. Older examples of animal figures with one or more separate legs usually appear on bases, while freestanding animals without bases or other support were produced mainly during the late nineteenth and early twentieth centuries.

Some animal figures were also decorated with glass eyes. This is most commonly seen in large dog, cat, and lion models of the late Victorian period and, as previously noted, very likely had more to do with decreasing sales than design or style interests.

Black Jackfield-type animal figures are elegant and rare. They are usually decorated with little more than gilt highlights. Black dogs are very collectible and are seen more frequently than other black animals like cats and cockerels, which command premium values.

Numerous goat groups were produced throughout the Victorian Era, nearly all of which included children or adults. Often, the Royal Children were portrayed seated on goats' backs. Even theatrical groups, like a rare Esmeralda and Gringoire group (from the play "The Hunchback of Notre Dame") included a goat at the actors' feet. The group illustrated here depicts a young girl and a goat set on a high embossed base highlighted in blue. 6". Mid-Victorian. Value: $100-$500. *Courtesy of Marla Chaikin, William Charles Antiques.*

Importantly, while Spaniels may be the best-known members of the Staffordshire animal world, significantly large numbers of other animal figures were manufactured and now represent an area of Staffordshire figure collecting that is increasing in popularity and value. For a time, other figure types appeared to be favored by collectors and, as a result, the animal "ornaments" that had been so generously produced were somewhat neglected. In recent years, however, Staffordshire animals have claimed the attention of collectors and dealers in much the same way that they certainly must have delighted eighteenth and nineteenth century purchasers. As a result, many collectors specialize and collect only animal figures and groups. There is something inherently emotive about these wonderful earthenware creatures whose seemingly infinite variety and delightful presence touch both the imagination and the heart.

Nearly every animal species was included in the figure makers' inventories during the eighteenth and nineteenth centuries. Potted for the most part in pairs, animal figures remind us of the animals Noah gathered into his ark, two-by-two. And just as Noah sought to protect and preserve each species, today's collectors protect Staffordshire's animal figures from the possibility of "extinction" for future generations of collectors to enjoy.

Inkwell in the form of a recumbent doe. Deer (harts and hinds) were potted frequently through all periods of figure production. 4.25". Circa 1860. Value: $100-$500

Stag and hound spill vase. Many stag and hound groups were produced during the 19th century in a range of styles. 8". Mid-Victorian. Value: $500-$1000. *Courtesy of Zane Moss Antiques.*

Well modeled figure in the manner of Thomas Parr of a boy in Scottish costume holding a giant stag. 10". Circa 1850. Value: $1000+.

Rare spill holder of a mare and foal in the manner of Thomas Parr. 6.50". Circa 1860. Value: $500-$1000.

Mare and foal by a stream, spill holder group. 12". Early to Mid-Victorian. Value: $500-$1000. *Courtesy of Zane Moss Antiques.*

Equestrian groups were produced in great abundance during the Victorian Era. Many portrayed royalty and military luminaries, but a large number also represented average folk in the time before automobiles replaced travel by horse. Illustrated at the left is the popular 9" group "Going to Market," which is usually paired with a "Returning Home" group. Value for the pair: $500-$1000. The titled "Duchess" group on the right is one of a portrait set depicting the Duke and Duchess of Cambridge. 10". Value for the pair: $1000+. *Courtesy of Anita L. Grashof, Gallerie Ani'tiques.*

Miniature group of a little girl and lamb. 2.75". Mid-Victorian. Value: $500-$1000. *Courtesy of Jane McClafferty Antiques.*

Shepherds and sheep group with extensive use of extruded clay to create a "grassy" setting. 5". Early Victorian. Value: $1000+. *Courtesy of Zane Moss Antiques.*

Pair of figures depicting children and swans in a seaside setting (note presence of shells). Left-hand figure 5.50", right-hand figure 5.75". Circa 1870. Value for singles or a pair: $100-$500.

Paired spill vase figures of a ram and a ewe. 5.50". Mid-Victorian (later versions of the same figures were produced by William Kent as late as 1955). Value: $1000+. *Courtesy of Zane Moss Antiques.*

Cow, calf, and milk boy (paired with a similarly posed milkmaid). 9". Mid-Victorian. Value for the pair: $1000+.

A very rare miniature group of a white and gold bird perched on the edge of a nest containing two speckled eggs. 1.75" (diameter), 2" (height). Mid-Victorian. Value: $500-$1000. *Courtesy of Jane McClafferty Antiques.*

Unusual figure of a dog attacking an eagle's nest. 6.50". Circa 1860. Value: $100-$500.

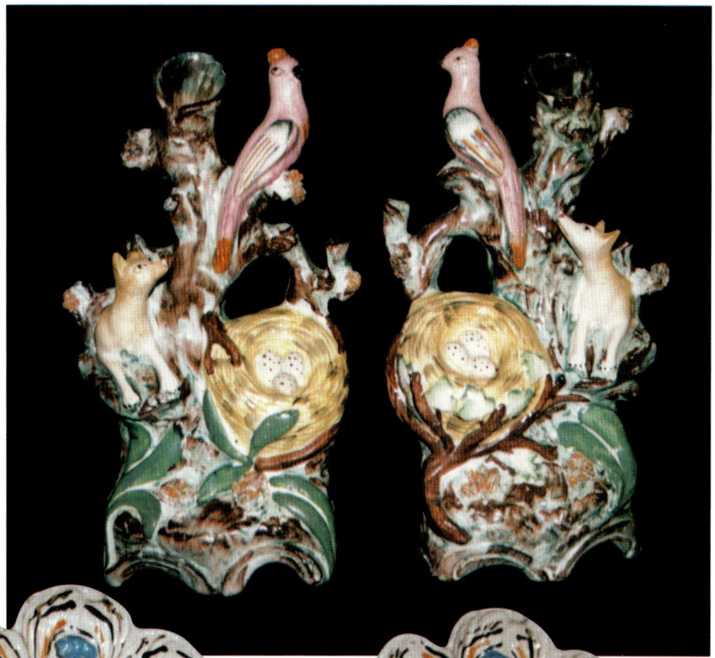

Superb paired spill vase groups comprised of foxes, nests filled with eggs, and birds. 9.50". Early Victorian. Value: $1000+. *Courtesy of Zane Moss Antiques.*

Swan and cygnet spill vase group. 4.50". Mid-Victorian. Value: $100-$500. *Courtesy of Jane McClafferty Antiques.*

Paired peacock figures with tails displayed. The backs of both are impressed, Copyright/Dec.10th 1901/T.H. Sandland." Circa 1901. Value: $1000+. *Courtesy of Zane Moss Antiques.*

Black and white rabbit on a grassy mound. 2.50" height, 3" width. Late 19th century. Value: $500-$1000.

Paired game birds possibly intended to represent ptarmigans (various grouses with feathered feet). 9.50". Mid-Victorian. Value: $1000+. *Courtesy of Zane Moss Antiques.*

Rare spill vase elephant, one of a pair. Possibly inspired by the Jumbo enthusiasm of the 1860s-80s (see Chapter Eighteen for details). Elephants were produced in a range of styles, including variations with spill vases. 5.75". Mid-Victorian. Value for the pair: $1000+. *Courtesy of Zane Moss Antiques.*

Spill holder with a zebra and its keeper. 6.50". Circa 1860. Value: $100-$500

Young man in Turkish costume riding a zebra. 7.50". Early or mid-Victorian. Value: $1000+. *Courtesy of Zane Moss Antiques.*

Rare large white cat wearing a collar and bell with traces of gold detailing remaining. 11". Mid 19th century. Value: $1000+.

Pair of red and white cats seated on pillows. Left-hand figure 7.25", right-hand figure 7". Circa 1890. Value: $100-$500. *Gift of Mrs. Beryl Russell and the late Major Phillip Russell, 1980. Collection: Ballarat Fine Art Gallery (Acc. No. 1981.6.A-B).*

With an eye on the prize – an amusing group of a cat lustfully watching the dog's meal, awaiting an opportunity to pounce. Researchers suggest that dog figures were produced at a ratio of 100-1 over cats, and most 19th century cat figures are considered highly collectible. 6" (height), 6" (width). Late 19th century. Value: $500-$1000.

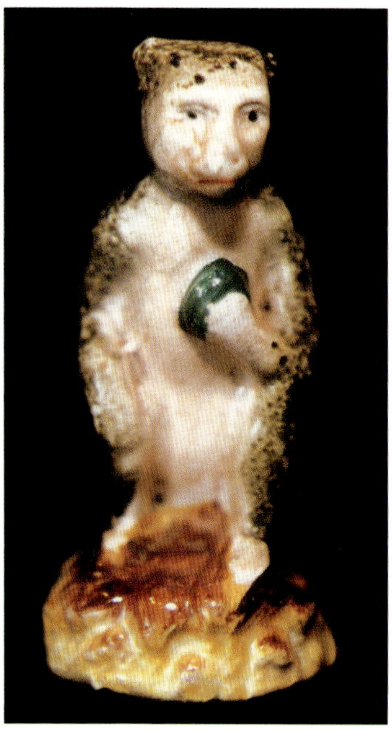

Small figure of a monkey holding a hat. 3.50". Mid-Victorian. Value: $500-$1000. *Courtesy of David P. Willis.*

Kent giraffe with palm tree in background taken from the same mold as earlier Victorian examples. Late examples like the figure illustrated may be identified by the stronger colors used in decoration. 5.50". Circa 1910. Value: $500-$1000

Rare miniature figure of a Terrier, not unlike today's Yorkshire Terrier (and reminiscent of England's most celebrated Yorkie, Huddersfield Ben, born in 1865); originally one of a pair. Terriers were used during the 19th century to chase rats and other vermin that are pests to humankind. In Yorkshire, they were used in the mines. They were also used for entertainment as rat catchers, and this figure may have been inspired by Billy the Rat Catcher (see Chapter Eighteen for details). All Terrier figures are rare and include a parent and pup group, recorded in red and white and brindle color variations (see Pope, pp. 154-155, figs. 2 & 3). 4". Mid-Victorian. Value for the pair: $500-$1000.

Poodle figures and groups were produced in quantity in a wide range of styles and sizes. Pictured here is a pair of large Standard Poodles with two separately molded front legs. 10". Mid-Victorian. Value: $500-$1000. *Courtesy of Anita L. Grashof, Gallerie Ani'tiques.*

Once enormously popular, the English Water Spaniel depicted in this figure is now extinct in Britain. Other models of the breed are recorded, including a puppy Water Spaniel seated on a cushion (illustrated in Chapter Six). 6". Early Victorian. Value: $500-$1000. *Courtesy of Marla Chaikin, William Charles Antiques.*

Crouching poodle with a rose in its mouth, finely modeled, decorated, and having a porcelaineous body. The unusual Rococo-style base is painted with bunches of delicate roses. 3" (height), 5.50" (length). Circa 1850. Value: $500-$1000.

Hound, resembling a Lurcher, at food bowl. Lurchers were cross-bred from Greyhounds and Terriers and, according to Pope, were associated with poachers and gypsies (Pope, 118). Well modeled and decorated. 4.50" (height), 4" (width). Circa 1850-55. Value: $500-$1000.

Poodles with baskets in their mouths. Possibly attributable to the Dudson Pottery due to the thick "fleece" coats applied to the dogs – a characteristic of that pottery's work and the porcelain bodies they used. The finer detail displayed in these figures was indicative of the more expensive figures produced by the pottery. Damage to the tails of both figures. Left-hand figure 3.75", right-hand figure 3.50". Circa 1840. Value: $500-$1000.

Rare and exceptionally well-executed recumbent dog, possibly a Harrier or "Hare Hound," a hunting dog known in Britain since the Middle Ages. 5" (length), 3.75" (height). Early Victorian. Value: $500-$1000. *Courtesy of Marla Chaikin, William Charles Antiques.*

Dalmatian figures were very popular during the 19th century and were modeled in a wide range of styles and sizes (seated and standing). Known as "Coach Dogs," Dalmatians were trained to run behind the rear axle of a carriage or coach and were considered the height of fashion. 6.25". Circa 1875. Value: $1000+. *Courtesy of Zane Moss Antiques.*

Slip-cast, spray-painted Pekinese pair with blue bows. The Pekinese was brought to Britain from China with the approval of Queen Victoria. This particular model was also produced in apricot/orange coloration. An earlier model dating to circa 1885 is recorded by Pope (p. 129, fig. 1). Some Pekinese pairs were made with inset glass eyes. 7.25". Early 20th century. Value: $500-$1000. *Courtesy of Anita L. Grashof, Gallerie Ani'tiques.*

Whippet and hare model, one of a pair (the "mate" carries a hare in its mouth). This example shows unusual black and white decoration and a Disraeli-like forehead curl. Whippets are usually seen in "fawn brown" colors, seated or standing or recumbent, and are recorded on cobalt and turquoise bases. One rare pair is recorded recumbent on arched gilt lined bases, and another is set on the lids of cobalt blue boxes. Whippets were also modeled with spill holders. 11". Early to mid-Victorian. Value for the pair: $1000+. *Courtesy of Zane Moss Antiques.*

Tall, spray-painted Collies; identified by Pope as "Rough Collies" and dated at circa 1890 (Pope, pp. 20-21, fig. 1). 13". Value: $1000+. *Courtesy of Anita L. Grashof, Gallerie Ani'tiques.*

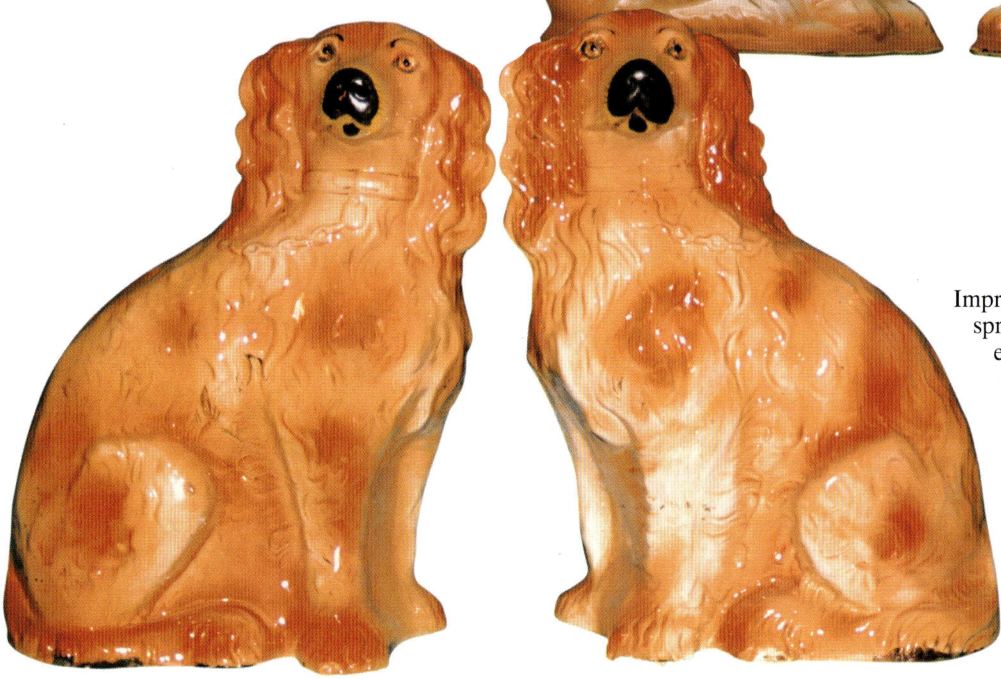

Impressively large dogs, apricot sprayed, with amber inset glass eyes. Although the breed is uncertain, these dogs have a commanding presence. 13". Early 20th century. Value: $1000+. *Courtesy of Anita L. Grashof, Gallerie Ani'tiques.*

Pair of inkwells featuring whippets resting on cobalt bases. 4" (height), 5" (length) both figures. Circa 1850. Value: $500-$1000.

Classically dressed children with their pet rats – an unlikely yet charming subject. The grape-leaf decoration around the bases features raised molding and painting. 5.50" left-hand figure, 5.75" right-hand figure. Circa 1870. Value: $500-$1000.

Very rare pair of spill holders depicting leopards. 7.75" each. Circa 1860. Value: $1000+. *Gift of Mrs. Beryl Russell and the late Major Phillip Russell, 1980. Collection: Ballarat Fine Art Gallery (Acc. No. 1981.51.A-B).*

Chapter Nine
British Royalty: Figural Commemoratives

When Princess Victoria, granddaughter of George III, acceded to the British throne on June 20, 1837, her youthful charm did much to restore the flagging spirits of a nation whose crown had been tarnished by the unpleasantness of earlier Hanoverians: their foreignness, their ineptitude, their excesses, and their general unattractiveness. Victoria's subjects were filled with a renewed sense of pride and patriotism, which would presage a reign of sixty-four years and Britain's glory as one of history's most powerful empires. For the potters of Staffordshire, Victoria represented the beginning of portrait figure production.

In those early days, Victoria bore no resemblance to later impressions of a stout, forbidding, and matronly woman who dressed in widow's weeds. Barely eighteen, the new queen was a small, blue-eyed, fair-haired girl, completely unlike the formidable monarch she would become and completely unaware of the impact she would have, not only on Britain, but on the whole world. Nor could she have guessed that "Victorian" styles in clothing, jewelry, ceramics, and furniture, along with a huge range of period collectibles, would, within one hundred years of her coronation, enjoy popularity unmatched by collectibles of any other era.

Early in her reign, as Victoria erased the memory of preceding Hanoverians and led her nation into global acquisition and a well-defined industrial age, popular sentiment was strong. Victorian royal commemoratives were as enthusiastically collected and prized then as they are today. Commemorative cups, plates, horse brasses, pitchers, plaques, and even mold-pressed glassware items bore the Queen's likeness. Early in the era, copies of Victoria's serpent engagement ring were fashionable and, later, other jewelry items including bar brooches engraved with the year of her diamond jubilee came into vogue.

Victoria was a woman of contrasts, and so was the period of her reign. Not unlike our own place in history, the Victorian era was a time of extremes. The aristocracy became increasingly affluent and the middle classes were offered greater opportunities for advancement than ever before. However, conditions among the poor worsened: the appalling conditions of child labor and the widespread establishment of workhouses and poorhouses underscored their abject poverty. Regardless, the Victorian age was a decorative one, best remembered for its ornamentation, its resplendent embellishments, and the imposing image of the Queen for which it has been named.

The Staffordshire potters had already established themselves as preeminent in the field of ceramics and as masters of the earthenware "dialect" through which they created historical "documents" in pottery. They were a canny lot: industrious and industry-minded, and quick to capitalize on consumer interests and enthusiasms; and the interests of the Empire were firmly focused on its young and "photogenic" monarch. Victoria's accession saw a tremendous surge in portrait figure production. During the early 1840s, Victoria, Albert, and their growing family were held especially high in the hearts of the nation; and the potters, ever on the alert for a money-making opportunity, capitalized on this popularity by depicting the royal family in a wide range of portrait figure models.

There are numerous portrait models of Victoria in which she is depicted seated, standing, on horseback, and even holding a scroll and flag as she stands beside a lion. She appears in "queenly" poses as well as in more spontaneous "personal" moods. The earliest portrait figure of Victoria portrays the queen seated on a sofa. She holds an open book in her right hand. On the sofa next to her is a large, double-arched crown. The placement of the crown beside the queen rather than on her head suggests a production date before Victoria's coronation a year following her accession. This rare figure rests on a fairly elaborate, four-footed table base of the kind formerly attributed to Obadiah Sherratt. Two plaques on the base read "Her Majesty" and "Queen Victoria." According to Pugh, after Victoria acceded, the potters anticipated great demand for a Staffordshire figure of the new Queen. Pugh further remarks that the mold used for this figure was actually an adaptation of the mold used for a figure of Maria Malibran, a young opera singer who died in September of 1836. The mold for Malibran's figure was designed after an engraving by J. Rogers for the *Dramatic Magazine*, and was modified through the inclusion of a crown to provide the buying public with a model of Victoria by June of 1837. With time always being of the essence for the production of a topical figure, this recycling and re-titling of molds was a common practice among the enterprising potters; often one portrait mold was altered or simply "redecorated" in order to create a new personality from the old without the cost-intensive and time-consuming process of hiring an artist to design a new mold (Pugh A118).

Victoria married Albert of Saxe-Coburg on February 10, 1840, when she was twenty-one years old. The marriage was characterized by an intense and enduring love on Victoria's part that was less whole-heartedly returned by Albert. Although Victoria made him Prince Consort in 1857 and, although she bore him nine children, Albert never fully returned her love with the same blind passion. In 1840, however, such knowledge was the province of future biographers, and the potters commemorated the royal wedding with several portrait figures of the young bride and groom. Some of these figures are remarkable for the likeness they bear to the regal subjects while others (potted in the heat of the moment to capitalize on the royal nuptials) bear resemblance to any well-dressed young swains.

The earliest known commemorative portrait figures that can be definitely attributed to a particular potter are paired figures of Albert seated alone and Victoria seated and holding the Princess Royal. The impressed mark "LLOYD/SHELTON" is found at the back of each. John and Rebecca Lloyd worked at their factory in Shelton from 1834-52, and these figures most likely date to early in 1841, shortly after the Princess Royal was born.

The potters produced several paired figures of the Queen and her Consort, including one exemplary pair that depicts each seated on an ornate throne with a lion and a unicorn at each of their feet (Victoria holds the Prince of Wales). There are also many portrait figures of the royal children. Some of the most charming include Victoria as a new mother. In a few of these, she holds her first-born, the Princess Royal (Victoria Adelaide Mary Louise, born in November 1840) and, in others, she holds her first son (the future King Edward VII, born in November 1841). Many of these are paired with figures of Albert in a range of styles and poses. The royal family's domestic life appeared, early on, as the "stuff" of romance, and the Victorians, in their quixotic return to romanticism, made much of the new Queen's personal and royal life. Not to be undone by other commemorative industries, the Staffordshire potteries began to create portrait figure models of the Queen and her family that were eagerly purchased by cottage folk and by members of the rising middle class.

Of the various models of the royal children, although all were at some time represented, the most frequently featured are Edward and the Princess Royal, often in pony or goat carts, standing beside family pets, or seated on domestic animals' backs (the Princess Royal properly side-saddle). Many of these are untitled, but their early Victorian production dates (when the royal children were under ten years of age) and supporting details like clothing (including Prince of Wales feathers) strongly suggest that they are indeed of the "royals." One such model is a striking watch holder group in which two children are depicted with a greyhound, very likely Prince Albert's dog, Eos, which was painted by Sir Edwin Landseer in 1841. This watch holder group was probably modeled within a few years of Landseer's painting. A variation shows the children in a similar pose with a Spaniel, possibly intended to portray their mother's beloved Spaniel "Dash," painted by Landseer in 1836. Both appear in well-colored versions (probably the first issues) and in all white (most likely produced some years later). The design of a few portrait figures of the children can be traced to engravings. In one, the Prince of Wales sits on a black pony and is paired with the Princess Royal similarly posed. The source of this portrait pair was "The Young Cavalier," engraved by John Cochran after a painting by William Salter.

Consumer demand for figures of the royal children declined by the early 1850s, and one of the most outstanding portrait figures of the decade is an elaborate depiction of Victoria seated on a sofa with Albert to her right. This piece is so well made that it may have been produced for the *Great Exhibition* of 1851 (Pugh, A119). The Rococo base is decorated with a rose, a thistle, and a shamrock, presumably symbolic of England, Scotland, and Ireland.

As Victoria's reign progressed, her politics and personality came under closer and colder scrutiny. Joblessness and poverty increased among the lower classes, war blackened the horizon, and there was even an assassination attempt against the queen. The Staffordshire potters produced fewer royal family motifs and turned their attention to war heroes, political and theatrical personalities, and even criminals. In models dating to the middle years of Victoria's reign, she is portrayed as an "aside" to such persons as Napoleon III, and with the King of Sardinia, Victor Emmanuel II (1820-1878), who would later become the first King of Italy (1861-1878). There is a patriotic Crimean War piece that depicts Victoria standing between, and holding hands with, Napoleon III and the Sultan of Turkey, showing their alliance – indicative of the new "global" focus of the Victorian era when astute international and political affiliations became central to pottery-buyers' thinking. Britain had entered into an age that was the foundation of our own. No longer could a country stand isolated. In order to flourish, alliances that may have once have seemed tantamount to treason became essential to the survival of Britain's tiny but prosperous island.

Once past childhood, the royal children were portrayed, albeit less frequently and less charmingly, as adults. The Princess Royal, mother of Kaiser William II, is depicted in several figures that date to the time of her engagement in 1857 to Prince Frederick William of Prussia and to 1858 when they were married. Also dating to circa 1858 are figures (three each) of the Prince of Wales and Prince Alfred that commemorate their first commissions in the army and navy. In 1862, the year in which the Prince of Wales's betrothal to Princess Alexandra of Denmark was announced, Staffordshire portrait models of the prince and his future bride commemorated the event. (A later, titled, pair shows Edward as King and Alexandra as Queen.) In at least one case, molds used for Princess Royal portrait figures at the time of her engagement were altered and reissued to represent Princess Alexandra at *her* betrothal-time five years later. Additional portrait figures connected with the marriages of Victoria's other children were also produced.

Although she was essentially a simple woman at heart, Victoria's character was tinged with contradictions. She was capable of egotism and immoderation and held to her own views with extraordinary stringency. It may be true that Albert was the only human being she ever truly loved and, therefore, she revered him as a man of perfection – a consideration with which her subjects did not agree. In the light of Victoria's strong temperament, the encompassing power of her sovereignty, and Albert's inability to capture the collective heart of the realm as securely as he captured its Queen's, the Prince Consort died (of typhoid in 1861), as Evelyn Anthony described him, a "*disappointed and disillusioned man whose wife's adoration had never compensated him for his failure to win esteem in his adopted country*" (Evelyn Anthony, page vi). Victoria's acute mourning, however, had a penetrating effect upon the nation. Although there is no nineteenth century documentation to confirm the "legend," it is widely believed that Victoria's obvious grief and the mourning attire she wore until her own death in 1901 did not go unnoticed by the Staffordshire potters who began to produce Jackfield-type Spaniels and other figures in mournful black decoration. (See Chapter Three.)

The final pottery portrait of Victoria was one of a pair of monumental figures of the Queen and the Prince of Wales, produced to commemorate Victoria's Golden Jubilee in 1887. This figure shows Victoria standing with her hands folded at her waist, highlighted by a crown and veil, ermine-edged robe, a multi-flounced skirt, and the garter sash. The model is seen in versions that bear, alternatively, the gilt script titles "Queen of England" or "Queen of England and Empress of India," the latter including the dates of her coronation and jubilee. Ironically, these final tributes are undoubtedly copycat models and variations of a better-made original issue produced to commemorate Victoria's silver and diamond jubilees with additional title information added to later figures. With kudos to the potters, the earlier of these models depict Victoria with the golden brown hair of her youth, while some of those produced later suggest, with representative Staffordshire realism, the length of her reign symbolized by gray "Widow of Windsor" hair.

It is important to note that when Victoria first became queen, the potters swarmed to her royal person with an almost unbecoming eagerness. Toward the conclusion of her reign, they lacked the impetus and interest to even model a new figure in recognition of her spectacular and record-breaking longevity as a monarch. The potters' dismissal of the importance of Victoria's jubilee was symptomatic, undoubtedly, of both the public ennui with royalty and declining interest in Staffordshire portrait figures.

Although Victoria and her family were central to the potters' portrait figures, the potters indulged in a bit of historical license and produced a range of earlier "royals." Included were: King John signing the Magna Charta, King Henry V trying on a crown, Henry VIII trying on a wife, King Charles depicted variously with Nell Gwynn and Oliver Cromwell, looking affably towards each (not surprising in the first instance, but remarkable in the second), Richard III in moments of greater and lesser intrigue, equestrian portraits of William III and his wife Mary, and George IV seated on a sofa besides an ample and amiable Mrs. Fitzherbert. The extended Victorian royal family also merited a passing interest from the potters: The Duke and Duchess of Cambridge (Victoria's uncle and aunt), George the latter Duke of Cambridge (Victoria's cousin), the Duke of Clarence (Victoria's grandson and a Jack the Ripper suspect) and his betrothed Princess Mary of Teck, and Princess May who married George V, although George himself never made the cut.

Rare figure of Henry VIII and Anne Boleyn, taken from the cover of a music front based on an engraving by Brandard entitled "*First Book of Select Airs from Anne Boleyn.*" 10". Circa 1860. Value: $1000+. *Courtesy of Susan Bishop and Darcy McGroarty, Bishop and Daughter Antiques.*

The Staffordshire potters were observant artists and historians who, through the medium of simple earthenware, left numerous remarkable and important images of the British monarchy, most prolifically and importantly of Victoria and her family, for today's collectors. These portrait figures might be said to form a unique category of Royal commemoratives with a character all their own. Royal portrait figures are eagerly sought by current collectors and range in height from about five to seventeen inches, the most impressive, collectible, and costly being the largest pieces, particularly those that are titled. Models of the queen alone are especially desired and often comprise the centerpieces of royalty collections.

Victoria may no longer hold sway and sovereignty over the British Empire, but she remains the undisputed ruler of a folk-art and of an era. It is hard to imagine that one woman will ever again exert such influence on taste and style. How often has a young woman been awakened at an early hour to take up the reins of a glorious empire in her nightdress? Never again will one woman come under the tireless scrutiny of the greatest group of ceramic artists the world has ever known.

Titled group of "Charles & Cromwell" spill holder depicting Cromwell signing Charles I's death warrant in 1649. There is no known source for this large group, but it is probably theatrical. 15". Circa 1870. Value: $500-$1000.

Untitled portrait of Charles I (1600-49), originally paired with a matching figure of Oliver Cromwell. The son of James VI of Scotland, Charles I was King of Great Britain and Ireland. Civil War broke out during his reign, and Charles was defeated at the Battle of Naseby in 1645. He surrendered to the Scots in May of 1646 and was executed on January 30, 1649. The paired figures have been recorded with an 1851 Sampson Smith factory mark on their bases. 13". Mid-Victorian. Value for the pair $500-$1000; for either single $100-$500. *Courtesy of Anita L. Grashof, Gallerie Ani'tiques.*

The Prince of Wales and Princess Alexandra of Denmark (later Princess of Wales and then Queen Alexandra) at the time of their betrothal. Although the couple married in 1863, this figure was most likely to have been issued as a commemorative for their engagement. 7.50". Value: $500-$1000.

Titled paired figures of King William III (1650-1702) and Queen Mary II (1662-94). Mary was the eldest child of James II and Anne Hyde. She married William of Orange in 1677. They were declared King and Queen of England, Scotland, and Ireland in 1689. 9.50". Value: $500-$1000.

Titled in raised capitals "QUEEN" and "ALBERT" depicting Victoria and Albert, the prince Consort. Both figures 10.75". Circa 1840. Value for the pair: $1000+; for either single: $500-$1000.

Portrait of a youthful Victoria, entitled "Queen" in raised gilt capitals, depicting the new monarch seated on a horse; paired with a mounted portrait of Albert. Several pairs of these figures were produced in well-colored variants during the 1840s. 7.50". Early Victorian. Value for the pair: $500-$1000; for either single: $100-$500. *Courtesy of Anita L. Grashof, Gallerie Ani'tiques.*

Victoria and the Princess Royal and Albert and the Prince of Wales, later Edward VII. These glimpses into the family life of the Royals depict a family at ease: as indicated by the relaxed postures of both Victoria and Albert with their feet resting on stools, and the obvious affection for their parents as seen in the poses of the royal children. Britain had not yet soured in its love affair with the young queen, her consort, and their ever-burgeoning family and eagerly bought these intimate and sentimental portraits. Victoria 6", Albert 6.50". Circa 1845. Value for the pair $1000+; for either single: $500-$1000.

Portrait most likely the Princess Royal (originally paired with the Prince of Wales), seated side-saddle on the back of a goat. 5". Early Victorian. Value: pair $500-$1000, singles $100-$500. *Courtesy of Anita L. Grashof, Gallerie Ani'tiques.*

Prince of Wales with a toy ship and the Princess Royal with a parrot. Prince 6.75", Princess 6.50". Circa 1850. Value: pair $1000+; singles $500-$1000.

A figure group that very likely represents the Princess Royal standing next to the newborn Prince of Wales. This identification is open to conjecture, but the figure is, nonetheless, charming. 6.25". Circa 1845. Value: $500-$1000.

The Princess Royal and Prince of Wales sleeping under the protection of a guardian angel. Behind the figure is a copy of the engraving titled *"Guardian Angel"* by G. Dawe on which it is based. One of the great pleasures of Staffordshire collecting is the discovery of original sources. Often, the close resemblances of the figures to their sources serve as a tribute to the potters. 9". Circa 1845. Value: $1000+.

Although the woman and two children in this boat group remain unidentified, there has been some debate as to whether or not they might be Victoria, the Crown Prince, and the Princess Royal. There is nothing to support the theory, but the group is charming nonetheless. 10.50". Early Victorian. Value: $500-$1000. *Courtesy of Anita L. Grashof, Gallerie Ani'tiques.*

Very rare figure of the Prince of Wales by Thomas Parr based on an 1846 Xavier Winterhalter portrait of the Prince wearing a sailor suit, painted as a Christmas present for Albert from Victoria. Minton also used this figure as the source for a Parian statuette of the Prince. Later and cruder reproductions of this figure are common. 12". Circa 1850. Value: Parr originals $1000+, reproductions $100-$500.

Titled portrait pair of Queen Alexandra and King Edward VII. 12". Mid-Victorian. Value: $1000+. *Courtesy of Anita L. Grashof, Gallerie Ani'tiques.*

Titled portrait group of the Princess Royal (Victoria Adelaide Mary Louise, Victoria and Albert's eldest child) with Prince Frederick III of Prussia. They were married in 1858; Frederick became the Crown Prince of Prussia in 1861 and succeeded his father as Emperor on March 9, 1888 – a short-lived reign as Frederick died on June 15th of the same year. Victoria Adelaide, died in 1901, the same year of her mother's passing. 16". Mid-Victorian. Value: $500-$1000. *Courtesy of Anita L. Grashof, Gallerie Ani'tiques.*

Edward "Prince of Wales" and Victoria "Queen of England." This is the last known original portrait figure of the Queen as any later figures were based on this likeness, not on Victoria herself. The figure of Victoria was re-issued in 1887 and 1897 to commemorate her gold and diamond jubilees. These later issues may be identified by the fact that the 1887 figure bears the additional title "Empress of India," while the 1897 version is slightly smaller in size and of reduced quality. One late version depicts the aging queen with grey hair. Prince 17", Queen 16.50". Circa 1870s. Value for the 1870s pair: $1000+; for singles $500-$1000.

Portrait of an aging Queen Victoria, depicted with gray hair and titled "Queen of England & Empress of India/Crowned June 20th 1837." This figure was issued in commemoration of her Diamond Jubilee in 1897; the gray-haired version is not commonly seen. 17". Value: $500-$1000. *Courtesy of Anita L. Grashof, Gallerie Ani'tiques.*

Portrait group of the Princess Royal holding a Spaniel (possibly her mother's "Dash") and her brother Bertie produced in all-white with little attention to detail. As Victoria's reign lengthened, public interest in portraits of the Royal Family lessened, and groups like this reflected flagging public interest in Victoria, her family, and Staffordshire figures in general. 9". Late 19th century. Value: $100-$500. *Courtesy of Anita L. Grashof, Gallerie Ani'tiques.*

Chapter Ten

The Other Monarchy: Foreign Royalty, Politicians, and Explorers

By the 1850s, Staffordshire pottery portrait figures had gained an unprecedented popularity as aides to decorative, patriotic, religious, or social success. The potters eagerly engaged in production of an ever-increasing gallery of important persons. The potters (always with an eye on public opinion, taste, and the news-worthy) quickly realized that enthusiasm for the Royal Family was waning: something of an ongoing but "been there, done that" experience. With public boredom starting to collect around the British monarchy like cobwebs around a neglected ornament, the enterprising geniuses of North Staffordshire apparently decided it was time for a metaphorical "spring-cleaning" of their subject matter and began to cast further afield for marketable celebrities. So commenced the potters' and their public's dalliance, if not full-blown love affair, with the "other monarchy" – foreign royalty, British politicians, and explorers. These persons were godsends to the pottery figure trade and answered the potters' requirements for desirable subject matter in numerous ways: they were newsworthy, they were decorative, and they were patriotic. Invariably, they were linked with foreign military alliances and engagements, or foreign matrimonial alliances and wedding engagements involving Victoria's several children.

Should a catalogue of Staffordshire figures produced during the 1850s and 1860s exist it would read like a "Who *was* Who" of European Royalty. Colorful and newsworthy personalities like Louis-Philippe, King of France, who abdicated in 1848 and sought asylum in England under the alias of "Mr. Smith," were commemorated in earthenware figures to the delight of the pottery-buying public. A pair of figures that depict Victoria and Louis-Philippe show the Queen and King seated on circular gilt lined bases with lions at their feet. France was a popular source of inspiration for the "other" royals, and one of the most important Frenchmen depicted by the potters was Napoleon I (1769-1821) who was defeated at Waterloo on June 18, 1815 and banished to St. Helena where he died. Figures of Napoleon range from the monumental to the miniature – some in standing pose and others on horseback. Napoleon III was depicted in numerous figures, including alliance groups and with the Empress Eugenie (sometimes holding the infant Prince). Other foreign royalty figures included Victor Emanuel II (King of Sardinia 1849-61 and King of Italy 1861-78), Frederick Charles (Prince of Prussia 1828-1885), Leopold I and Louise-Marie (King and Queen of Belgium 1790-1865 and 1812-1850), William I (seventh King of Prussia and First German Emperor 1797-1888), Augusta (Queen of Prussia 1811-1890), Frederick William III (Crown Prince of Prussia, then second German Emperor 1831-1888), Prince Christian of Schleswig-Holstein (1831-1917), and Franz Joseph I (Emperor of Austria, King of Hungary 1830-1916). The potters cast their vision even further afield to the East in their search for royal "subjects," and Alexander II (Czar of Russia, 1818-1881), Marie-Alexandrovna (Empress of Russia 1824-1880), and Nasr-Ed-Din (Shah of Persia 1829-1886), joined the coroneted ranks. For their roles in wars, coups, alliances, inter-marriages with the British royal family, or, as in the case of the Shah, as proponents of the spread of the "British way of life" to "uncivilized heathens," all earned the potters' attention and merited collection by the Victorian public.

As well as being a period characterized by royal re-alliances, the Victorian Era was also one of major change in politics and diplomacy. Constant activity in Victorian politics saw the change from politics characterized by nepotism to politics in which negotiation was fundamental. The Empire was, at all times, teetering on the edge of belligerence and conflict, where the skills of statesmen and politicians were not, as popular portrayals presented, solely for use as barbed and belittling repartee in the Houses of Commons and Lords. British diplomats, statesmen, and politicians did not always acquit themselves honorably, or avoid the occasional undignified imbroglio. On the whole, however, they managed themselves and their nation in a manner that elicited tolerance (if not always admiration) from the population on constitutional matters.

Victoria acceded to the throne amidst political unrest and demands for electoral reform that resulted in riots by groups of dissidents like the Chartists. The young queen turned to her Prime Minister, the avuncular Lord Melbourne, for advice and inspiration, and so did the potters of Staffordshire in their attempts to answer the demands of *their* subjects (the pottery-buying public). Lord Melbourne (1779-1848) who achieved unilateral approval for the manner in which he introduced the newly crowned Victoria to her sovereign duties, was the first of many prime ministers to draw the potters' attention. Sir Robert Peel, Victoria's second prime minister and popular subject of the potters, was famous for, as Home Secretary, his formation of a new police service ("Bobbies" or "Peelers") in 1822, his repeal of the Corn Laws in 1846 opening up hitherto protected British agriculture to free-trade, and his spectacular Hyde Park riding accident death in 1850. Other prime ministers who captured the interest of the potters included Benjamin "Dizzy" Disraeli (prime minister 1874-1880 and part-time novelist under whose tutelage Victoria aspired to the status of "Empress of India," and England purchased the Suez Canal), William Gladstone (prime minister 1868-1874, 1880-1885, 1886, 1892-1894, the "Grand Old Man" of British politics, paired with a figure of his wife by the potters), and Arthur Wellesley, the Duke of Wellington (prime minister 1828-1830 and hero of Waterloo).

Other politicians drew the attention of the Staffordshire potters and were rewarded with portrait figures for their contributions to the statesmanship and fashion-sense of the period: the Chartist radical Thomas Slingsby Duncombe, known as "the best-dressed man in the House" joined the more notable and noteworthy like Anthony Ashley Cooper, the Seventh Earl of Shaftesbury, member of parliament and distinguished philanthropist. Shaftesbury opposed slavery, fought for the reform of lunacy laws (1829), the protection of factory workers (1833), the protection of colliery workers (1842), chimney sweeps, and of child laborers; he also helped establish "ragged schools" for the children of the poor. Shaftesbury was rewarded with numerous figures commemorating his noble campaigns: one of the most fascinating and rare being a portrait of the statesman himself and a small child posed beside a discarded pick, shovel, and harness of the kind worn by juvenile mine workers. Another politician and economist, Richard Cobden, the "Apostle of Free-Trade," earned ceramic immortality through his principal role in the repeal of the Corn Laws and his philosophies of anti-interventionism and free-trade.

Politicians from the other side of the Irish Sea also drew public interest and generated several portrait figures. The Irish Republican Daniel O'Connell, known as "The Liberator," was a leader of the agitation for the rights for Catholics. He was elected as a Member of Parliament in 1828 but was denied taking a seat because of his Catholicism; however, after the Catholic Emancipation Bill was passed, he assumed his seat in 1830. O'Connell was also Lord Mayor of Dublin (1841), and he was among the staunchest advocates for a free Ireland. Another Irish politician, Charles Stewart Parnell, president of the Irish National Land League, was jailed in 1881 for his open opposition of Gladstone's Land Bill for Irish land settlement, reached agreement with the British government with whom he forged the "Kilmainham Treaty" for Home Rule, and was accused of criminal activities through his involvement with the Land league, charges for which he was acquitted after a Royal Commission. Thomas Sexton, initially a "Parnellite" Member of Parliament, also drew the attention of the potters through his commitment to the cause of Irish Home Rule. William Smith O'Brien, parliamentarian and campaigner for the improvement of poor relief and education in Ireland, joined O'Connell's Repeal League and in 1848 led an abortive uprising against British rule. He was charged with treason and transported to the penal settlement of Tasmania. O'Brien captured the potters' imagination because of his "criminality" (the actual insurrection took place in a cabbage patch!) and the romance of both his sentence and his relationship with his wife, Lucy, with whom his portrait figure is frequently paired.

American statesmen and politicians also interested the potters and the pottery buyers. Presidents George Washington (1732-1799, first American president), Thomas Jefferson (1743-1826, who secured the prohibition of the slave trade), and Abraham Lincoln (1809-1865 admired for an anti-slavery stance) all had their portraits made in earthenware. So, too, did the American statesman, philosopher, and scientist Benjamin Franklin (1706-1790).

This group is identified by the Hardings as the Crown Prince in a boat at Windsor Castle (Harding, Book One, p. 184, fig. 579). It is also considered by some to be a depiction of Prince Charles Edward Stuart, better known as Bonny Prince Charlie or the "Young Pretender," seen escaping to Skye by boat after the Scottish defeat at Culloden in 1846. 7.50". Circa 1850. Value: $500-$1000. *Courtesy of Susan Bishop and Darcy McGroarty, Bishop and Daughter Antiques.*

Italian soldier, patriot, and statesman Giuseppe Garibaldi (1807-1882) was a favorite among the potters. Garibaldi devoted his life to revolutionary activities, first in South America where he fled to escape a death sentence in his home country, and then in Italy after his return in 1848. Forced to leave Italy again, Garibaldi sought shelter in New York, returning to render assistance to Victor Emmanuel in 1859. With the aid of his "Red Shirts," a rag-tag group of a thousand ill-armed rebels, Sicily was freed from the grip of an occupying military force nearly 25,000 strong, after which they turned their sights to Naples. When Victor Emmanuel was proclaimed King of Italy in 1861, Garibaldi declined all rewards, but was warmly received in England as the hero of Italian independence. The potters were quick to portray him, most particularly Thomas Parr who modeled a large, life-like, and finely detailed figure of Garibaldi standing beside his horse.

The Victorian Era was a time for leaders, and the Victorian people were profoundly interested in monarchs, politicians, and adventurers, the latter managing to stir public attention through their daring-do, patriotism, and the pseudo-science to which they subscribed in their adventures. Exploration was part of the Kingdom's international presence as well, and the potters responded with portrait figures of explorers. These figures included the titled, paired portraits of Sir John and Lady Franklin (see Chapter Sixteen). Sir John, who entered the Navy when he was fourteen years old and fought in the Battle of Trafalgar, spent his early years exploring the arctic coast of Canada. Awarded a knighthood in 1829, he sailed in 1845 in search of the North-West Passage and disappeared. His wife financed five ships in an attempt to find him, but despite numerous searches no word was received until 1854 when a boat containing the remains of his crew and a note stating that Sir John had died on June 11, 1847 were discovered.

Louis Napoleon on horseback with three of the horse's legs molded free; the base is titled in raised gilt capitals. 11". Mid-Victorian. Value: $1000+. *Courtesy of Madelena Antiques.*

Very rare portrait of the French Royal Family, including an enthroned Eugenie, Empress of France, and the Prince Imperial. 7". Circa 1855. Value: $1000+.

Other explorers who caught the potters' attention included Captain James Cook (1728-1779) who, while in the command of the "Endeavour" on an expedition to observe the transit of Venus, circumnavigated the coast of New Zealand and discovered the East Coast of Australia. His voyages also included expeditions to discover how far southward the Arctic reached, and to discover a passage round the coast of North America. Other explorations took Cook to Hawaii where he was killed by natives. A portrait figure depicting Cook seated at a chart-strewn table is based on a painting by Nathaniel Dance and is purported to be one of the most complicated figures ever modeled by the potters. Sir Richard Francis Burton (1821-1890), along with his wife Lady Isabel Burton (see Chapter Sixteen), was also a Victorian explorer of note. Burton and co-explorer Speke set out to discover the sources of the Nile in 1856 and in 1858 discovered Lake Tanganyika. Burton assumed consular duties after 1861 that led him to postings around the world. During their travels, Burton and his wife, Lady Isabel, co-authored numerous popular accounts of their activities. Figures of Burton and his wife show them sporting a strange hybrid attire of a combination of Arabian and Western styles perched atop equally strangely disproportionate camels – exotic, exciting, and exactly what the pottery-buying public required of their explorers.

The nineteenth century was a time of great vitality and variety. The potters were able to tap into the remarkable diversity and the unquenchable curiosity of the Victorian people in creating figures that tell us today of the "other monarchy" – the foreign royalty, the politicians and statesmen, and the explorers who powered their century toward some of the most profound and far-reaching change the world has ever known.

Napoleon patriotically held captive beneath the British lion; originally one of a matched pair. 9.50". Produced around the time of the Anglo-French war scare in 1860 (see Chapter Eleven for details). Value for a pair: $1000+; for a single: $500-$1000. *Courtesy of Madelena Antiques.*

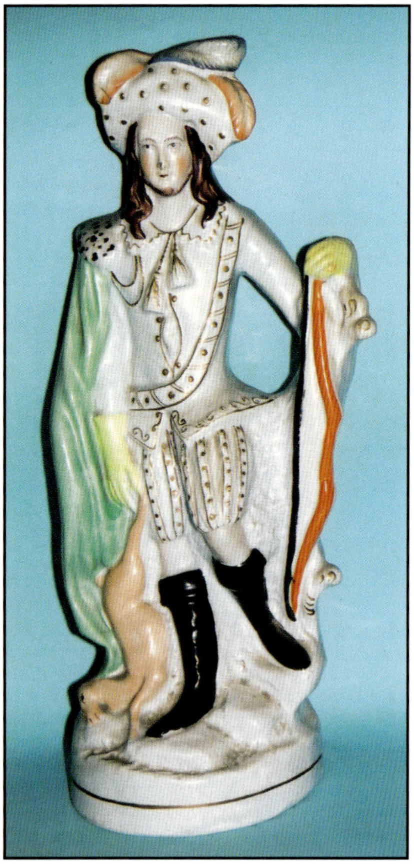

The “other monarchy” included, to some extent, various members of the aristocracy and the privileged elite. Here is a figure of a nobleman hunting game. 16". Circa 1870. Value: $500-$1000.

Portrait group titled “Lion Slayer” representing the “king” of big-game hunters and explorers – Roualeyn Gordon-Cummings (1820-1866). Cummings was educated at Eton and served in the Madras Cavalry from 1838-40. In 1843, he became an explorer and sportsman in South Africa; his fame was so great that some of his hunting trophies were displayed at the Great Exhibition of 1851. His museum at Fort Augustus attracted large Victorian audiences, and reminiscences of his travels were published in the very popular *Five Years of a Hunter's Life in the Far Interior of South Africa*. This group is also seen in well-colored variations.16". Circa 1855. Value: $500-$1000. *Courtesy of Anita L. Grashof, Gallerie Ani'tiques.*

Finely modeled and decorated figure of a man in Eastern dress by Thomas Parr frequently identified as the explorer Dr. C. L. Meryon, although this identification has yet to be substantiated. Meryon was the physician and traveling companion of the eccentric explorer Lady Hester Stanhope who traveled extensively throughout the Middle East and Holy Land during the early 19th century (see Chapter Sixteen for details). 9.50". Circa 1860. Value: $1000+.

Possibly another portrait figure of the big-game hunter and explorer, Roualeyn Gordon-Cummings. 11". Circa 1855. Value: $1000+.

Paired portrait figures of Queen Victoria and French King Louis-Philippe (who sought asylum in England under the alias of "Mr. Smith"). 7.25". Circa 1845. Value: $1000+. *Courtesy of Roy W. Bunn Antiques.*

Anthony Ashley Cooper, Seventh Earl of Shaftesbury (a member of parliament and philanthropist) was instrumental in the abolition of child labor, the reform of lunacy laws, and the protection of factory and colliery workers. He opposed slavery and was responsible for the establishment of the Board of Health of the 1840s to improve the lot of the poor and needy. Shaftesbury was also a keen supporter of the "Ragged Schools" that helped make education available to all. Shaftesbury is depicted with a child colliery worker in this figure: the pick, shovel, and miner's harness providing the necessary clues to identification. 10.25". Circa 1850. Value: $1000+.

Arthur Wellesley, First Duke of Wellington, military leader, and "elder statesman" who led the overthrow of Napoleon at Waterloo; prime minister 1828-1830, and most famous military commander of the 19th century. His funeral at St Paul's in 1852 was sited as one of the most spectacular pageants of the Victorian Era. It is likely that this figure was made to commemorate his death. 13". Circa 1852. Value: $1000+.

"A. LINCOLN." A very rare portrait of Abraham Lincoln, sixteenth President of the United States, mounted on horseback. Lincoln, originally a lawyer, was elected to his first term of office in 1861, a moth prior to the outbreak of the American Civil War. He was elected to his second term in 1865. As well as being intended for the American market, figures of Lincoln also sold well in Britain due to his abolitionist stance. Lincoln's 1865 assassination by John Wilkes Booth at Ford's Theatre in Washington DC very likely inspired production of this figure. 15.50". Circa 1865. Value: $1000+.

Sir Robert Peel (1788-1850) entered Parliament at the age of 21 and served as the Secretary for Ireland and then as the Home Secretary. He introduced the first government-run police service in Britain in 1822 as prior to his introduction of trained police, known as "Peelers" or "Bobbies" in his honor, law-enforcement was privately run and subject to corruption. Peel served two terms as Prime Minister (1834-35 and 1841-46) and as such carried through the repeal of the hated "Corn Laws" in 1846. He died in a riding accident in 1850 and it is likely that this figure was made to coincide with that event. 7.50". Circa 1850. Value: $1000+.

To the authors' knowledge, this uniformed man with his lady is a previously unrecorded group possibly representing one of Robert Peel's "Peelers" or "Bobbies." 9". Mid-Victorian. Value: $100-$500.

Richard Cobden was a philosopher and economist who was elected as a parliamentarian in 1841 and became known as the "Apostle-of-Free-Trade." Loved by the poor, he founded the "Anti Corn Law League" to open up the import of cheaper grain in order to help make food cheaper for the needy. Cobden was opposed to the Crimean War and openly supported the North during the American Civil War for its anti-slavery philosophy. Cobden remained in parliament until his death in 1865. This figure possibly dates from the repeal of the Corn Laws in 1846. 6.50". Circa 1850. Value: $1000+.

One of a series of Thomas Parr portrait figures of the Italian patriot and soldier Giuseppe Garibaldi who won the admiration of the British public through his heroic victory in the campaign for the liberation of Sicily and Naples in 1860. His men, dressed in red shirts or civilian clothes and armed with muskets scavenged from a rubbish dump, captured public imagination, and earned for Garibaldi and his men the title of "Red Shirts." When Garibaldi visited England in 1864 (after a failed coup attempt on the king of Italy, Victor Emmanuel, for whom he had previously fought), he was warmly welcomed as the liberator of Italy. 9.50". Circa 1860. Value: $1000+.

"PEACE ON EARTH GOODWILL TO ALL MEN" reads the scroll held by the angel bestowing a blessing on the peace between Ireland and Britain. This figure was made to commemorate the signing of the Kilmainham Peace Treaty of 1882 that was brokered by the English and Irish leaders Gladstone and Parnell. Figures of the two statesmen were made to accompany the figure. Interestingly the figure was modified in 1902 to mark the end of the Boer War: the woman with the harp became a bearded Boer while Britannia was transformed into a Union Jack waist-coated John Bull. 12.75". 1882. Value: $1000+.

Group depicting Queen Victoria with the King of Sardinia and a Greyhound. The title appears in gold raised capitals. Victor Emmanuel II (1820-1878) was King of Sardinia (1840-1861) and the first king of Italy (1861-1878). 14". Mid-Victorian. Value: $1000+. *Courtesy of Anita L. Grashof, Gallerie Ani'tiques.*

Group portraying Napoleon Bonaparte III, Queen Victoria, and Abd-ul-Medjid on a base titled "France . England . Turkey" in raised gilt capitals. This group's subject was also produced in smaller versions and in a variant "mirror" group titled "Turkey . England . France." 11.25". Circa 1854. Value: $1000+. *Courtesy of Anita L. Grashof, Gallerie Ani'tiques.*

Chartist radical politician Thomas Slingsby Duncombe, known as "the best-dressed man in the House," is seen here elegantly posed beside a pillar. Duncombe presented a Chartist petition (titled *"The Peoples' Petition"* which held 3,315,752 signatures *"of the industrious classes of this country"*) to Parliament in May 1842. The petition would strike a cord with most voters today: it asked for, in short, nirvana: more honest and representational government, improved wages and conditions for factory and farm workers, fairer taxes, fairer policing and a reduction in unjust arrests and detentions, reductions to military expenditures, an acknowledgement of judicial and Church corruption, better services for children, the poor, and the sick, and a reduction in bureaucratic "fringe benefits," quoting in support of this claim, *"That your petitioners have also learned that his royal Highness Prince Albert receives each day the sum of £104.2s. whilst thousands have to exist upon 3d per head per day."* Unfortunately parliament failed to deliver on most of the petition's requests. This figure most likely dates from the presentation of the petition. 8". Circa 1842. Value: $1000+.

This figure is titled "Old English Gentleman" but is, in reality, a portrait of American statesman Benjamin Franklin. The figure also appears erroneously titled "Washington" (see Pugh, p. B202, fig. 23B and Harding, p. 61, Book One). 9". Circa 1860. Value: $500-$1000 *Courtesy of Nick Harding* (A & N Harding, *Victorian Staffordshire Figures 1835-1875*).

Arthur Wellesley, first Duke of Wellington (1769-1852); distinguished for military service and Commander-in-Chief from 1842 until his death in 1852, Wellington was also a politician and statesman, having served as Prime Minister from 1829-30 and Foreign Secretary under John Peel from 1834-35. He died sitting in a chair at his home, and it has been suggested that this figure was produced at that time with a paired figure of Wellington with his head slumped to his left. (See Chapter Eleven for details.)12". Circa 1852-60. Value: $500-$1000. *Courtesy of Nick Harding* (A & N Harding, *Victorian Staffordshire Figures 1835-1875*).

Chapter Eleven
War: The Potters as Patriots

"War: what is it good for? Absolutely nothing!" were lyrics in a popular 1970s protest song. Protesters of the 70s decried war as worthless and evil, but the nineteenth century Staffordshire potters found that war was good for thousands of pottery figures. At any time throughout Victoria's long reign, British soldiers or sailors could be found fighting somewhere in the world. Nineteenth century Britain was a ruthless imperial power that used its troops to help maintain a hold on colonies while suppressing the activities of rivals. The military also served to police the empire and to curb civil unrest (even on Britain's home shores), as a civilian police force was not established throughout the United Kingdom until after the Police Act of 1856.

Like almost every other aspect of Victorian society, the military, too, felt the impact of technological and social advances. Prior to the Crimean War (1853-1856), the army was poorly managed and organized pretty much along the lines of an old boys' club. More soldiers died during that war from starvation and disease than from enemy action, and after such a rout not only were medical services overhauled, but supplies, weaponry, discipline, and organization were also upgraded to more progressive and professional standards. The military became an occupation that generated pride in its servicemen and in the public. Officers and soldiers, in the space of a four decade period of service, saw duty in more than a dozen locations around the world from India, to Africa, to the Pacific, to China, and even in Europe.

As Victoria's empire continued its expansion, technology continued to play its role in the process through the transformation of the British military. The "Royal Engineers" pioneered balloon flight in military engagements, the use of signaling (including the revolutionary use of the telegraph), canal building, railways, docks, and survey mapping the Empire – roughly one quarter of the globe. War brought conquest and bloodshed, but it also brought progress and thousands of Staffordshire pottery figures made in tribute to England's then largest employer.

As well as bringing trade, employment, and flow-down technological developments, war also wrought tremendous social change. It brought travel, respectability, wealth, prestige, and power to ranks of non-commissioned soldiers and officers who, without it, would have faced unemployment, social ostracism, and destitution. War necessarily touched every family in Victorian Britain in some manner. Most families had a least one member who served in the military; and many suffered bereavements or maimings of loved ones through active duty. In short, war was ubiquitous, a fact of life that brought the military into every home: through family members in service, through newspapers, journals, patriotic artwork, *and* through Staffordshire figures.

War was not, however, the unconditional success of Victoria's rein: the Crimean War was undoubtedly its most unmitigated disaster, a horror compounded by the atrocities of the Boer War where civilians were identified as targets in campaigns, bringing to military conflict for the first time the concept of "collateral damage." The causes of these wars were longstanding – economics, religion, and nationalism. The justifications leaned heavily on standard excuses: people needed to believe in their rectitude and necessity. Too much was invested in the Empire not to defend it. Failure to support Britain in war was a failure to support the "British" way of life and England's moral, social, and religious superiority.

Even war cannot undermine the importance of hearth and home as captured in this rare insight into the Victorian domestic life of an officer and lady. 7.50". Circa 1850. Value: $500-$1000.

Reminders of wartime horrors were unwelcome on the mantelshelf, but tokens of its heroism and victories were produced by the potters of Staffordshire in the thousands and were eagerly purchased by the public. Few pottery figures depicted suffering and maimed servicemen; the most notable is a pair of figures known as *The Chelsea Pensioners*. Unlike the more sanitized and common group *The Wounded Soldier*, the pensioners were depicted as amputees who were forced to live on the nation's charity at the Chelsea home for disabled ex-servicemen. The figures are neither attractive nor desirable reminders of war and are unlike most "war" figures produced in the potteries. While the potters were sometimes subversive in their dealings with, and depictions of, other aspects of Victorian society, it is unusual that they appeared to be such keen proponents of the government and the status quo in their ennobling depictions of war.

The savage rebuff to Victorian pride inflicted by the defeats of the Crimean campaign did little to diminish the enthusiasm of the government or the people. Not only did the potters redouble their efforts and verve in the production of figures like those depicting the 1860 Anglo-French war, but they also rekindled old victories by resuscitating heroes like Wellington, Nelson, and Admiral Robert Blake, a parliamentarian, who was appointed Commander-of-the-Fleet in 1649, was victorious against the Dutch and died en route to England after destroying the Spanish West Indian Fleet in 1657. Even great opponents like Napoleon Bonaparte merited resuscitation in clay. There was nothing like a war to generate remarkable Staffordshire figures, and those inspired by the Anglo-French War were no exception: a figure depicting Napoleon III with the symbolic British lion recumbent on top of him was so popular that it was produced for three decades and is still highly valued today (see illustration in Chapter Ten). Also related to the Anglo-French war scare is a group titled *V. Rifles* in raised gilt capitals, which commemorates the enlistment of over 130,000 Volunteer Rifles. The group depicts a pair of soldiers standing at each side of flags, a drum, a bugle, and an inanimate clock.

An allegorical figure representing "War" by Thomas Parr. The use of symbols in the details of this figure is sophisticated and indicates that the potter did not underestimate the public's understanding of what are, to most modern viewers, seemingly esoteric decorative details. Note the skull under War's feet. 6.50". Circa 1855. Value: $1000+.

Reverse of the Parr figure of "War" showing a cauldron and battle standards.

Another military figure from across the Channel and depicted by the potters was Pierre Joseph François Bosquet, the French Marshal who led troops at Alma, Balaclava, and Sebastopol and was wounded while commanding an attack on Malakoff. François Certain Canrobert, a French Marshal who supported Napoleon III in the coup of 1851 and served in the Crimean War before being named Commander-in-Chief of the French forces, was taken as a prisoner of war during the Franco-Prussian War of 1870. The potters produced several figures of Canrobert in mounted and standing poses, one of which was part of a series that included Lord Raglan, Abd-ul-Medjid (Sultan of Turkey), and Omar Pasha. Omar Pasha was actually Michael Latas, who served in the Austrian army, converted to Islam, and became Abd-ul-Medjid's writing master. Later governor of Lebanon, Pasha crossed the Danube with 60,000 troops in 1855 and was instrumental in defeating the Russians at Eupatoria. Another French portrait figure subject was the Duc de Malakoff (Jean Jacques Pellissier, 1794-1864) who served as a general during the Crimean War and was commander-in-chief before the Battle of Sebastopol.

After storming Malakoff, he was awarded a marshal's baton and was made the Duc de Malakoff. He was the French Ambassador to England from 1858-1859.

As already identified, living with the likelihood of war and with war itself were acknowledged elements of Victorian life, and patriotism ran high in Victorian Britain. Figures designed to commemorate national pride, as well as figures that put forward a more personal sense of involvement in Britain's military supremacy, received high marks from buyers and record the history and heart of their time. Among the wars and conflicts of the era were the first Opium Was between China and Britain (that began in 1839 and lasted until 1842), the Maori revolt against British colonists (1843), the Anglo-Sikh War (1845, second war in 1848), the Basuto War between Britain and Native South Africans (1851-53), the Crimean War (1854-56), the Anglo-China War (beginning with the British fleet's bombardment of Canton and the Persian occupation of Herat that signaled the onset of the British-Persian War (both 1856), the Indian Mutiny (1857), the American Civil War which generated much interest in Britain (1861-65), the Abyssinian Expedition and the Fenian outrages in Ireland and Manchester that followed the Great Hunger of 1846 (both 1867), armed expedition of Ethiopia and the capture of Magdala (1868), the Franco-Prussian War (1870), and the British-Zulu Wars in South Africa (1879). All of these coincided with the height of Staffordshire figure production and popularity, and each gave rise to related figures.

Among the British military heroes most enthusiastically commemorated by the potters was Horatio Nelson (Viscount Nelson, Duke of Bronte, 1758-1805). Nelson was born in Norfolk to the rector of the parish, and he entered the Royal Navy in 1771. In 1796, he was appointed Rear Admiral, and in 1797 an injury sustained at Santa Cruz resulted in the amputation of his right arm. In 1798, he lost the sight in one eye during an attack on the French fleet in Aboukir Bay. His illustrious career culminated in a naval battle with the French fleet during which he chased Villeneuve (the French commander-in-chief) to Cape Trafalgar where English victory was assured but Nelson was killed. Several figures depict Nelson's death while others show him standing, dressed in uniform and wearing a cocked hat with his right sleeve tucked into his jacket. One group, produced in five and a half inches and three and three quarter inches, shows Nelson with his ship "The Victory." Nelson also appeared in a series with figures of Napoleon Bonaparte and The Duke of Wellington.

French soldier with rifle and backpack by Thomas Parr. 11.25". Circa 1855. Value: $1000+.

Napoleon Bonaparte captured the Victorian imagination, as indicated by the numerous figures depicting him. Such fascination is curious, as it seems tinged more with admiration than enmity. 8.25". Circa 1860. Value: $1000+.

The Duke of Wellington (Arthur Wellesley, 1769-1852) was the third son of the Earl of Mornington and was born in Dublin in 1769. Educated at Eton and Pegnerol's Military Academy, he joined the British Army in 1787 as an ensign in the 73rd Regiment. By 1803 he had been appointed chief political and military agent in the Deccan and South Mahratta states where he settled considerable unrest and was awarded a knighthood for his service. He resigned his command and returned to England in 1806. After serving as a Member of Parliament for Rye, he was appointed Chief Secretary for Ireland in the following year. The threat of French invasion resulted in Wellington's return to the military and several victories over the French. He was appointed Ambassador to Paris in 1814 and in 1815 he defeated Napoleon at Waterloo. He served as Prime Minister from 1828-30 and Foreign Secretary under John Peel from 1834-35. He died sitting in a chair at his home (Walmer Castle) in 1852. Among the most popular British military and statesmen, the potters portrayed Wellington on horseback, standing, and in busts formed as jugs and tobacco jars. Figures of Wellington were paired with Nelson and Bonaparte and were incorporated into series that depicted the three men. Many Wellington figures are titled in gilt script. One of the most striking is *Up Guards and At Them* – derived from Wellington's battle cry at Waterloo, recorded by his biographer, Sir Herbert Maxwell as "Stand Up, Guards." In another figure, Wellington is portrayed mounted on his favorite charger, Copenhagen, with his right arm raised and holding a telescope. In this figure, unlike later versions, Copenhagen is correctly colored as a chestnut. The most poignant Wellington figures are those in which he sits cross-legged in a chair with his right arm resting on the arm of the chair and his head resting on his left hand. The eleven and a half inch figure is set on a gilt lined Rococo base (sometimes found with the title "Wellington" in raised gilt capitals). In one version, Wellington's head is upright; in another, it is slumped to his left, suggesting the hero's death. These figures were very likely produced when Wellington died.

Rare, small version of Thomas Parr's "Omer Pasha – Success to Turkey." Born Michael Latas in Croatia, Latas served in the Austrian army, but deserted; in Bosnia he converted to Mohammedanism, and fought for the Ottoman army. He was made governor of Lebanon in 1842. Latas, now Omer (Omar) Pasha, led an army of 60,000 in 1853 and routed the Russian invasion of the Danubian Principalities. Omar Pasha continued his campaign, arriving in the Crimea in 1855, and defeating the Russians at Eupatoria. 6.75". Circa 1855. Value: $1000+.

Vivandière group depicting a warrior on horseback and a woman in eastern dress posed before a mosque-like structure. Vivandières were women who sold provisions to soldiers during the Crimean War. 8.25". Circa 1855. Value: $500-$1000.

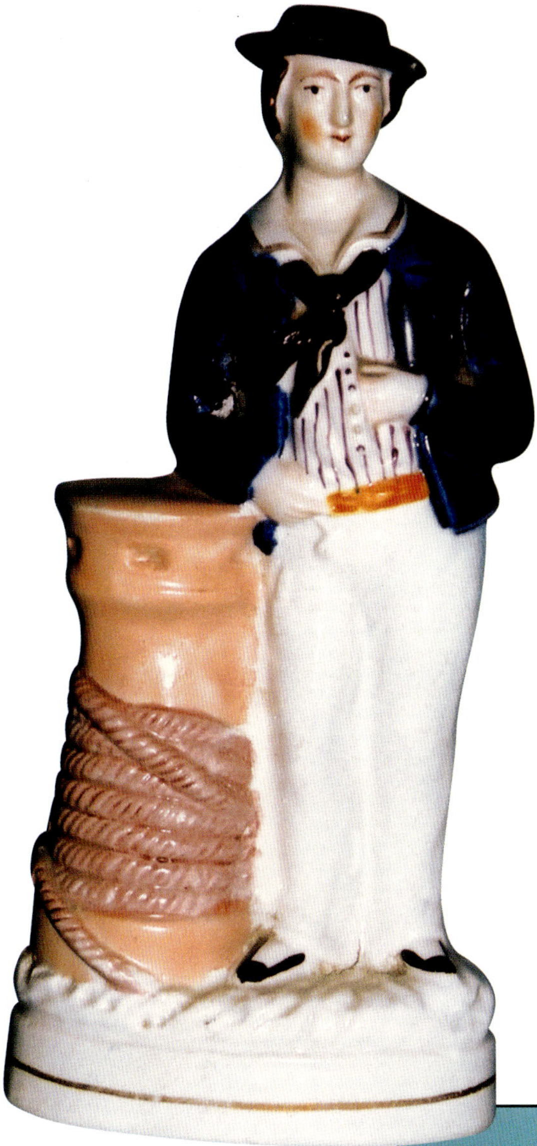

Rare figure of a sailor leaning against a bollard. This figure is sometimes identified as a portrait of Queen Victoria's second son Prince Alfred. 8.25". Circa 1850. Value: $1000+.

The potters' patriotism is again evidenced in this figure claimed by some to be one of the royal children with a drum and pennant and mounted on the back of a stag. 10.75". Circa 1850. Value: $500-$1000.

A very rare Crimean War figure titled "Ready and Willing" depicting a sailor leaning against a cannon. This famous figure helped play a part in the potters' patriotic recruitment drive. 11.50". Circa 1855. Value: $1000+.

Admiral Sir Charles Napier (1786-1860) was depicted in several figures, most of which show him standing on oval bases that are titled with his name. Napier entered the Royal Navy in 1800 and participated in the West Indies operations of 1806-09. In 1813, he joined an expedition to America and, in 1833, he was asked to command the Portuguese fleet. During the Syrian War of 1840, he attacked the Sidon and was awarded a knighthood. He served as a Member of Parliament and as Commander-in-Chief of the Baltic Fleet during the Crimean War. Unfortunately, after taking Bomarsund, a shortage of gunboats resulted in a halt to his progress. Arguments with Sir James Graham (First Lord of the Admiralty) ended in Napier's dismissal.

Lord Raglan (Lord Fitzroy James Henry Somerset, First Baron, 1788-1855) entered the British Army in 1804. In 1808 he was appointed Wellington's aide-de-camp. Raglan lost his right arm in the battle of Waterloo and returned to England as a Member of Parliament for Truro. He was Military Secretary at the Horse Guards from 1827-52, after which he was raised to the peerage. In 1854 he served as field marshal and led an expeditionary force to the Crimea just before the onset of the war. In September of 1854, he helped defeat the Russians at Alma, but after months of warfare, a horrendous winter, and unsuccessful attacks on Malakoff and the Redan, Raglan became ill and died of dysentery in 1855. The potters, inspired by Raglan's military career and by an engraving that appeared in *Cassell's Illustrated Family Paper* in 1854, produced several titled figures of Raglan on horseback (and two standing). Two mounted figures are paired with figures of Sir George Cathcart. Cathcart, an aide-de-camp at Waterloo and other campaigns against the French, later commanded the Fourth Division in the Crimean War; he was killed in a cavalry charge on November 5, 1854. Raglan was also depicted with Marshal Arnaud (War Minister under Napoleon III, Commander-in-Chief of the French forces during the Crimean War, and assistant to Raglan during the battle at Alma). An 1855 engraving entitled "The Late Lord Raglan" appeared in *The Illustrated London News* and is believed to be the source of an extremely rare figure of which only two examples are known.

War heroes remained popular and, while wars and skirmishes dotted Victoria's reign, the potters complied with purchaser demand. Sir James Simpson, who served with the Grenadier Guards during the Peninsular War of 1812-13 and was later Chief of Staff during the Crimean War, became Commander of the British Troops in the Crimea following Lord Raglan's death. Simpson was awarded a knighthood in 1855 for his Crimean War service and the capture of Sebastopol, and was recorded in large figures – standing on a gilt lined base with his name in raised gilt capitals as well as on horseback holding a flag (also titled in raised gilt capitals on a gilt lined base). Sir George Brown, who served in the Peninsular War of 1851 and received a knighthood in 1852, was represented in a titled figure in which he appears mounted above a cannon and holding a flag. Wounded in the Peninsular War and awarded a knighthood for his service in the Second Sikh War of 1848-49, the immensely popular Sir Colin Campbell commanded the Highland Brigade in the Crimean War and was honored for victories at Alma and Balaclava. At the outbreak of the Indian Mutiny in 1857, Campbell was made Commander-in-Chief of the British forces in India and received a Baronetcy that same year. The potters produced numerous figures of Campbell. These including several titled pieces that show Campbell on horseback or standing on oval and Rococo gilt lined bases. Other Indian Mutiny figures include Sir Henry Havelock and Highland Jessie (see Chapter Sixteen).

This dramatic and rare figure of the death of Horatio Nelson depicts the great sailor being supported by his officers Hardy and Beatty on the deck of his ship "The Victory" in 1805 after having been fatally shot while engaging the French at the Battle of Trafalgar. Nelson's remarkable naval career commenced in 1770 when he was only twelve years old and culminated in his elevation to the rank of vice-admiral. His illustrious career spanned decades and included engagements from the West Indies to the Mediterranean. During this time he was injured and lost sight in his left eye (hence the trademark green-baize eye patch to protect Nelson's eye from the sun), received major abdominal injuries, and had his right elbow shattered by grapeshot. Nelson, with no more than the standard shot of rum, survived the amputation of his arm, high and near the shoulder, but suffered phantom pains from the lost limb for the rest of his life. 7.25". Circa 1860. Value: $1000+.

The Crimean War resulted in a large number of figures, one of the first being a group in which two men are seated at a barrel reading a newspaper headlined "War." The commencement of the War in March of 1854 inspired the potters to create a new wave of British Royalty figures as well as figures of foreign allies. Napoleon III of France, his wife the Empress Eugenie, the Sultan of Turkey, and the King of Sardinia were all potted. The short-lived alliance between England, Turkey and France fell under suspicion when Napoleon III annexed Savoy and Nice in 1860. It was during the Crimean War that the potters produced the greatest number of naval and military figures and groups – including figures of the British Royal Family, allies, and portraits of important naval and the military personalities. Among these, there are figures of at least four English admirals, ten English commanders, and four French commanders. Various alliance groups, including some that depicted Napoleon and Albert, were produced in quantity in a range of sizes and decorating styles. A group titled *The Allied Powers* (noted in Chapter Nine) includes Napoleon III, Queen Victoria, and Victor Emmanuel II. There are also groups that depict Victoria, Abd-ul-Medjid, and Napoleon. These were produced variously with Rococo and gilt lined bases, all of which are titled *Turkey, England, France.* Individual models of Victoria, Napoleon, and Abd-ul-Medjid stand on titled bases with raised gilt capitals. Victoria was also depicted in groups with Napoleon (titled *Queen Emperor*) and with Victor Emmanuel (one of which is titled *Queen & King of Sardinia* in raised gilt capitals; illustrated in Chapter Ten). The potters even portrayed Florence Nightingale (1820-1910, the *Lady with the Lamp,*) for her work as a pioneer nurse (see Chapter Sixteen). Such was the fascination with the Crimean conflict that even the sights of famous battles such as the forts of Malakoff and Sebastopol were captured in clay.

Spill holder of a sailor fare-welling his lass who, for the sake of the "war effort" has taken on her beloved's duties as fisherman. Pottery patriotism focused on the feminine sensibility. 8.50". Circa 1860. Value: $100-$500.

A jug in the manner of Thomas Parr depicting Nelson standing in front of the Union Jack and a cannon, clearly showing his missing right arm. Contemporary Victorian examples of this figure are rare, but later 19th and 20th century versions are plentiful and are easily identified by the title "NELSON." 11.50". Circa 1860. Value: $1000+.

"SCOTLAND'S PRIDE" takes patriotism to the Hebrides with this handsome portrait of a kilted soldier with flag and cannon. 10.50". Circa 1860. Value: $1000+.

A later military luminary who, like the Crimean War itself, was celebrated for his failure was General Charles George Gordon, who served in campaigns in the Crimean at Sebastopol and Redan (1855), in China against Peking and the Taipings (1860) where he gained his nickname "Chinese Gordon," and as governor of equatorial Egypt (1873). Gordon was killed at the hands of the Mahdi's rebels during the 317-day siege of Khartoum (1885). His death in the Sudan generated public outcry against the government's ineptitude and failure to reinforce troops at the outpost. The Staffordshire potters assisted in raising the hue and cry and produced three figures of the statesman and soldier; a well-modeled sixteen-inch portrait of the hero, titled in crimson script, is now remarkably rare.

Figures and groups of non-portrait naval and army personnel were produced in quantity and, undoubtedly, served to console and cheer those whose loved ones were in service or at war. Sailors were presented in various poses: standing with anchors at their feet, with hands on their hips, carrying flags, standing in boats, with cannons, and standing near roped bollards. Soldiers were represented with flags, swords, guns, cannons, and drums. Sleeping soldiers (and sailors) and mounted soldiers were also produced. There is even a patriotic group in which a woman and child are depicted seated – the woman's right arm rests on a pair of flags and a cannon is placed at her feet. One of the most unusual is a group that depicts enigmatic bat-holding cricketers in military uniforms.

Servicemen were frequently portrayed with their wives or sweethearts, some in moving poses that suggest the sadness and fear of wartime separation. Among the most touching figures and groups are *Mother's Last Gift* (depicting a sailor and his mother who is handing her son a Bible) and paired figures of a girl and a sailor standing beside gravestones. Figures depicting foreign military personnel include Scottish soldiers. A noteworthy group is one in which a soldier sits cross-legged next to a table paired with a figure of a seated sailor whose right leg is missing. Also noteworthy are: *Brothers in Arms* (a group of an English soldier with his arms around a French soldier), *Ready and Willing* (showing alternatively a soldier or a sailor prepared to serve), *The Soldiers Farewell* (a group of a soldier and his lady whose head rests on the soldier's shoulder), and *The Soldiers Return* (in several versions that depict a soldier reunited with his lady).

"Sir Charles Napier" went to sea at the tender age of only thirteen and received his first command at age twenty-two. Prior to his triumphs during the Crimean War, where he commanded the Baltic Fleet, he led campaigns in the Mediterranean, led the ascent of the Potomac, commanded the Portuguese fleet and restored Portugal's monarchy, was the "Hero of the Sind" during the Crimean War, was made an admiral but was demoted for insolence. He sat twice in parliament where he campaigned for reforms to the navy. Napier was also, according to his contemporaries, slovenly, eccentric, imprudent, shrewd, excitable, and vain. He was also described more fondly by the same observers as being frank and truthful, fun-loving, self-confident, daring, energetic, and possessed of "an indomitable will." In short, Napier was a military hero. This figure very likely dates to his death in 1860. 16.50". Circa 1860. Value: $1000+.

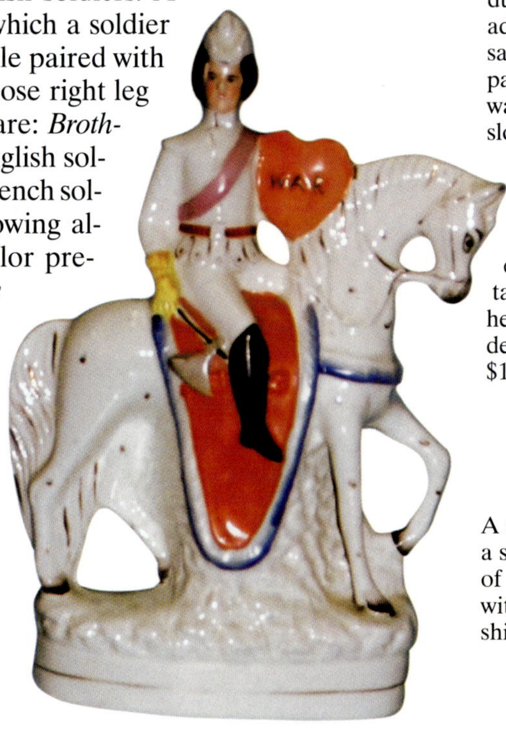

A mounted soldier, carrying a battle axe, and holding a shield that, rather ironically, is formed in the shape of a heart and reads "War." This figure is matched with a corresponding figure that has "Peace" on the shield. 12". Circa 1870. Value: $1000+.

Along with war heroes and everyday sailors and soldiers, the potters recorded the "fighting spirit" with portrait figures of a few non-British personalities who commanded the headlines of the time. Prince Bismark, Duke of Lauenburg, known as "The Iron Chancellor" was portrayed on horseback with a titled base in a series that included General von der Tann, Prince Frederick Charles of Prussia, and Count von Helmet Moltke. Moltke (1800-1891) was responsible for reorganizing the Turkish army and assisted in victories against the Danes during 1863-64, against the Austrians in 1866, and during the Franco-Prussian Wars in 1880. The Count was represented in a figure that was produced in fourteen and half inch and thirteen inch sizes in which he is shown mounted and wearing a tall plumed hat. The figures are titled in raised gilt capitals. Hungarian Lajos Ferenc Kossuth (1802-1894) also captured the potters' imagination. Kossuth came from an impoverished family of the lower gentry and began his political career as a parliamentary reporter. Publication of anti-government literature resulted in a three-year prison term during which he learned the English language. After his release from prison, Kossuth founded the daily "*Pesti Hirlap*," which he edited in a spirit of political reform. Already known in Hungary as a radical, he generated a loyal following among the lesser nobility. Following the beginning of the Hungarian Revolution in March 1848, Kossuth realized that his goals could only be achieved through armed revolution. In July of 1848, he delivered a speech that resulted in huge numbers of the *honvéd* (defenders of the homeland) rallying to embrace his views. A new Hungarian cabinet was formed, and Kossuth took the lead in a national movement to fight for freedom as elected head of the defense committee. On April 4, 1849, the National Assembly dethroned the House of Hapsburg, and Kossuth became governor of independent Hungary. Russia quickly provided aid to the Hapsburgs, the tables were turned, and Hungary was again defeated. On August 13, 1849, Kossuth was forced to emigrate. In 1851 he moved to England and continued his involvement in activities geared toward liberation of Hungary from Austria. Three figures of Kossuth are recorded; the source of one was a Louis Antoine Jullien engraving that appeared in *The Illustrated London News*. More exotic, perhaps, than Moltke and Kossuth was Gholab Singh, a Sikh chieftain, who assisted the British in the Sikh Wars. Singh was despised by his countrymen and distrusted by the English. He became the Maharaja of Jammu and Kashmir following his aid to Britain and traveled to England with his son, Ranbir, as bodyguard in 1846. Obviously intrigued with Singh's notorious reputation, the potters issued paired figures of the father and son on horseback.

Figures in the content area covered in this chapter represent a substantial portion of all Victorian Staffordshire figures. Perhaps because these represented the most crucial news of the day and the concerns of most citizens, they achieved unqualified popularity among consumers. In their own time, they "told the stories" of current events; today, they offer "figural biographies" of the personalities that shaped the course of war, politics, and policies.

Believed to be a portrait of Prince Alfred made to celebrate the successful passing of his examination as naval cadet and his appointment to the "Euryalus" in 1858. This rare and well executed figure is attributed to Thomas Parr. 12.75". Circa 1858. Value: $1000+.

Tobacco jar in the form of a bust of the Duke of Wellington. Wellington's hat is the lid of the jar. 10.5". Circa 1870. Value: $500-$1000.

"WAR" proclaims the newspaper headline to two gentlemen relaxing in a pub. Whether this was a call to arms by the potter or a chastisement to the un-enlisted remains unclear. 8.25". Circa 1850. Value: $500-$1000.

Soldier and sailor commemorating the River War of 1898. The soldier's uniform has been identified as that of the 21st Lancers. 12". Circa 1898. Value: $1000+.

Very rare and highly colored portrait pair of Sir Robert Henry and Lady Florentia Sale. Sir Robert was a British colonel who, after various campaigns, took command of the British retreat from Kabul in 1842. Lady Sale was with him at the time, was taken captive, and was rescued with her party by Sir Richmond Shakespeare – a harrowing experience recorded by Lady Sale in *Journal of the Disasters in Afghanistan* (1843). 8". Value for the pair: $1000+. *Courtesy of John and Barbara Gair, Castle Antiques.*

"GORDON." This is a rare purple-titled portrait of General Charles George Gordon who perished in the siege of Khartoum. Gordon had been a member of the Royal Engineers and fought and was wounded during the Crimean War. He received more fame, however, as "Chinese Gordon" for his role in the capture of Peking and his command of Chinese troops to suppress the Taiping Rebellion. Gordon was sent to Egypt in 1884 to represent England and to attempt to quell rebellion in the Sudan being led by the "Mad Mahdi," a fanatical and murderous religious leader. Gordon, a great strategist and leader, led the defense of Khartoum that lasted 317 days, waiting for relief that never came due to duplicity and ineptitude on the part of Prime Minister Gladstone and his cabinet. Gordon was killed in 1885 during the siege and became a popular martyr for those in opposition to Gladstone's government. 15.25". Circa 1885. Value: $1000+.

The ultimate price of war: these figures of children mourning at gravesides date from the Crimean War. Similar figures on which the gravestones are marked "A Sailor" or "A Soldier" may also be found. Each figure 8". Circa 1850. Value: $500-$1000.

Another side of war: the "BEGGING SAILOR" returned from war and was discharged from duty into the arms of his loving and penniless family. This, and a number of similar figures, evidenced the public's dissatisfaction with the meager pensions awarded injured war veterans. Those who did not sustain physical injury had no claim to compensation for loss, trauma, or family dislocation. The potters were never pacifists; they were protestors! 17". Circa 1860. Value: $1000+. *Courtesy of Susan Bishop and Darcy McGroarty, Bishop and Daughter Antiques.*

Chapter Twelve
Never-Never Land: Children

It has been argued that the concept of "childhood" is an academic perception created by philosophers like Rousseau or a sentimental notion designed by Victorian poets and prose writers to cash in on the newly affluent, indulgent, and slightly guilt-ridden middle classes. Prior to publications by Rousseau and other Humanist philosophers during late eighteenth century, children were regarded as miniature adults to be tolerated until they reached maturity and full economic (or biological for female offspring) productivity. Toys were luxuries, clothing an adaptation of grown-up dress, formal education unheard of for other than very few, and work a given in the lives of most young people.

During the mid-nineteenth century, industrialization saw a dramatic change in labor economics and the development of a non-manual laboring class. Perhaps the emergence of this new moneyed class brought about the relaxation in class structure that admitted well-paid, new working "gentry" to refined society. Conditional with admission to "polite" but not "refined" society came aspirations and social affectations borrowed from their social "betters." One of the most important refinements to be cultivated was "childhood," and the entire "estate" of childhood was sentimentalized and cherished in art, literature, and popular culture.

"Childhood" required a new philosophy and mindset, special arrangements, special equipment, and special rules. Among the upper classes, much attention was paid to the care and raising of children. In general, children, especially girls, were idealized as innocent and pure. Wealthy children were pampered but had little contact with their parents. Most spent considerable time under the care of nursemaids, nannies, and governesses in home nurseries where all their needs were anticipated and attended to.

The middle classes now paid increased attention to the diet, education, moral and social development, and entertainment of their progeny that had hitherto never been awarded. Like wealthy children, they played with commercially produced toys – hoops and boards games for boys and girls, and gender-specific playthings like dolls for girls and toy soldiers for boys. Middle class children were afforded the opportunity to be "childish" and to occupy their time and minds with childish things.

Unlike the offspring of the wealthy and middle classes, economically underprivileged children were not permitted the extravagance of immaturity, irresponsibility, and play. If they enjoyed any playtime at all, their toys were homemade and their games were simple. Most poor children faced working days that saw them rise before dawn six days a week and trudge off to paid employment in conditions worse than those we pillory in the sweat-house factories of Third-World countries today. They were not categorized as children but, rather, as cheap labor, and they worked in factories alongside their parents.

Although young lower class girls sometimes stayed home in the capacity of cooks and housekeepers, their siblings and parents sought work in factories, and most spent their childhoods as day laborers or apprentices. These "fortunates" of the laboring class had employment and lodgings. The unlucky were designated as "charity" cases and were allocated to workhouses. Many factory owners acquired children, called pauper apprentices, from orphanages and workhouses and reduced them to the status of property. A figure group that depicts two poorly clad children holding hands is a reflection of the plight of orphans of the time. The source for this figure was Felix Miller's marble statue "The Orphans," which was featured in *The Illustrated London News* in February of 1847.

A trio of figures titled *The Red Maid . Bristol*, *George Muller's Orphans . Bristol*, and *Colston Boy . Bristol* comprise a set of two individual figures and a centerpiece. The Red Maid depicts a young girl dressed in the uniform of the Red Maids School in Bristol, and the Colston Boy is a figure of a young boy carrying a Bible and wearing the Colston uniform. The centerpiece represents a boy and girl standing side by side and wearing the George Muller uniforms. George Muller was a German immigrant whose early life of dissolution was turned around when he became a minister and opened an orphanage in 1832. Over time, Muller increased his operations and by 1886 had established residences for over 2000 destitute and orphaned children at Ashley Down. Muller provided a high standard of education for boys and girls. Boys remained at the facility until they were fourteen years old at which time they were provided with jobs. Girls remained at the home until they were seventeen when they went into domestic service, nursing, or teaching. Poor children and orphans who were taken in by philanthropists like Muller fared better than others of their kind. They were fed, clothed, and educated. Their childhoods were vastly different from those of upper class children but better by far than the children who were acquired by factory owners or who were left to the streets and crime (a common condition in Victorian cities as described by Charles Dickens and illustrated by characters like the Artful Dodger).

It was not uncommon for boys and girls from age five up to work in the rough environments of iron mines, coalmines, gas works, shipyards, construction, match factories, nail factories, and potteries. Some of the smallest children were used as chimney sweeps, and many died before they reached adulthood. Parliamentary acts to regulate the employment of workhouse children in factories and cotton mills to twelve hours per day had been passed as early as 1802 and 1819, but these did not come into immediate practical application. In 1831, "Short Time Committees" began to demand a ten-hour day. In 1833, a royal commission established by the Whig government suggested that children between eleven and eighteen years of age who worked in the textile industry should only be permitted to work up to twelve hours per day; children from nine to eleven should be allowed to work eight hour days, and children under nine should not be permitted to work at all. Unfortunately, this act did not apply to other industries and occupations.

In North Staffordshire, scores of children worked in the potteries. Pottery production (considered by contemporary standards to offer improved and enlightened employment conditions) placed children in an environment polluted with heavy metals, dampness, dust, and toxic fumes. The rooms in which they worked were either stiflingly hot (in the case of oven workers) or cold and damp (in the case of mold-runners). Pottery workers were sickly, prone to consumption, asthma, pulmonary diseases, rheumatism, and other ailments that resulted from exposure to harmful materials, inadequate ventilation, lack of exercise, and poor nutrition. Samuel Scriven's report provides a comprehensive study of conditions child workers endured in the potteries. One child, eight year-old Josiah Bevington, stated: *"I have been a mould-maker a year. I work for George Stanaway. He gives me 2s. a week; we work very near every day. I carry the moulds from the worker to the hot-house and back again. I come about six o'clock, sometimes five, to light fires. Father's a dipper. He got no work to do. I have one sister at work; she gets 3s. a week, as paper-cutter. I get meal and water for breakfast, and tatoes for dinner; sometimes a bit of bacon; I don't get enough; I could always eat more if I had it. I've got no more clothes than what I have on. I can't read and write a little; can sign my name...."*

Most children who worked in the potteries, like their counterparts throughout England, had little time for normal childhood play. Children labored until after dusk when they walked home, dirty and exhausted, through grime and smog choked streets to their meager evening meal of "tatties" and bread – possibly the only sustenance they had taken all day apart from breakfast. Meat was an unattainable luxury for most poor families, and was only enjoyed once or twice a week by the slightly better off.

Before implementation of the "New Factories Act" of the mid-nineteenth century, it was unlikely that the young workers would have been lucky enough to punctuate their arduous twelve-hour days with a brief stint in the classroom to be drilled in basic letters and numbers. For most of these children, Sunday school was their only chance to attain rudimentary skills in reading, writing, and arithmetic. By 1840, only about twenty percent of the children in London had any formal education. Within the next twenty years that number increased, but educational opportunities depended upon the children's gender and their parents' financial circumstances, social class, religion, and values. Elementary schools (run and funded by different organizations and means) were known variously as normal schools, infants schools, boarding schools, parish schools, district schools, and village schools. These were often crowded, and discipline was stern. Paired figures known as *Good Child* and *Naughty Child* (modeled after Belgian statues shown in the Great Exhibition of 1851) suggest the importance attached to child obedience in nineteenth century Britain.

Often identified as "The Lion Warrior" this spectacular figure depicts a classically attired father and son engaged in archery lessons and attended by a lion. Drawn from Victorian ideals and imagination rather than any fragment of historical fact, this is still an imposing piece of statuary. 16.50". Circa 1860. Value: $1000+.

Another figure of similar mood is known as *The Dunce and the Good Scholar*. This group portrays a seated girl holding an open book and a standing boy holding a slate at his side, wearing a dunce's cap, and standing on one leg – a common punishment in Victorian-Era schools. In the classroom, students were required to sit quietly in their seats. When an adult entered the room, they were expected to stand. Students lined up in an orderly fashion when entering and leaving the school, and the schoolmasters demanded curtsies from the girls at the end of the day. Discipline was often enforced through corporal punishments that included hitting students' knuckles with rulers and caning students' palms. Disobedient students' names were entered in a "punishment book," which was used as a reference for future employment. In boarding schools, discipline was even more stringent, and in some boys' schools, severe treatment (including beatings and partial starvation) was standard. Figure groups pertaining to education are rare; most remarkable among them are paired figures in which a boy and girl sitting on rockwork bases hold oversized books. Another is a tulip-form spill vase group in which a boy and girl are seated on each side of the spill; they hold open books with a slate between them, suggesting the growing importance of literacy in Victorian Britain. Free education, however, was virtually nonexistent until the 1890s and, during the preceding decades, the customary fee was between one and four pence per week, which few poor families could afford.

Previously unrecorded, to the authors' knowledge, a Thomas Parr group of a boy, girl, dog, and donkey. This charming group belies the serious and hardworking lives that poor Victorian-era children faced – unlike the privileged children of moneyed families. 9". Circa 1850. Value: $500-$1000.

If this is an accurate depiction of everyday life for over seventy per cent of Victorian youth, was it one accurately replicated by the potters of Victorian Staffordshire in their figural works? Not surprisingly, it was not. The potters understood their purchasers' ideals, and they depicted an image of childhood that drew from a lost, but romanticized, bucolic past and from the pampered lifestyles of the "rich and famous." Queen Victoria's children were favorite subjects and were often depicted with pets that ranged from dogs to ponies and goats. While figures of children and dogs (Spaniels in particular) were relatively ubiquitous, children were also represented with swans, peacocks, and exotic birds as well as with every imaginable four-legged creature from rabbits to rats and from donkeys to circus animals.

A well modeled and beautiful figure, "FIRST RIDE" expresses the Victorian desire for wish fulfillment. A mother, undoubtedly of the working class, has time to teach her small son to ride. In reality, most working mothers could neither afford leisure time away from work to be with their children, nor could most urban working class families, then most of the population of Britain, afford to buy and keep a horse. 12.25". Circa 1850. Value: $1000+.

Kennel groups are especially charming, and groups in which a dog stands ready to rescue a child from danger propose a flavor of the dramatic so dear to Victorian hearts. Equestrian models of children were made in quantity, as were figures of children astride or beside unrealistically large dogs. Children in prayerful poses reflected the religious inclinations of nineteenth century Britain – two of the most outstanding are children with crosses and a mother and child kneeling together in prayer. Guardian angels were popular and, among related groups, the Princess Royal and future Edward VII were portrayed asleep with an angel watching over them.

The depiction of childhood in occupations or labor is rare (although figures of adults at work, albeit sanitized, were popular). Notable exceptions may be found in the figures of *AM* and *PM* that depict a youthful bootblack and newspaper seller respectively. A young crossing-sweeper, juvenile muffin seller, and milk-boy join this very rare pair of figures as possibly the only known portraits of child employment. These figures depict cheerful, well dressed, and amply fed children in ruddy good health who suffer none of the illnesses and privations so often documented in interviews with young workers of the time.

Children with a rabbit and hutch posed beside a faux clock. Playmate or ingredient? The latter would have been much more likely for the 19th century families who invested in this pottery. 7.25". Circa 1860. Value: $100-$500.

A grim, but realistic depiction of childhood: given the infant mortality rate in Victorian Britain it is not surprising that the potters were forced to address high numbers of deaths among children. Between 1836 and 1842 alone, influenza, typhus, typhoid, and cholera reached epidemic proportions and claimed one in five children. Malnutrition and diseases like influenza, smallpox, diphtheria, measles, whooping cough, and tuberculosis killed tens of thousands of children during this same period without being considered "epidemic." This figure represents an angel holding a wreath and standing over a dying, or dead, child. The symbolism of the attendant angel and wreath was common in much Victorian art, and it is not surprising that the potters adopted it. 6". Circa 1860. Value: $500-$1000.

Spill holder depicting two children bird-nesting. 6.50". Circa 1845. Value: $100-$500.

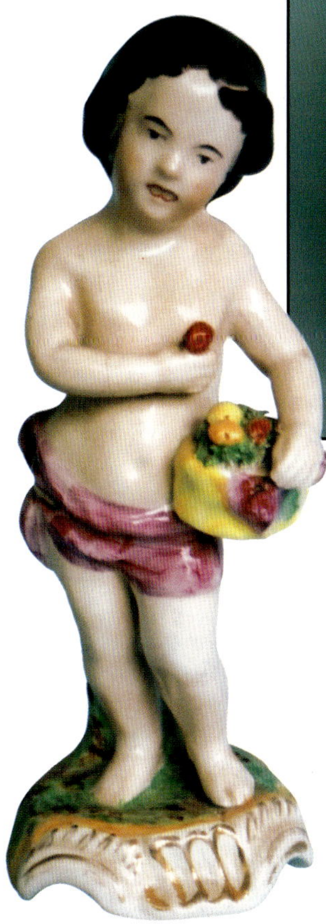

This Cupid fruit-seller by Kent presented both a classicized and romanticized image of the child for the Victorian public: well-fed, handsome, and rosy. 9.25". Early 20th century. Value: $100-$500.

The most popular groups of Staffordshire figures depicting childhood are undoubtedly those of country children either at play wrestling, climbing, bird-nesting, romping with dogs, or engaged in some gentle manual labor such as filling water jugs, collecting windfalls, or riding to and from market on horseback. One remarkable and highly desirable figure titled *First Ride* shows a small boy astride a horse and supported by his mother. It is a beautiful figure and one in which the potters sought to make solid another myth of childhood: that of the ever-present and nurturing parent. Another anachronism taken on by the potters was that of the extended family. Figures such as *Grandmother's Hope* and *Grandfather's Joy* show grandparents comfortably reading to their grandchildren and children proudly presenting their toys for inspection. Unfortunately these delightful images are untrue: family structure had changed with industrialization, nuclear families eked out their meager livings in towns and cities having left those unable or unwilling to adapt to the new work and the new lifestyle on their farms and in their villages. Workers could not afford to support, feed, and house the aged matriarchs and patriarchs so fondly depicted by the potters. The second reason for this subject matter being one drawn from the potters' imaginations is the mortality rate for working class people – put simply, it was unlikely that the majority would ever make it into the grand old ages depicted by the potters.

Advancements in printing and lithography techniques resulted in publication of numerous illustrated children's books. Widespread juvenile illiteracy and equivalent poverty, however, rendered these beyond the pale of lower class children. Although children's literature experienced its coming of age during the Victorian era with masterworks like Charles Kingsley's *The Water-Babies*, Lewis Carroll's "Alice" books, George MacDonald's *At the Back of the North Wind*, and J. M. Barrie's somewhat later *Peter Pan*, the potters of Staffordshire steadfastly ignored these sources as inspiration for their figural subject matter. This exclusion is an interesting insight into which children were doing the reading during this period: obviously not those of the working class. Exceptions to the ostensible "ban" on children's literature as a source of inspiration for figures by the potters are a few works inspired by nursery rhymes and fairy tales, including "The Cat and the Fiddle," "Mother Goose," and "Red Riding Hood," but these were most likely directed at more affluent and middle class buyers and never intended for working class children whose parents could ill afford them. In this instance, the potters captured something of the reality of the world of the average Victorian child.

If Staffordshire's potters were to create figures of today's Western-world youth, we might find earthenware models of children at computers, talking on cell phones, playing organized sports, and "hanging out" at malls. Sadly, there would also be figures of children committing very adult-like crimes. The sophistications of our twenty-first century would have been unimaginable to both the children and the potters of nineteenth century Britain. In any century, though, childhood is an ephemeral time – a never-never land that is universally remembered as infinitely precious and far too quickly lost. The potters recognized that and left us wonderful ceramic documents that speak not of the realities of the poor, but also of the spontaneity and innocence that are fundamental to childhood in every era, in every time.

Unusual spill holder featuring a toga-clad girl with a sheep. 10". Late 19th century. Value: $100-$500.

Porcelain candle-holder with applied flowers depicting the "Babes in the Wood." "Babes in the Wood" was popular as a stage play and moral nursery tale throughout most of the Victorian era. There are many variants of this particularly fine version. 5.50". Circa 1845. Value: $500-$1000.

Two children fetching water. This figure has been repaired and there is some doubt as to the accuracy of the repair to the neck of the jug. 7.50". Circa 1860. Value: (as shown) $100-$500.

Previously unrecorded figure of a child attempting to part a puppy from its mother who, in retaliation, is attempting to part the child from its clothing. The original source of this figure is yet to be identified, but the vignette was also used in an advertisement for chocolates during the 19th century. 10.50". Circa 1860. Value: $1000+.

Very rare and well executed porcelain figure of a girl and doll. The figure has sometimes been identified as the Princess Royal, but this identification is, as yet, unsubstantiated. 6.25". Circa 1840. Value: $1000+.

Rare group of three children playing balancing games. 9.50". Circa 1850. Value: $1000+.

Young boy resting with his dog. 5.50". Circa 1850. Value: $500-$1000. *Courtesy of Zane Moss Antiques.*

Young girl with a lamb. 5.50". Circa 1850. Value: $500-$1000. *Courtesy of Zane Moss Antiques.*

Thomas Parr group "Happy as a King" based on the popular painting by William Collins and the widely available Pears Print on the same subject. 7.25". Circa 1850. Value: $1000+.

Reverse of "Happy as a King" laying rest to the popular misconception that the 19th century Staffordshire potters concentrated only on the "flatback." The reverse of the figure is highly detailed and encourages viewing "in the round."

This small boy seated on a large dog is an interesting observation of 19th century fashion. In line with early Victorian custom, which insisted that young boys of the more privileged classes wear dresses and leave their hair long until they were about six years old, the child wears an off-the-shoulder style of frock often seen in painted portraits of the period. 4.5" (length), 3.50" (height). Circa 1840. Value: $500-$1000.

A very attractive group featuring a small boy riding a large dog while an older girl leads the hound. 12". Circa 1850. Value: $1000+. *Courtesy of Susan Bishop and Darcy McGroarty, Bishop and Daughter Antiques.*

Equestrian group of a young girl seated side-saddle on a white mount and carrying sheaves of wheat or corn; title "HOME" in raised capitals. 11". Mid-Victorian. Value: $100-$500. *Courtesy of Anita L. Grashof, Gallerie Ani'tiques.*

Watch holder depicting children climbing in a grape arbor. An attractive concept, but one that would have held little relevance for the children of large industrial towns like Birmingham, Manchester, London, and even in The Potteries, where arbor climbing would have been unheard of and trees would have been more valued as fuel for industry, heating, and cooking than as playthings for children. 12.50". Circa 1860. Value: $500-$1000.

Children in the labor force spent limited spare moments during working hours (should their employers be that generous and progressive) or attended Ragged Schools – the only opportunity they would ever have to gain basic skills in literacy and arithmetic – where learning was conducted in an atmosphere of urgency and exhaustion. This humorous admonition of a reluctant scholar depicts the boy wearing a dunce cap and standing on one leg, common punishments in Victorian schools. 8". Circa 1860. Value: $500-$1000.

Girl with a shawl wrapped around the shoulders of a very large Great Dane modeled and decorated in the manner of Thomas Parr. 10". Circa 1860. Value: $1000+. *Courtesy of Susan Bishop and Darcy McGroarty, Bishop and Daughter Antiques.*

Children and animals are a time-honored and natural combination, and Staffordshire's potters were conscientious in producing thousands of animal and children figure groups. Often the animals were modeled in large scale to highlight the small size of the children. In this group, a young girl (the Princess Royal) is seated properly side-saddle on the back of a St. Bernard. The paired figure depicts the Crown Prince. The potters' shorthand and a clue to the identity of the children are indicated by the inclusion of Prince of Wales feathers. 9". Circa 1848 (as dated by Pope, pp. 150-151). Value for the pair: $1000+. *Courtesy of Marla Chaikin, William Charles Antiques.*

Young girl seated on the back of an over-sized Setter that carries a basket of flowers in its mouth; paired with a young boy similarly posed. 10.75". Mid-Victorian. Value for the pair: $1000+. *Courtesy of Zane Moss Antiques.*

Young girl standing beside a large Afghan Hound; one of a pair with a young boy similarly posed in the left-sided group. Also recorded in other colors. Pope dates this model to 1875 (pp. 12-13, figs. 1 & 2). Value for the pair: $1000+. *Courtesy of Marla Chaikin, William Charles Antiques.*

Chapter Thirteen
Religious Figures: The Potters' Amen

Among the various "theme" figures produced by Staffordshire's potters, religious motif pieces have long been among the least celebrated and, until recently, not enthusiastically sought except by specialist collectors. Genre items of a sort, figures in this category of Staffordshire collecting are beginning to achieve the elevated status of other figure types – like their secular counterparts, they reflect the history and human feelings of their time.

North Staffordshire was dominated by potting firms, pubs, and churches. Religious and social reform was felt, but widespread poverty, humble living conditions, and drunkenness persisted among the working classes. While the Church of England was well attended by the gentry, many of the potters and pottery workers were Nonconformists. Some followed the Methodist teachings of John Wesley, some were Baptists or Presbyterians, and others attended the Unitarian Chapel at Newcastle under Lyme. In general, Staffordshire was a mixed bag of denominational leanings.

During the last quarter of the eighteenth century, potters like Ralph Wood and others produced noteworthy religious figures. Some were earthenware decorated with colored glazes and others were pearl glazed earthenware with overglaze enamel decoration. *Elijah and the Ravens*, *King David with Harp*, an early *St. George and the Dragon*, *St. Peter*, *St. Paul*, and a particularly striking figure of a peasant at prayer were among the religious figures of this period. Such figures were not surprising. Interest in religious matters ran high in Staffordshire, and many of the potters were deeply involved. For example, in 1788, pottery luminary Enoch Wood formulated, with others, codes of conduct for observing the Sabbath and a pledge to see that laws pertaining to drunkenness were enforced. In 1790, Wood served as a churchwarden and, from 1801-34, he was an officer of the Methodist Sunday School in Burslem.

Around this time, worldly vicars were subject to a watchful public eye. Beginning late in the eighteenth century and during the early nineteenth century, local sentiment toward wayward clergymen was recorded by the potters who delivered clever ceramic "floggings" in *The Drunken Parson* Toby jugs and in the first issues of earthenware groups like *The Vicar and Moses* (or *The Parson and Clerk*). In one of these groups, a paunchy cleric is depicted asleep in his pulpit above a clerk who was apparently called Moses. Another group shows a drunken vicar being escorted home by his clerk. Among the best-known pre-Victorian Staffordshire figures that poke fun at the clergy are the various *Tithe Pig* groups that depict a farmer surrendering to a vicar his tithe (one tenth of his goods, including a litter of pigs) while his wife offers the clergyman her tenth child. Another anecdotal group with "church" implications was modeled in response to the New Marriage Act of 1823 that attempted to stop clandestine marriages. However, couples could still marry outside of the church in Scotland (i.e., in Gretna Green, the nearest town north of the English border) where it was sufficient to state their wishes before witnesses of any kind to be considered married.

Early nineteenth century figures included St. Sebastian and St. Barbara, and the theological virtues of Faith, Hope, and Charity were introduced in classical forms. *The Virgin and Child* with overglaze painted decoration was made by Enoch Wood circa 1820-30 and may have been intended for the Continental Roman Catholic market. Undecorated pearlware figures excavated from under the pavement outside Burslem Old Town Hall included *The Pieta*, *The Virgin and Child*, *Christ* (or an Apostle), and *Elijah and the Ravens*. These, too, were made circa 1820-30 by Enoch Wood, who was also responsible for the now-famous bust of John Wesley and a bust of the Virgin Mary.

During the period from about 1810-30, Old Testament representations including *Scriptures Preserved Jeremiah, The Widow of Zarephath*, and *Abraham Sacrificing Isaac* were produced along with New Testament figures like The Holy Family's *Flight into Egypt*, its companion *Flight from Egypt*, and *Christ Teacheth Nicodemus*. These are characterized by bocage and belong to the Walton School class of figures discussed in Chapter Five. Noteworthy among the religious bocage figures are depictions of the New Testament Gospel writers – Saints Matthew, Mark, Luke, and John. A bocage figure of St. Peter portrays the saint kneeling on one knee and holding the keys to the Kingdom of Heaven in his hand (a rooster and a book, presumably the Bible, appear to his left). St. Paul was represented with a sword that recalls his pre-conversion persecution of Christians and his letter to the Ephesians (6:7) in which he metaphorically calls the Word of God "the sword of the spirit." While these figures lack the sophistication of Continental bocage porcelains, they express meticulous attention to scriptural details. Other religious bocage groups include *Jesus Praying* (in Gethsemane), a crucifixion group (marked with Walton's name), *Faith* (holding a purple luster cross), and a version of the *Tithe Pig*.

Several religious figures that date to around 1825-30 were mounted on table bases. (See Chapter Five). These include a Christening group and a *Christ in Gethsemane* bocage variant. Others in this style were entitled *Abraham Stop* (including text from Genesis 22), *Peter Rising the Lame Man . Acts Ch. 3*, and *Samuel Anointed David . Samuel Ch. 16*.

In 1851, the Vatican established Roman Catholic dioceses headed by bishops, an action that generated "no popery" campaigns in England. A group of figures produced by Thomas Parr denigrating Catholicism and suggesting Protestant superiority and purity were issued around this time and included representations of Ridley and Lattimer and of Archbishop Cranmer being burned at the stake. There was also an anti-catholic group in which a young woman holding a moneybag inscribed with the sum of £10,000 stands before a kneeling priest as the priest offers her a veil. This figure's source was a cartoon that appeared in an 1851 issue of *Punch* – a satirical statement that suggests the priest's exchange of a nun's veil for the money. Perhaps the most striking Protestant versus Catholic figure groups are paired figures known today as *Popery and Protestantism*. One depicts a priest resting his right hand on a chained Bible. His left hand holds a scroll that reads, *"Either we must root out the Bible or the Bible will root us out. The translators of the English Bible are to be abhorred to the depths of Hell. It would be better to be without God's law than without the Pope, Dr. Troy, Archbishop of Dublin, 1816."* Behind the scroll are the words, *"He that*

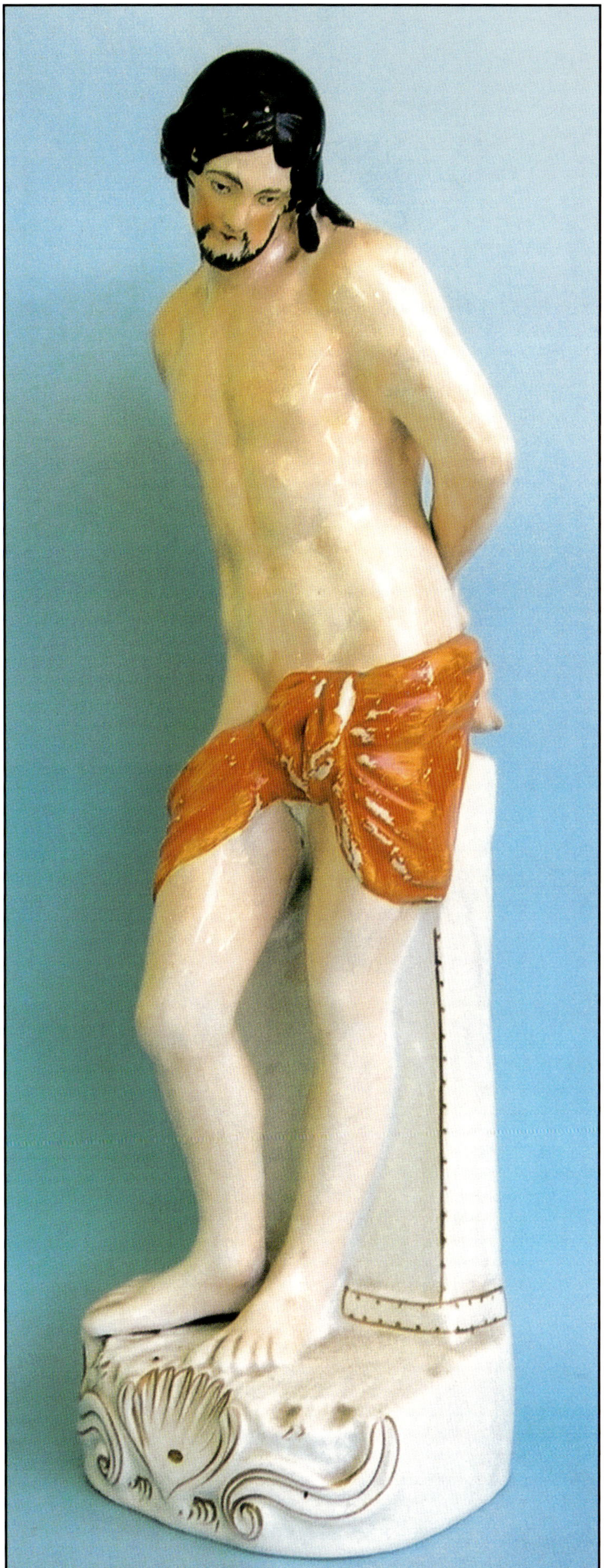

This figure of Christ with his hands tied behind his back, known as "Ecce Homo" or "The Flagellation," is based on a bronze sculpture from the collection of Louis XIV held in the Louvre, Paris. This figure represents the cross-over from high culture to everyday life frequently wrought by the Staffordshire potters, enabling access to art, otherwise denied to the working classes. The figure displays a high level of skill on the part of the modeler who sculpted the master figure from which the mold was taken. 15.75". Circa 1860. Value: $1000+

committeth his conscience to the keeping of another is no longer a free man. Freedom of conscience and freedom of thought are essential to the freedom of a nation. Therefore a nation of Catholics is a nation of slaves." The paired figure depicts a woman who holds an open Bible in her left hand and a scroll in her right. The scroll reads, *"Search the Scriptures, John 5:39. Prove all things. Thes. 5:27. Let the word of Christ dwell in you richly. C3.16. To the Law and to the Testimony, if they speak not according to this word it is because there is no light in them. Isa. 8.26."* Behind the scroll, an inscription states, *"The Bible, the open Bible is the Religion of Protestants. It is everything else from God, free as the air we breathe. It spurns alike indulgences and penance."*

A group inspired by the Old Testament account of Abraham and Isaac (Genesis 22). In this spill holder, Abraham is seen preparing a sacrifice for God while Isaac collects firewood to assist with the sacrifice. Isaac is unaware that God has instructed his father, Abraham, to offer Isaac as a sacrifice, and the dramatic tension in clearly reflected in this group. 11". Circa 1860. Value: $1000+.

Samuel and Eli of the Old Testament based on a painting by J.S.Copley. Copley's painting was adapted to a print and appeared in the 1861 edition of Rev. John Brown's *Old Testament* and in the popular reader *Family Devotions*. Such was the popularity of the image that it was further adapted into a pattern for needlework and sold as a "kit." 12.50. Circa 1860. Value: $1000+.

As the century moved forward, diminishment of anti-Catholic fervor was reflected in portrait figures of Pope Pius IX, St. Vincent de Paul, Cardinal Manning, St. Joan of Arc (possibly modeled from a "Joan of Arc Waltz" music front by Chas Dalbert), and even St. Patrick (presumably for the Irish and Irish-American market). One figure shows a nun kneeling in prayer under an arbor that is topped by the head and wings of an angel, and another shows a monk and a nun standing at either side of a watch holder with a church door below and a figure of the Blessed Mother and Child above. Small figures, about three and a half inches in height and made to serve as candlesnuffers are believed to be portraits of Sister Mary Margaret Hallahan and Père Bernard Moulaert. Interestingly, a figure titled *Sacred Heart of Mary*, probably modeled by a non-Catholic, should have been titled, according to Catholic dogma, *Immaculate Heart of Mary*. Along with these, figures and groups like *Moses*, *David with the Lamb of God*, *Daniel and the Lions*, a new version of *St. George and the Dragon*, *The Madonna and Child*, and *Jesus* (with the Sacred Heart exposed and paired with the *Sacred Heart of Mary*) were added to Staffordshire's growing repertoire of religious figures.

Children figured prominently in Victorian-era figures, and religious groups were produced that depict children with guardian angels or kneeling beside crosses. Also included were numerous representations of Christ and the Virgin Mary, several of which included holy water stoups. Holy water stoups were often modeled to show Christ crucified with angels at his sides. Usually one or two angels' heads were incorporated to decorate the fronts of the stoups. A variation of the portrayal was modeled with two women standing, crossed-legged, on each side of a holy water stoup that is topped with a crucifix on which one hand of each woman is placed. An unusual holy water stoup figure portrayed Christ standing with his arms crossed at his chest and looking upward; angels with outstretched wings were placed beside him, and two angels' heads were molded into the stoup. In one monumental figure, Christ was depicted at the pillar about to be scourged (Matthew 27:26). This figure was produced in fifteen inch and sixteen and three quarter inch versions and is known as *The Flagellation* or *Ecce Homo* (behold the man). A smaller figure depicts Christ in the moments before his crucifixion: he wears a loin cloth, his hands are bound in front, and drops of blood are painted on his forehead beneath a crown of thorns. Superb among the Christ figures are *Forbid Them Not* and *Suffer Little Children to Come Unto Me*, each of which is a variant on the Gospel texts of Mark 10:14 and Matthew 19:14. In a lovely thirteen and three quarter inch group, Christ was modeled kneeling in prayer and surrounded by five angels. Christ was also modeled in several groups with the woman of Samaria and, in one group, restoring sight to the blind man.

Other figures of the period included a set of the Gospel writers – Matthew, Mark, Luke, and John – each figure colored with cobalt blue and titled with gold indented capitals in the Alpha style. Similarly modeled and decorated figures of Christ and the Virgin Mary were also produced, undoubtedly as a series by the same factory. Old Testament figures of the period included several versions of *Daniel and the Lions*, *Rebecca at the Well* (spelled "Rebekah" in titles and in some versions portrayed with Abraham's servant), *Abraham and Isaac*, *Lot and His Daughters*, *Jacob and Rachel*, a watch holder of *Moses Holding the Tablets Containing the Ten Commandments*, *Moses and the Serpent* (Numbers 21:8-9),the *Prodigal Son*, *Ruth* (with Boaz and alone), *Sampson and the Lion*, *Samuel and Eli*, *Saul Presenting His Daughter to David*, *Saint Winifride*, and *St. Pierre* (with the title in French and presumably produced for the French market). An untitled group traditionally called *St. Agnas* depicts a seated woman with her arm around a child who stands reading from a book. While the potters may have intended the book to be the Bible or a prayer book, there is no documentary evidence to support the presumed title, and it is unlikely that the figure represents the Catholic Saint Agnes who was martyred in Rome at the age of twelve or thirteen during the persecutions of Diocletian (circa 314). *Flight to Egypt* remained popular and was potted without bocage as well as in a white and gilt version that shows the Holy Family in much the same manner as earlier groups of the same subject. Versions of the three theological virtues (Faith, Hope, and Charity) were popular and were produced in Victorianized versions and well as in more classical representations. Related figures included *Band of Hope* (which commemorates the Band of Hope formed in 1847 as a temperance organization for children) and figures that represented Faith, Hope, and Charity as the motto of the Independent Order of Good Templars.

The Staffordshire potters were keen businessmen, adept at capitalizing on consumer interests. Accordingly, they took an ecumenical approach to their religious portrait figures as they recorded the broad scope of both local and national religious persuasions. The Quakers were represented by William Penn and Joseph John Gurney; the Methodists by several figures of John Wesley; the Calvinists by William Huntington and Rev. John Elias; the Baptists by Rev. Christmas Evans and Rev. Charles Spurgeon; the Congregationalists by Dr. Thomas Raffles; the Presbyterians by Henry Cooke; the Church of England by Rev. Edward Goulburn; and the American Revival Missionaries by Dwight Lyman Moody and Ira D. Sankey. "General" William Booth, originally a revivalist and Methodist preacher, founder of the Salvation Army received pottery accolades in the form of a very well modeled bust for his role as champion of the urban poor through his establishment of Christian missions in Whitechapel in 1865 that rapidly spread throughout the country.

This figure, in the manner of Thomas Parr, is often considered to have been inspired by the Old Testament as depicting a rather voluptuous "Rebecca at the Well" attired in the potter's romantic and revealing version of Old Testament garb. The Hardings, however, identify the source of the figure as a Minton figure of "Arabia," possibly modeled as the paired figure for a similarly posed male dressed in Eastern attire and holding a water jug near a well (see Harding, Book 2, p. 299). 9". Circa 1860. Value: $500-$1000.

Extremely rare and previously unrecorded figure drawn from the Old Testament account of Abraham's servant and the woman at the well. This figure is by Thomas Parr and interestingly utilizes elements of two already known figures: the palm "bocage" employed on several of Parr's animal groups, and the figures from another group. 9". Circa 1860. Value: $1000+.

The New Testament account of The Holy Family's "Flight into Egypt" (Matthew 2:13) to escape Herod's massacre of the innocents is the subject of this spill holder. 9.50". Circa 1860. Value: $1000+.

A subtly colored and finely modeled large figure of the Virgin Mary and the Baby Jesus modeled in the style of Thomas Parr. 14". Circa 1850. Value: $500-$1000.

In general, religious art appeals to a limited audience. Collectors may include Staffordshire's religious figures in their collections for variety, but there are few who focus exclusively on these items. Such pieces are relatively rare, especially those from early production periods. Current values are high and continue to climb. Collectors and dealers may not attach a spiritual spin to Staffordshire figures, but religion *was* an integral part of eighteenth and nineteenth century life and, while many of Staffordshire's religious figures are stirring stuff in their own right, they are infinitely more fascinating when understood in their historical and sociological contexts. Amen!

Small and unusual vine shrouded "shrine" protecting a group of the Virgin and Child. 5.75". Circa 1870. Value: $100-$500.

Previously referred to as "David and the Lamb of God" these paired figures again represent the cross-over from high culture to everyday life that was often and successfully achieved by the Staffordshire potters. The authors have discovered a pictorial source for the pair (pictured center); titled on the card's reverse "Hearken unto the Prophet." Sadly no acknowledgement of the original artist is given on the card. Left-hand figure 7.25", right-hand figure 7.50". Circa 1850. Value for the pair: $1000+; for singles $500-$1000.

The Virgin Mary defeating Satan, as symbolized by the serpent and apple under her feet. The imagery of the serpent and apple are sourced to the Old Testament account of "The Fall" in Genesis 3: contrary to God's command, Eve, tempted by the serpent, ate an apple from the tree of knowledge and gave fruit from the same tree to her husband Adam. 11". Circa 1870. Value: $100-$500.

Christ and the Woman of Samaria featured in front of a spill holder in the manner of Thomas Parr. The potters made many versions of this popular New Testament subject, this example being one of the most attractive. 13.75". Circa 1850. Value: $500-$1000.

This figure of St. Sebastian is a Kent reproduction of a pre-Victorian pearlware portrayal of the death of Saint Sebastian who was martyred for his Christian faith. The young saint was tied to a tree and shot with arrows; faithful to the story, the potters made sure that wound-marks from the arrows are present on the figure. 10". Circa late 19th century. Value: $500-$1000.

Saint George (Patron Saint of England) and the dragon, although in essence more patriotic than religious, was a popular subject for the potters and found a ready market. Because the potters were ecumenical in addressing the needs of their public, hagiography featuring a range of popular saints came within their repertoire as much as did portraiture of Non-Conformist preachers and philosophers. 7.50". Circa 1860. Value: $500-$1000.

Another version of "Saint George and the Dragon." 10". Mid-Victorian. Value: $500-$1000. *Courtesy of Anita L. Grashof, Gallerie Ani'tiques.*

Angels were as popular a source of spiritual solace as they were of decorative relief in Victorian times. Here the potters have a surprisingly bare-breasted angel watching over two sleeping children. This spill holder most likely depicts the story of "Babes in the Woods" where the angel is poised to take the dying children's souls to Heaven. 9". Circa 1860. Value: $500-$1000.

This group of a seated woman and a child reading from a book is often considered to portray St. Agnes (curiously spelled "Agnas" in most listings), a 4th century Roman martyr. According to Catholic tradition, the St. Agnes honored by the Church was martyred at the age of twelve or thirteen in circa 314 AD when Diocletian began his persecutions. Her symbol is the lamb, and her feast day is January 21. Although the association persists, there is nothing in this group to suggest a relationship to the saint, and no sources have as yet been discovered to explain the popular identification. Nevertheless, this remains a charming figure. 7.50". Circa 1860. Value: $100-$500.

Portrait figure of the philanthropist, writer, and Quaker minister Joseph John Gurney (brother of the prison reformer Elizabeth Fry) who played a prominent role in the abolition of slavery, prison reform, and the abolition of capital punishment. Gurney died in 1847, and this very rare figure was probably made in commemoration of his death. 11.50". Circa 1847. Value: $1000+. *Courtesy of Susan Bishop and Darcy McGroarty, Bishop and Daughter Antiques.*

This figure of a woman and child at prayer provides a simple yet beautiful depiction of the active presence of religion in the lives of the everyday people in 19th century Britain. 8". Circa 1850. Value: $1000+.

This small and graceful figure of a woman kneeling at a prie-dieu and reading a Bible records the presence of prayerful devotion and the prominence of religion during the Victorian Era. 4". Circa 1840. Value: $100-$500.

One of a pair of rare and remarkably controversial figures produced by Thomas Parr representing, alternately, the faiths of "Protestantism" and "Popery" (Catholicism). Parr, with a very obviously Protestant market in mind, chose to represent that religion as a beautiful and virtuous young woman and depicted her with scriptural excerpts and observations on the virtues of Non-Conformist religion. "Popery" is represented by an elderly cassocked priest accompanied by far less flattering scriptural quotes and theological observations. This pair of figures forms part of a pro Non-Conformist series of figures by Parr. 9". Circa 1850. Value for either single or for the pair: $1000+.

Reverse of "Protestantism" showing the theological tract used in support of the Protestant religion.

"BAND OF HOPE" is a beautiful and rare figure celebrating the virtues of temperance. The Band of Hope Temperance Society was founded in Leeds in 1847 with the intention of saving children before they were tempted into alcoholism. The "demon drink" is seen in this spill holder as a snake being deflected by the shield of Temperance herself. 14". Circa 1850. Value: $1000+.

Sampson and the Lion, based on the Old Testament account of Sampson in the vineyards of Timnah, recorded in Judges 14:5-10. 12.75". Mid-Victorian. Value: $1000+. *Courtesy of Zane Moss Antiques.*

Rare portrait figure of the eccentric preacher Reverend William Huntington S. S., who became a preacher after minimal education and a varied career that included stints as a servant, gun-maker, coachman, gardener, and tramp. During his time as "jack-of-all-trades," Huntington also seduced and made pregnant the daughter of a Kentish tailor and developed a liaison with a serving girl. By 1769, William, by now a preacher, had added the initials "S. S." ("Sinner Saved") to his name in an attempt to circumvent any potentially damning public revelations of his more liberal past. As a Calvinistic Protestant minister, Huntington established the "Providence Chapel" in London in 1783 and published *God the Guardian of the Poor*. 8.50". Circa 1850. Value: $500-$1000. *Courtesy of John and Barbara Gair, Castle Antiques.*

Bust of John Wesley (1703-1791), an evangelical preacher who, after rejecting the "high church" tradition, became founder of the Methodist faith. During his ministry, Wesley traveled extensively throughout England and reached many small industrial towns, which helped him become the favorite of miners and other laborers who felt little kinship with the Church of England. Numerous figures of Wesley were made during the nineteenth century. 10.50". Circa 1850. Value: $500-$1000.

St. John from a set of bocage figures depicting the four gospel writers: Saints Matthew, Mark, Luke, and John. Later versions of the set were produced without bocage, most notably the Alpha factory-style set titled with gold indented capitals. Approximately 7.5". Circa 1820-30. Value: $500-$1000.

The Widow of Zarephath with circular bocage, paired with "Elijah and the Ravens" (see Chapter Five). 9.25". Circa 1820-30. Value (as shown with restoration in progress on damaged hands) $500-$1000, (undamaged) $1000+.

This figure of St. Peter (missing its original bocage in this example) was very likely paired with a similar figure of St. Paul. The St. Peter figure is depicted holding the "keys to the kingdom of heaven," while St. Paul is holding the "sword of the spirit." 7.5". Circa 1820-30. Value for singles: (as shown and undamaged) $500-$1000.

Rare titled figure of St. Patrick, Patron saint of Ireland, undoubtedly intended for the Irish Market. 11". Circa 1870. Value: $500-$1000.

Group of Christ and two children entitled "Forbid Them Not" and based on the New Testament Gospel according to Matthew (19:14). 12.50" Mid-Victorian. Value: $500-$1000.

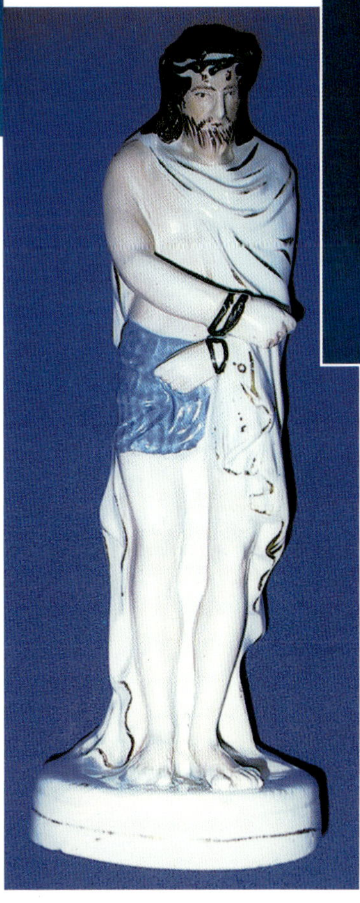

Christ bound and wearing a crown of thorns. The source of this figure is scripture: "Pilate then had Jesus taken away and scourged; and after this, the soldiers twisted some thorns into a crown, and put it on his head..." (John 19:1-2). 9.25". Mid-Victorian. Value: $500-$1000.

Paired, titled figures of American evangelists Dwight Lyman Moody (1837-1899) and Ira David Sankey (1840-1908). Moody was born in Northfield, Massachusetts and opened a Sunday school in Chicago. He teamed up with Sankey to write hymns and together they made visits to England. Sankey was born in Edinburgh, Pennsylvania; his printed collections of hymns are recorded to have sold over 50,000,000 copies. These figures are recorded in four sizes (see Harding, pp. 89 and 124, Book One), with the examples shown being the tallest. 17". Circa 1870. Value: 1000+. *Courtesy of Nick Harding* (A & N Harding, *Victorian Staffordshire Figures 1835-1875*).

Chapter Fourteen
Literary and Theatrical Figures: Pen and Stage

The statues and plaques in Westminster Abbey's Poet's Corner bear silent witness to Britain's love of language. In Victorian times, that love was as much a matter of good upbringing as it was of art. Literary luminaries aside, it was a social imperative that well polished ladies and gentlemen pen the occasional poem or story.

Literature's place in genteel society, and the impulse to create and share it, extended to the working classes by the mid-nineteenth century. Industrialization in Britain wrought ruthless and pitiless changes on the lives of rural workers. Wrenched away from their agricultural heritage and mythos, these displaced groups became what we now know as the urban working classes. This dislocation left a vacuum in their lives that they sought desperately to fill. By the mid-nineteenth century, printed literature had supplanted the oral folk tradition that formerly sustained rural social life and identity and helped form the emotional, educational and moral experience of its listeners.

The move to a printed norm was supported in the 1830s, a period widely regarded by educationalists as "the Dawn of Literacy," through the passing of a succession of acts of Parliament, investigative committees, and special educational grants. One of the most important acts was the "Factory Act" of 1844, which attempted to protect children between the ages of eight and thirteen by limiting their working hours and obliging employers to provide "schools" for their young employees.

Although illiteracy remained widespread among the poor, literacy rates among the working classes gradually increased through the next decades aided by the establishment of day, evening, and Sunday schools like "The Ragged School Union" in 1844. These schools aided the spread of literacy, and their limited lending libraries made available a precious and hitherto unattainable and expensive commodity to workers – books. The introduction of cloth binding as a substitute for leather during the 1830s further served to make books more affordable for the working classes, and ongoing advances in printing techniques made illustrated texts and newspapers more available to an increasingly literate society that sought escape, education, and entertainment. The ever-pragmatic Staffordshire potters tapped into these phenomena and produced thousands of pottery figures derived from literary sources.

By the 1850s, the British print media had undeniably become an arbitrator of popular taste and culture. Poetry, novels, plays, bibles, prayer books, magazines, and newspapers provided the potters with an almost endless source of subject matter for their figures. Sometimes this inspiration even extended to the potter transfer printing whole verses of poems or sections of prose on their figures to add literary authenticity.

Virtually any writer or work of literature lit by the spotlight of Victorian favor provided subject matter for Staffordshire's potters. Writers whose contribution to literature remains acknowledged today – Shakespeare (modeled at least ten times including figures based on Peter Scheemaker's statue in the Poet's Corner), Byron, Johnson, Milton, Sir Walter Scott, Robert Burns, Voltaire, Rousseau, the Brownings, and Harriet Beecher Stowe – joined forces with the more bizarre mediators of Victorian taste like Letitia Elizabeth Landon and the spectacularly untalented and sentimental poet Eliza Cook, to be forever captured by the potters as tributes to their prominence in Victorian thought and taste.

Pre-Victorian figure of a woman representing "Comedy." 5.75". Circa 1810. Value: $500-$1000.

The potters also modeled numerous literary characters. Among the many were Uncle Tom, Little Eva, and Aunt Chloe (from Harriet Beecher Stowe's *Uncle Tom's Cabin)*, "Highland" Mary Campbell (from poems by Robert Burns), Byron's Maid of Athens (portraying Byron's real-life muse, Theresa Macri), and Dog Tray (based on Stephen Campbell's 1836 poem "The Harper"). Harrison Ainsworth's novel, *Rookwood*, which detailed the exploits of highwaymen Dick Turpin and Tom King, led to a number of theatrical productions and several figures of Turpin and King (see Chapter Fifteen).

Along with models of the great bard himself, earthenware images based on characters from Shakespeare's plays gained favor by the mid-nineteenth century, and engravings in the Tallis "Shakespeare Gallery" (1852-1853) gave rise to a range of noteworthy figures produced by the Parr and Kent group. In these figures, the talented potter, most likely Thomas Parr himself, enabled fairly exact and instantly recognizable copies of the original engravings.

Other literary characters portrayed by the potters include John Anderson and his wife ("My Jo"). Figures of Tam O'Shanter and Souter Jonnie were based on poems by Robert Burns, some inspired by James Thom's sculptures used on the Burns monument at Ayr. Robinson Crusoe (after Daniel DeFoe's novel) possibly paired with Man Friday are rare, with the presumed Man Friday figure as yet uncataloged. Six figures representing characters from Dickens' *Nicholas Nickelby* are recorded as are depictions of Ali Baba and Morgiana from *Arabian Nights*, which was first performed in 1806 at Drury Lane (John Banister as Ali Baba) and in 1818 at Covent Garden (John Liston in the title role). Figures of the "Babes in the Wood" were popular and were based on a mid-seventeenth century ballad from Thomas Percy's *Reliques of Ancient English Poetry*. This poem was dramatized numerous times by the Victorians and tells the story of a brother and sister whose evil uncle sought to kill them and obtain their estate when the children's father died. The uncle hired two men to kill the children, one of whom had second thoughts, killed his partner, and left the children to die in the woods where a robin covered their bodies with leaves. George Coleman's play, *Jealous Wife*, remembered mainly from extant nineteenth century playbills, gave rise to a titled figure, and even lady Godiva (celebrated in Tennyson's "Godiva") appeared in a rare Parr Factory style figure of the infamous lady riding bare-breasted on her horse. A 1787 novel by Nernardin de St. Pierre that tells the story of the doomed lovers Paul and Virginia was the inspiration of several Victorian lyrical dramas, and the potters portrayed the title characters in various figures. R. B. Sheridan's 1775 comedy involving Captain Absolute and Lydia Languish (niece of Mrs. Malaprop) was recorded in a figure titled *The Rivals*. Cervantes characters Don Quixote and Sancho Panza were portrayed in titled figures – Sancho mounted on a donkey and Quixote mounted on a horse. Versions of these characters were produced in the Parr Factory style, and others were manufactured into the twentieth century.

The Bible and devotional texts like the 1861 edition of Rev. John Brown's *Old Testament* and the reader *Family Devotions* offered a wealth of subjects for the potters. Newspapers and magazines were popular and accessible, and publications like the *Illustrated London News*, *Cassell's Illustrated Family Paper*, and *Punch* brought literature to a wider public. Illustrated stories, poems, and serialized novels fueled interest in contemporary authors' works and provided the potters with characters that were readily adapted to pottery figures. Children's literature was also represented with figures of Red Riding Hood, Cinderella and her Prince (modeled after actors Mrs. Edwards and Luigi Lablanche), the Cat and the Fiddle, Mother Goose, Old Mother Hubbard, Mr. Punch with his dog Toby, Robin Hood, and characters from Aesop's fables like "The Fox and the Stork."

Portrait of the poet Eliza Cook whose verse, sentimental to the point of being mawkish, had a very strong following among Victorian "connoisseurs" of poetry. *Eliza Cook's Journal* and *Jottings from My Journal* were published in 1860 and 1861, and it is likely that this figure dates to the release of these, her two most popular volumes. 6.25" Circa 1860. Value: $1000+.

Stage performances also took on the guise of potters' muse. The book *Tom & Jerry* by Pierce Egan became a three-act operatic performance that resulted in character portraits of Billy Waters, African Sal, and Dusty Bob. The dramatization of literary works like Byron's poems "The Bride of Abydos," "The Corsair," and "Mazeppa" led to the production of lithographed playbills illustrating characters from the works. These playbills were eagerly seized upon by enterprising potters and used as yet another source for their figures.

Titled portrait figure of the once very popular, but currently much derided Miss Cook. 11". Circa 1860. Value: $1000+.

Portrait figure of William Shakespeare whose works were immensely popular during the Victorian era for rich and poor, the scholarly and less literate alike. 7.50". Circa 1850. Value: $500-$1000.

Unidentified group of an elderly woman, cat, and cockatoo. There is a nice set of clues to assist with identification, but as yet none has been made and the group is simply referred to as "The Old Maid." Because the figure is paired with a group of an elderly gentleman taking tea that has been sometimes identified as "Mr. Dick Taking Tea" from Charles Dickens's *David Copperfield*, it is likely that this group has some Dickensian association. Perhaps "Aunt Betsey?" A group of figures modeled in a manner similar to this figure are often attributed to the "Alpha Factory." 7". Circa 1850. Value for the pair: $1000+; for either single: $500-$1000.

A faux clock group featuring William Shakespeare, Hamlet, and Lady Macbeth. These fake clock figures were popular among the less wealthy as few could afford the luxury of clockwork timepieces or of multiple timepieces; and the head of the household would undoubtedly be in possession of any watch the family owned. Faux, or inanimate, "clocks" gave the illusion that a clock could be afforded to grace the mantle. A popular belief persists that the time at which the decoration of a figure was completed was the time the enameller chose to put on the clock face. Since few enamellers would have been able to afford watches this is unlikely. This figure is based on an engraving that appeared in the *Illustrated London News* in 1848 of a clock to be made in the more expensive medium of Parian designed by the famous sculptor John Bell. 10.25". Circa 1850. Value: $1000+.

Achieving parity with literary character figures is an array of identifiable portrait figures of popular actors and actresses in their onstage roles. John Phillip Kemble was shown as Hamlet, David Garrick as Richard III, James Quin as Falstaff, William Charles Macready as Shylock, Isabella Glyn as Lady MacBeth, and Mr. Williamson as Wackford Squeers from Dicken's *Nicholas Nickelby*. Ada Isaacs Menken, mistress of the poet Swinburne, was modeled strapped to a wild horse as she appeared in the stage version of Byron's "Mazeppa," and Edward Askew Sothern was modeled wearing the drooping whiskers and monocle he brought to the role of Lord Dundreary in "Our American Cousin." Other actors depicted by the potters include: Susan Cushman, Sarah Egerton, Edmund Falconer, Fanny Elizabeth Fitzwilliam, Mary Glover, James Henry Hackett, Charles John Kean, Edmund Kean, John Liston, Jenny Marston, Charles James Matthews, Agnes Kelly Anderson, Frederick Robinson, Sarah Kemble, Edward Askew Sothern, Charlotte Elizabeth Vandenhoff, and Lucia Elizabeth Vestris. (See Chapter Eighteen for additional related illustrations.)

Staffordshire's literary figures serve very much the same function for today's collector as they did nearly a century and a half ago; they excite and educate and are a permanent acknowledgement of the power and importance of literature in reflecting and informing the experience of everyday life.

"Winters Tale" depicts the actors Jenny Marston and Frederick Robinson in the lead roles of "Perdita" and "Florizel" in Shakespeare's play of the same title as the figure group. Pictured behind the figures is the potter's source of inspiration: one of seven engravings from the 1852-53 Tallis "Shakespeare Gallery" used by Thomas Parr to create a series of finely modeled and extremely hard-bodied figures. 12". Circa 1855. Value: $1000+.

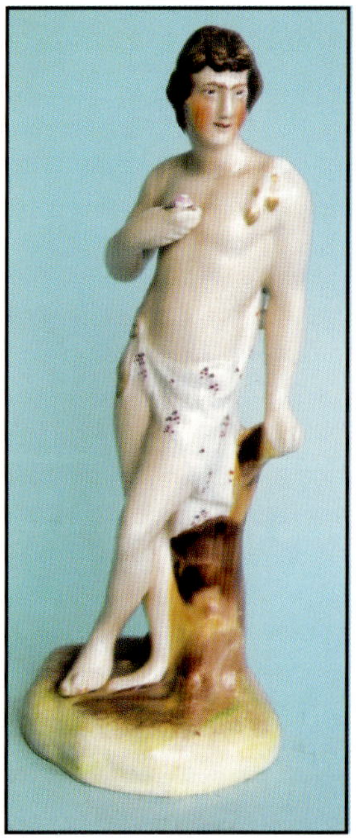

Again perhaps not one the main players, but this roguish and handsome young gentleman would make a dashing Oberon. He is also part of Parr's season series. 6.75". Circa 1850. Value: $500-$1000.

Staffordshire figures invite imagination. Perhaps not Titania herself of Shakespeare's *A Midsummer's Night Dream*, this lovely fairy is definitely ethereal enough to be an attendant sprite. (She is, in, actuality, part of a set of the seasons by Thomas Parr.) 7". Circa 1850. Value: $500-$1000.

Very rare portrait figure of Charlotte Van Denhoff as Juliet based on an engraving from the Tallis Gallery dated 1852. 7.75". Circa 1855. Value: $1000+.

Romeo and Juliet by Thomas Parr again derived from the Tallis series of prints. Transfer printed on the base of this figure is a verse from the play that reads: *"Jul: Oh thinkst thou we shall ever meet again? Rom: I doubt it not; and all those vows shall serve for sweet discourse for times to come."* The players in this instance are the American Cushman sisters, Charlotte and Susan, the former of whom was known to play "trousers roles" (a Victorian eccentricity in which women played male roles on stage). Seen behind the figure is the Tallis print on which it is based. Copies of this figure were made from the late 19th until the mid 20th century, but these lack the elegance and subtleness of earlier figures. 10.25". Circa 1855. Value: $1000+. (See close-up of the transfer printed excerpt in Chapter Three.)

Faux clock group of the actors Mrs. Sarah Siddons as Lady Macbeth and John Kemble as Hamlet. 8.75". Circa 1860. Value: $500-$1000.

Arbor group depicting the lovers Jessica and Lorenzo from Shakespeare's play *The Merchant of Venice*. 9". Circa 1860. Value: $500-$1000.

"Topsy & Eva" from Harriet Beecher Stowe's anti-slavery novel, *Uncle Tom's Cabin*, published in serial form in the *National Era* (1851-1852) and in book form (1852). This very rare group is posed in front of a lithograph from the cover of a music sheet entitled "Topsy's Song." 9". Circa 1855. Value: $1000+.

Mid-1850s Berlin woolwork of Topsy and Eva derived from the same source as the Staffordshire group: the music sheet "Topsy's Song." This crossover between decorative and domestic arts provides an insight into the all-encompassing nature of popular taste in Victorian Britain.

Close-up of "Topsy and Eva."

Uncle Tom and Eva resting on bales of cotton. 11.25". Circa 1855. Value: $1000+.

Arbor group in the manner of Thomas Parr that depicts Eva teaching Uncle Tom to read. 6.75". Circa 1855. Value: $500-$1000.

Rare figure of Aunt Chloe from *Uncle Tom's Cabin* incorrectly titled "Topsy." 8.25". Value: $1000+.

Little Red Riding Hood with a very non-threatening wolf. Although the reason for the Victorians' fascination with this particular fairy tale is unclear (Freudian delving aside), numerous versions of this particular tale found their ways into homes. 7". Circa 1860. Value: $100-$500.

Porcelaineous group of Mother Goose, the Goose, and a golden egg in Mother Goose's hand. A charming and well modeled nursery rhyme-inspired group. 7.75". Circa 1850. Value: $1000+.

Previously unrecorded pictorial source for a number of "Little Red Riding Hood" figures popular during the 1850s. These figures varied in size from less than 5" to in excess of 15" and saw equally significant variations in the quality of decoration and modeling. In all examples, however, the potters remained faithful to the original, even in the reduced proportions of the wolf to his juvenile companion and her stern expression.

Spill holders representing Aesop's fable the "Fox and the Stork" in which the two animal antagonists discover the significance of the concept of "each to his own." These figures are particularly well modeled and colored and feature fine Rococo bases. Left-hand figure 6.75", right-hand figure 7". Circa 1840. Value for the pair: $1000+; for singles $1000+.

Classical mythology had always retained its popularity among the learned and well-read, but as books became more affordable during the mid 19th century due to improvements in the printing process, publishing increased exponentially and versions of famous myths came into print. Thus, "The Classics" became accessible to a far larger proportion of the reading public. Subjects like the abduction of the young shepherd Ganymede by the god Zeus (in the form of an eagle) portrayed in this figure became familiar to the public, and the potters, ever entrepreneurial and eager to please, created figures in response to consumer interest. 7.25". Circa 1850. Value: $500-$1000.

Classical literature again provided subject matter for the potters in the tale of "Androcles and the Lion." Androcles, an escaped slave, while hiding in a cave, discovered a lion with a painful, swollen paw and removed a thorn that was causing the problem. Androcles was captured and sentenced to certain death in an arena contest with a lion. As it transpired, his adversary in the arena was the same lion on which he showed pity, and the lion, in gratitude, refused to attack. So impressed were Androcles's masters that they freed both him and the lion. A similar group was produced in which Macombo was depicted in the role of Androcles (see Chapter Eighteen for more information on Macombo). 7.25". Circa 1850. Value: $1000+. *Courtesy of John and Barbara Gair, Castle Antiques.*

Robert Burns led as romantic a life as the lines he set to paper. A self-educated farm-laborer, he was born the son of a poor farmer. Burns published a small book of poems in 1786 that earned for him the then staggering sum of five hundred pounds. Now acknowledged as Scotland's greatest poet, Burns set to courting not one, but two, women. It was Mary Campbell who became the romantic subject of much of Burns's work. Although Burns died in 1796, the romance of his works was such that his popularity never diminished during the 19th century. Burns is pictured here with his "Highland Mary." 6.50". Circa 1860. Value: $100-$500.

Spill holder featuring Burns and Mary in a tryst, accompanied by a verse from Burns's poem "Highland Mary." This figure also exists in a well-colored form. 12". Circa 1860. Value: $100-$500.

John Anderson, the subject of Burns's poem "Dear Jo" that tenderly explores the nature of ageing and relationships. 5.75". Circa 1860. Value: $100-$500.

Lord Byron and the Maid of Athens. The "Maid of Athens," Theresa Marci, was the eldest daughter of the British Consul to Athens with whom Byron stayed in 1809 and who inspired the "Maid of Athens" poem. Byron was so taken with Theresa that he even named his boat in her honor; the public was so taken with his poem that it was set to music. Other figures and a bust of Lord Byron are also recorded. 9". Circa 1860. Value: $500-$1000.

John Gilpin was the subject of a humorous poem by the poet William Cowper in 1785. The unfortunate Mr. Gilpin (a real person!) hired a horse to take his wife to Edmonton to celebrate their twentieth wedding anniversary, but the unfortunate draper lost control of the animal, which galloped off with John clinging to its back. The poem was adapted to an Astley's hippodrome spectacular in 1844, from which this figure probably dates. 6.75". Circa 1844-45. Value: $500-$1000.

The "Cat and the Fiddle" of nursery rhyme fame. 4.25". Circa 1860. Value: $100-$500.

Couple reclining on chaises reading. Both 9" (length), 9" (height). Circa 1870. Value: $500-$1000 pair.

Chapter Fifteen
Rogues and Renegades: The Criminal Element

Confess! We're all fascinated by the seamy, the notorious, and the outré. Crime and infamy sell. Fancy experiencing a frisson of horror every time your eyes met those of the cold-blooded murderer perched on your mantelpiece? The Victorians and their predecessors did. They were so chilled and thrilled by the crimes of their day that they crowded their mantelshelves with a motley assortment of murderers, embezzlers, conmen, rogues, and crime-scenes that gazed down malevolently into the everyday lives of their hosts.

The fascinating aspect of crime is not necessarily the blood and gore (although a little of that never goes astray) but the glimpses it provides into others' loves, habits, vices, and weaknesses. In eighteenth and nineteenth century England, the ingenious North Staffordshire potters were eager to feed the public's morbid and lucrative interests.

During the late eighteenth and early nineteenth centuries, improved transport, newspapers, broadsheets, and traveling exhibitions increased access to information and news and brought about the equivalent of today's "information revolution." Broadsheets (ephemeral, cheap, and produced in the thousands) were long sheets of paper printed on one side with text and crude woodcut illustrations on single subjects – official announcements, songs, current events and, most significantly, sensational crime reports. Sold by local bookshops or peddled by itinerant hawkers, these were the flyers and posters of their time. Broadsheets were often pasted on the walls of public houses and meeting places so that even those who could not read were treated, through the recitations of their more lettered companions, to visions of dreadful crimes and misdeeds.

Another phenomenon that fed the public's appetite for the criminal was the move of Madame Tussaud's famous waxworks to England where she started touring in 1802 and set up a permanent museum in 1835. During those decades, the public's taste for depictions of crime was firmly established and was quickly translated, along with a pantheon of favorite villains from preceding eras, into Staffordshire figures by the potters.

Perhaps one of the first groups to immortalize infamous acts was "Roman Charity," decorated in the early colored glaze style and dating to the 1770s. The group portrays Cimon, a political dissident of Classical times, who was imprisoned without food or water and left for dead. His daughter, Pera, a symbol of filial devotion, breastfed him during daily visits and saved his life. Versions of the saga appeared in broadsheets and were also adapted as a late eighteenth century play staring Mrs. Siddons. In the 1820s, Cimon and Pera were also depicted in a dramatic and explicit tableau on a table-like base of the type formerly attributed to Obadiah Sherratt (see Chapter Five).

Lucrezia Borgia was one of the next to be "captured" by the potters – this time by Enoch Wood – the "Father of the Potteries." Lucrezia (1480-1519) was the illegitimate daughter of Pope Alexander IV. She was renowned for her excesses, incestuous offspring, and her prowess with poisons. Along with her equally notorious brother Cesare, she skillfully eliminated anyone who attempted to thwart Borgia family interests. In an opera by Donizetti she accidentally murders her own illegitimate son and, driven by guilt and remorse, takes poison and dies. Wood's enamel painted figure is a languorous and lovingly rendered nude Lucrezia in her death throes on a Roman-style couch that would send more feelings than just a shiver of guilt through her 1790s male viewers.

Descended from a noble family and a royalist by sentiment, Charlotte Corday was another femme fatale whose deadly interest in the French physician and Revolutionary leader Marat enticed the potters to immortalize her in clay. Inspired by the Girondins, their opposition to the execution of King Louis XVI, and the more extreme policies of the French Revolution, Corday gained an interview with Marat and assassinated him while he was in his bath. (Marat suffered from a skin disorder that required frequent long immersions in baths, and Charlotte seized upon such a vulnerable moment to stab him through the heart.) Corday was arrested on the spot and sent to the guillotine. Lakin and Poole's 1790s Staffordshire figure of Charlotte and Marat is notable for its remarkable resemblances to the actual subjects, the fact that Marat (in the interests of decorum?) is portrayed fully clothed (not in his bath), and the length of its title: *"The Assassination of Marat, by Charlotte Corde [sic], of Caen, in Normandy, 1793."*

The 1828 Red Barn Murder was the crime of the season when William Corder was alleged to have shot, strangled, and stabbed Maria Marten, the daughter of the local mole-catcher, and to have buried her body under the floor of a barn. Corder was arrested, tried and hanged, but not before the public was horrified into buying a series of figures (see illustrations in Introduction) featuring groupings of Maria, Corder, the trial judge, and the Red Barn itself (complete with various outbuildings and livestock). After his execution, Corder's body was dissected, and his skin was gruesomely used to bind a copy of Curtis's account of the murder. The book once belonged to George Creed, the surgeon who conducted the dissection, and Creed inscribed the book as follows: *"The binding of this book is the skin of the murderer William Corder taken from his body and tanned by myself in the year 1828. George Creed Surgeon to the Suffolk Hospital."* Today, in a St. Edmondsbury museum, various Corder-Marten items, including Corder's skull and the book bound in his skin, are available for public viewing. Like the color of the Barn itself, the history of the crime remains splendidly sinister.

The 1834 publication of Harrison Ainsworth's *Rookwood* (followed by Victorian ballads and plays) resulted in figures of infamous highwaymen Dick Turpin and Tom King who had terrorized travelers a century before. Turpin was an innkeeper's son who became highwayman Tom King's partner on the Cambridge Road. In 1735, Turpin and King stole a horse at Epping Forest and took it to Whitechapel where a constable attempted to arrest King. Turpin fired at the constable, missed, and killed King. Turpin escaped but was caught four years later in Yorkshire where he was hanged for horse theft. Various potters created paired figures of the duo – King on a white horse, and Turpin on his famous mare Black Bess.

Lucrezia Borgia, considered a mistress of the arts of poisoning and intrigue by some and as a victim by others. This superbly modeled figure of Lucrezia, as imagined on her deathbed by Wood and Caldwell, is simultaneously tragic and titillating. 11" (length), 7.50" (height). Circa 1800. Value: $1000+.

By the time Victoria was crowned in 1837, greater dissemination of illustrated news allowed both the literate and the illiterate opportunities to be better informed than ever before. The notorious remained newsworthy, and even the staid and seemingly conventional Victorian sensibilities were not immune to the lure of the headlines and a fascination with humanity's darker side.

Intense interest in the strange and protracted case of Gloucester draper Jemmy Wood was prompted by press accounts of Wood's huge cash estate, his will, a dubious codicil, and disclosures of unusual conduct. Legal proceedings stretched from 1837 until 1844, during which the potters produced several figures of Jemmy that ranged from seven and a half inches to fourteen inches in height.

An 1848 murder that involved West Norfolk farmer James Bloomfield Rush was sensationalized in the press and recorded by the potters. Rush's Potash farm was mortgaged for £5000 to Isaac Jermy of nearby Stanfield Hall. On November 28th, two days before Jermy planned to foreclose, Rush shot and killed Jermy and his son, wounding Jermy's daughter-in-law and servant Eliza Chastney in the process. Emily Sandford, the governess Rush hired to care for his nine children, and whom Rush seduced, gave evidence against him. After a six-day trial and a fourteen-hour closing speech, he was found guilty and was publicly hanged on April 21, 1849 on a bridge over the moat at Norwich Castle. The potters responded with paired figures of Rush and Sandford and architectural figures of Potash Farm, Stanfield Hall, and Norwich Castle.

In 1849, White Hart landlord Frederick George Manning and his wife Maria were convicted at the Old Bailey for the murder of Patrick O'Connor, Maria's former lover. Maria and Manning invited O'Connor to dinner, murdered him, and hid his body in a hole they had dug in their floor. Depicted in paired, titled figures by the potters, Frederick and Maria were hanged on the roof of Horsemonger Lane Gaol on November 13, 1849.

Previously unrecorded figure of a naked woman stretched out on a chaise. Close examination reveals that the placement of the figure's legs and arms are identical to those of early figures of Lucrezia. The attempt at copying the chaise from the more complicated Wood and Caldwell prototype is obvious and, therefore it is likely that this figure represents a Victorian interpretation of the original masterpiece. This identification is based on the observations of the authors alone, as there is no additional evidence to support the theory. The upsurge of public interest in the Borgias was undoubtedly brought about by the staging in 1847 of Donizetti's opera "Lucrezia Borgia" at Covent Garden. If this voluptuous figure is to be believed, the Victorian perception of the feminine ideal had certainly "fleshed out" since the time of Wood and Caldwell. 4.25" (length), 3" (height). Circa 1850. Value: $500-$1000.

Following the 1840s crime wave, the arguable romance of smuggling offered a source of inspiration and the potters created figures of Will Watch, a smuggler and privateer who was well known to Victorians. Portrayed in typical pirate attire, the potters provided Watch with a pistol, a gun, and a backdrop of brandy casks,

In 1850, Australian Frank Gardiner was arrested and jailed for stealing horses. Several arrests, escapes, and releases later, he joined a group of bushrangers and participated in a gold robbery. Gardiner eluded capture until February 1864 when he was arrested, tried in Sydney, and sentenced to thirty-two years imprisonment. Good conduct, agreement to leave Australia, and the fact that he'd never committed murder gained him an early release in July 1874 when he immigrated to San Francisco and lived, apparently crime-free, until his death. Titled figures of Gardiner are rare and were probably made from modified Turpin molds.

William Palmer, a Rugeley physician and member of the Royal College of Physicians, was suspected of the poisoning murders of his wife and brother in August 1855. When a friend, John Parsons Cook, died in December of the same year, Cook's stepfather initiated an investigation that resulted in Palmer's arrest. Palmer was tried and convicted at the Old Bailey for Cook's murder and was hanged in June 1856. An eleven-inch titled figure of Palmer and a building titled "Palmer's House" were modeled by the potters.

A rogue of a different kind: Mazeppa, stealer of hearts and ladies' favors. Ivan Stepanovitch Mazeppa, a Polish Cossack commander, was caught making love with the wife of a local nobleman. As his punishment, Mazeppa was tied naked to the back of a wild horse that was whipped into a fury and then released. Mazeppa was rescued by Ukrainian peasants and eventually came to the notice of Czar Peter the Great who made him the Prince of the Ukraine. By 1709 Mazeppa had outlived his fealty to the Czar and joined the King of Sweden to fight against Russia. When they lost, Mazeppa was forced to flee for his life and into the poetry of Byron who immortalized the miscreant's story in verse. These figures are most likely to have been inspired by the Astley's Hippodrome production of the saga that dated from the 1830s and starred the American equestrian Ada Isaacs Menken in the leading role (see Chapter Eighteen). Costuming, to say the least, would have proved a challenge to Victorian propriety. 6" (length), 5.50" (height) both figures. Circa 1850. Value: $1000+.

On August 7, 1866 William Collier was publicly hanged at Stafford Gaol for the murder of his neighbor, Thomas Smith. When Smith caught Collier poaching on his property, Collier shot Smith in the head and beat him with the gun until the barrel broke. A rare figure generally accepted as representing Smith and Collier shows them beneath an arbor – Collier holds the barrel of a gun in his left hand and clutches Smith's lapel with his right while a dog lunges at Collier's leg.

The story of the Tichborne claimant was a curiosity of its time. Lady Tichborne, widow of the tenth baronet, was convinced that she recognized Arthur Orton as her eldest son (believed to have been lost at sea). Lady Tichborne persuaded Orton, who had immigrated to Australia, to return to England. In 1871, she supported him in an attempt to dispossess his younger brother. The potters immediately produced a fifteen-inch figure entitled "Sir R. Tichborne." Orton lost the 103-day legal battle when perjury was established and he was sentenced to fourteen years of hard labor.

Along with new versions of eighteenth century figures like *Roman Charity* and *Lucrezia Borgia*, the Victorian potters also depicted William O'Brien, an Irish parliamentarian convicted of high treason and transported to Tasmania; Russian conspirator Pavel Pestal (1794-1826), about whom a Victorian song contained words that he reputedly scratched on a dungeon wall the night before his execution; George Hudson, the "Railway King," who became a millionaire through fraud; Mary Anne Talbot, a.k.a. John Taylor and the "British Amazon" who masqueraded as a man and actually served on British warships; and even Robin Hood, the greenwood outlaw-hero of Nottingham's Sherwood Forest. Based on a story from a French collection of fairy tales assembled by Charles Perrault and translated by Robert Samber, a very dramatic figure group depicts Blue Beard with a young woman kneeling in supplicant pose on a cushion beside him. The woman very likely represents Fatima who, having accepted Bluebeard's proposal, was given the keys to his rooms and instructed not to unlock one room in particular. Fatima's curiosity got the better of her, and she unlocked the room to discover the bodies of Blue Beard's former wives. When Fatima was found by Blue Beard, she dropped the room key into the wives' blood and begged for mercy. However, before Blue Beard was able to murder her, her brothers arrived and killed the villain.

The potters were comprehensive, but not just anyone who ran afoul of the law was fair game for the kilns. One criminal, conspicuously absent, was Jack the Ripper whose 1888 unsolved reign of terror in London's Whitechapel stalked into the Victorian psyche and remains to haunt our own. Figure making was still active during the late 1880s, but why the Ripper was never represented in earthenware remains as much a mystery as his identity. Perhaps the potters limited themselves to solved crimes, or maybe the Ripper slashings were too horrific for even the enterprising potters to record.

Diavolino, the dashing bandit from the 1846 ballet "*Caterina, ou La Fille du Brigand*" ("Caterina, or the Daughter of the Bandit") composed by Jules Perrot. Perrot, who also danced the role of Diavolino, stared with Lucille Grahn as "Caterina" to tell the ripping yarn of an orphaned girl (and her dashing lieutenant) who took up banditry on the outskirts of Rome. The ballet's tour de force, according to critics, was a scene in which Caterina and her all-female band of bandits danced with shouldered rifles. 10.50". Circa 1850. Value: $500-$1000.

Stop thief! A stealer of hearts and kisses is being made to feel the pointy end of a father's wrath in this delightful comical group popularly known as "Courting Under Difficulties," which demonstrates the potter's skill in the group's remarkably economical modeling. 11.50" as pictured. Circa 1860. Value: $500-$1000.

A contemporary drawing of Potash farm, the property owned by the murderous James Bloomfield Rush, but mortgaged to one of his victims, Isaac Jermy, for the then astounding sum of five thousand pounds.

"Stanfield Hall" where, in 1848, James Rush fatally shot Isaac Jermy and his son, and wounded his daughter-in-law and their housemaid when Jermy threatened Rush with foreclosure. 8". Circa 1846. Value: \$500-\$1000.

Contemporary print depicting Stanfield Hall on which the previous figure was based.

Contemporary portrait of William Palmer to which the Staffordshire portrait figure of Palmer bears a remarkable resemblance.

One-time surgeon William Palmer who poisoned his wife, brother, and his best friend John Parsons Cook. Only after Cook's stepfather instigated an inquiry into his death did it come to light that Palmer owed significant gambling debts, and suspicion was raised over the previous deaths. Palmer was tried, found guilty of Cook's murder, and hanged in 1856. 11.25". Circa 1856. Value: $1000+.

Emily Sandford, the mistress who was promised marriage by James Rush if she ever bore him a child. Sandford gave evidence as to Rush's whereabouts at the time of the murders and it was largely on her testimony that he was convicted. 6.25". Circa 1846. Value: $100-$500.

Contemporary sketch of William Corder, who murdered Maria Marten in 1826 and buried her body in the "Red Barn" at Polestead. As if Corder's crime was not horrific enough, after his execution, his skin was used to bind a book. The book, his skull, and other gruesome mementos were presented to West Suffolk General Hospital and may be seen today in a St. Edmondsbury museum.

Titled "CORDER," this portrait figure of William Corder records a somewhat less than accurate likeness of the murderer when compared to contemporary drawings. 6.50". Circa 1826. Value: $100-$500. *Courtesy of John and Barbara Gair, Castle Antiques.*

Contemporary portrait of Maria Marten who was bludgeoned to death by William Corder and whose body was buried at the Red Barn. The location of Maria's body was said to have come to her mother in a dream, no doubt adding to the public's fascination with the gory crime (see Introduction for an illustration of the table base portrait group of Corder and Marten).

Contemporary view of the infamous Red Barn (see Introduction for an illustration of the Red Barn table base group).

Contemporary view of Maria Marten's grave.

Contemporary depiction of the execution of William Corder that was attended by thousands of onlookers. Close examination of the crowd reveals not only smartly dressed spectators as well as the less affluently attired, but shows women and children, and a food vendor (lower left) plying his trade amongst the crowd. Executions were grand entertainment indeed!

A contemporary view of the scene inside the Red Barn where Maria Marten's body was discovered. No detail associated with the murder, no matter how small or mundane in appearance, escaped the eye of the media and the public.

Frederick George Manning and his wife Maria who, between them, murdered Maria's former lover Patrick O'Connor in 1849. After first inviting him to dinner (!), the two then murdered O'Connor, buried his body under the floor of their kitchen, and looted his lodgings. The Mannings were found guilty of murder and hanged – an event witnessed by Charles Dickens who paid two guineas per ticket to gain a good view of the execution. Manning 9.25", Maria 9". Circa 1850. Value: Pair or singles $1000+.

Two of many Dick Turpin groups, always paired with a matching figure of Tom King. Dick Turpin (1706-1739) was the son of an innkeeper in Hempstead, Essex, who became a highwayman and the partner of Tom King (b.?-d.1735). Turpin accidentally shot and killed King during an escapade in Epping Forest. The exploits of Turpin and King captured the British imagination when Harrison Ainsworth's book *Rookwood* was published in 1834; numerous theatrical productions followed. *Left:* 10". *Right:* 8.75". Mid-Victorian. Value for either single: $500-$1000; for either Dick Turpin paired with Tom King: $1000+. *Courtesy of Alex D. Pinto.*

Dick Turpin's hapless highwayman partner Tom King. 8.75". Mid-Victorian. Value for the single: $500-$1000. Value paired with Dick Turpin: $1000+.

Arthur Orton (alias Tom Castro) the "Tichborne Claimant" and obese butcher from Wagga Wagga in Australia who sought to lay claim to the title and fortune of the 11th Baronet of Tichborne. The real heir was believed to have drowned off the coast of America in 1854, but when the still-grieving Lady Tichborne saw Orton she immediately declared him her son who had been missing for seventeen years. A court case in 1871, lasting nearly three months, found against the claimant who was then arrested for fraud and faced another court session that lasted over six months. Orton was found guilty of "imposture" and sentenced to fourteen years imprisonment and hard labor; however, he was released in 1884. In 1895 he confessed to his attempted scam, but not before he had made a successful career for himself as an attraction in traveling sideshows. The Staffordshire figure depicting Orton is both accurate and unflattering.

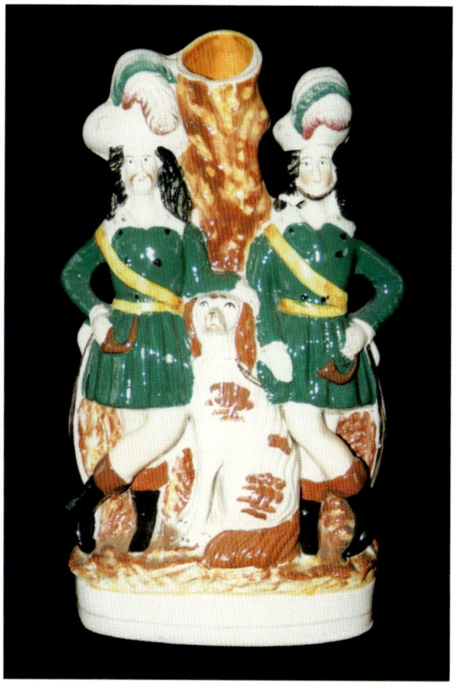

Robin Hood and Little John. While this group is not titled, it is considered by many to represent Robin Hood and Little John, characters from the ever-popular tale of the outlaw/hero of Sherwood Forest. Numerous other groups of similar design, in titled, well-colored, and white and gilt versions, have been recorded. In Medieval England, many thieves were known as "Robin Hoods," but the Greenwood champion who stole from the rich to give to the poor was, in Victorian times as now, the only "Robin Hood" to successfully and enduringly capture romantic imagination. 12". Mid-Victorian. Value: $100-$500.

Chapter Sixteen
Admirable Pottery: The Hero

"Heroes" have always been important in societies. They provide role models for us to respect, to admire, to emulate, and onto whom we are able to project our own fantasies of bravery and fame. They are larger-than-life, more daring, braver, and more generous than the common cast of humankind.

Industrialization and increasing secularization during the nineteenth century saw the role of the hero become more important in English society. For many of the poor working under-classes, religion was no longer able to offer the comfort and role models it had in the past. To the disenfranchised, formal religion was a vehicle by which the governing classes coerced and alienated the poor. The age-old need for a protector, and the impulse to mythologize, led this large section of society, the victims of industrialization, to seek out new role models and new heroes to enrich and direct their lives. The devout and the royalist found heroes in kings, queens, saints, and clergymen, but others sought inspiration from less conventional personalities. Today we have cinema and comic book superheroes, but these only provide us with escapist "junk-food." True spiritual sustenance comes from heroes like those who fought to save the trapped in the horrendous aftermath of the World Trade Center attack of September 11, 2001. These were the types of heroes the Victorians reached for in their need to believe in the innate nobility of humankind, and these were the heroes the potters captured in all their nobility, vision, and humanity.

Heroes themselves, as key players in Britain's dominance of the world ceramics trade, Staffordshire's potters possessed unrivaled aptitude in tapping into the interests of the pottery buying public with an acuity that would shame most modern marketing companies. Amazingly, their ability to hone in on popular taste was sometimes surpassed by their ability to produce figures within remarkably short time frames in order to capitalize on their heroes' popularity. As noted in Chapter Six, the record for lightning-fast production must go to the figure of hero James Braidwood, Superintendent of the City of London Fire-Engine Establishment, which was on the market less than a week after Braidwood's death in the most disastrous fire in London since the Great Fire of 1666. Braidwood applied scientific methods to firefighting and his success was such that he became a popular figure with the London public who gathered and cheered him as he rode to fight fires. Braidwood's gallantry was widely reported in the press and his death was mourned by the Londoners whose lives and property he had helped save. Thanks to the potters' quick thinking and quick potting, mourners were able to purchase portraits of their hero and figures of firemen by which to remember Braidwood's bravery and sacrifice. Considering the amount of time taken to design and create an original from which molds were struck, and then producing numerous figures through casting, drying, firing, glazing, and re-firing multiple times before transporting and marketing, the timeline achieved by the Staffordshire potters in 1861 is remarkable. Given modern technology, production techniques, communications, and conveyance systems, it is unlikely that such a time frame could be bettered today.

The potters more than captured the common man as hero *for* the common man. They went a remarkable step further: the common woman as the hero. Historical stereotypes suggest that Victorian women were lovely and lilting – they made effective use of those wonderful fainting sofas, and some even placed leeches behind their ears to drain the color from their faces to affect the popular pallor. In general, women were expected to be subservient to men in all realms of life except childbearing. Fortunately for women and despite the best efforts of the opposite gender, Queen Victoria's long reign, with its national and international successes, brought about a slow change in women's compliant roles.

Married middle class women were expected to remain at home, although opportunities to work outside the home increased, and the topic of "working women" was much debated. In a country where amplified industry and a stable economy were hallmarks of the time, it became less unusual, if not the norm, for women to seek employment outside their homes. A woman's earning potential, however, was sometimes seen as a threat to masculine financial domination. A writer for *The Lady's Review of Literature, Art and Social Economy* wrote in 1860, *"The plan of training young women with the idea of their getting their own living...would, I think, prove very disastrous to society...."* The same writer states, *"This masculine sort of woman will not gain husbands."*

For most Victorian women, making a suitable marriage and raising a family were vitally important and integral to their roles in society. Unmarried women with no money of their own were "singularly" oppressed. Younger working-class women turned to domestic service. The better educated were able to obtain positions as governess to the children of the wealthy. Scores of poor women secured employment that consisted of shoveling coal, making bricks, and forging iron. In North Staffordshire, their roles in the potteries consisted of the arduous and monotonous jobs of transferring patterns onto china and hand painting earthenware figures. Some women turned to the theater, to music halls, and even to the circus where the spotlights were not restricted to men and a greater degree of freedom was possible. Poor women, however, especially those who were not married and those who had children to support, faced long hours in factories or the alternatives of abysmal workhouses and poorhouses. Those who chose not to die on the streets sometimes "took to the streets," and prostitution was common among women of the lower strata of society.

In a society more given to patriarchy and misogyny than equal opportunity, the Staffordshire potters provided unusual and unique insights into women's endeavor and achievement that extended beyond the traditional Victorian vehicles for infamy and notoriety of the boudoir, parlor, pantry, nursery, or footlights. The reasons for this break from an exclusively masculine perception of the world are multitude: changes to laws that permitted women to own and inherit property, increased employment of women outside the home and consequent increased female income, improved literacy among women, growing sensitization to their rights, and, importantly, a woman on the throne of the mightiest empire on earth.

Whatever the cause of the potters' interest in the female hero, the resultant figures are fascinating. Two of the most popular female pottery heroes are Grace Darling and Florence Nightingale. In 1838, Darling set out in a rowboat from the coast of Northumberland where her father was lighthouse keeper and saved four men and a woman from drowning in a shipwreck. The dramatic figures created in her honor depict Darling and her father setting out to sea against a backdrop of a lighthouse and rugged cliffs. Nightingale took a group of nurses into the battlefields at the outbreak of the Crimean War in 1853 to care for the wounded. Her changes to laundry, kitchen, and nursing hygiene standards revolutionized the conditions of military hospitals and saved uncountable lives. Long after Nightingale's pioneer nursing reforms, the potters depicted Edith Cavell, who nursed both Allied and German troops who were injured during World War I. After being court-martialed, Cavell was executed by the Germans for aiding the escape of Allied soldiers in 1915 from prison camps. Although a remarkably late portrait figure, it depicts Cavell with the dignity and courage worthy of her place beside other Staffordshire heroes.

Britannia and the lion of England – perhaps the ultimate heroes of the British Empire. The trident in Britannia's hand is original and made from painted metal. The figure was made in the manner of Enoch Wood. 14.25". Circa 1810. Value: $1000+.

Grace Darling, the heroine of the shipwreck of the steamer "Forfarshire" that sank off the coast of Northumberland. Grace accompanied her father, the lighthouse keeper on the Farne Islands, out to the wreck in a small boat and helped rescue five survivors. Sadly Grace died of consumption four years later in 1842. The public was captivated by the story of Darling's heroism: etchings and songs depicting her bravery became popular, and even a rose was named in her honor. 7.50". Circa 1845. Value: $500-$1000.

The theme of "war" had always provided the potters with a rich cast of male heroes, but women were not ignored. In 1857 Jessie Brown, popularly known as "Highland Jessie," the wife of a soldier stationed at Lucknow during its famous siege, experienced a vision in which she heard the sound of reinforcements approaching. Jessie's "vision" rekindled hope and managed to rally the troops at the fort until the bagpiped reinforcements of her dream arrived. Jessie is depicted by the potters posed next to her husband Corporal Brown, an altogether romantic notion, but one that does not overlook Jessie's role in the defense of the British colonial outpost of Lucknow. Flora MacDonald, a farmer's daughter, played a significant role in the Jacobite uprising in the Hebrides in 1746 when she helped Prince Charles Edward flee from the Battle of Culloden and to reach safety at Skye. Flora's loyalty to the Scottish monarchy saw her imprisoned for treason in the Tower of London, but soon released under the "Act of Indemnity" of 1747. Portrait figures of Flora depict her as a slight young woman variously helping the prince aboard a rowboat, or wading ashore, presumably having seen her royal companion make good his escape. War also provided another group of female heroes for the potters: Vivandières. These women helped supply British and allied troops with provisions during the Crimean War. The potters created numerous different versions of the subject making the soldiers variously British, French, or Turkish, and the woman attired in either European or Eastern costume.

Philanthropists were a rich source of subject matter for figures, including those produced of Elizabeth Fry and Lady Jane Franklin, who were both pioneers in prison reform. Fry, after visiting Newgate Prison in 1810 and on discovering the horrific conditions in which women and children, both tried and untried, were held, devoted her life to English prison reform and founding hospitals and charities for the homeless. Franklin, equally disturbed by the conditions endured by female convicts in the Australian penal settlement of Van Diemens Land devoted much of her life and wealth to improving the conditions in which women prisoners were held. When her explorer husband became lost while seeking the North West Passage, Franklin financed search parties to find him and his crew. Franklin was herself a dedicated explorer having lead expeditions in Syria and the Tasmanian wilderness, and this passion, coupled with her backing of numerous expeditions of discovery, earned her the founder's medal from the Geographical Society in 1860. It would be naïve to assume that the Staffordshire-buying public of the nineteenth century was not unaware of, or concerned by, prison conditions, so it is not surprising that the potters found ready markets for figures depicting these admirable women.

Previously unrecorded figure and possibly a portrait of the Scottish hero Flora MacDonald who aided Bonnie Prince Charlie in his escape from the English forces by providing him with a boat in which he managed to sail to safety in Skye. This figure bears a resemblance to other figures identified as MacDonald, and the fact that she is barefoot and carrying her shoes also fits nicely with the aspect of the rescue in which she waded into the water to help cast off the Prince's boat. 6". Circa 1850. Value: $500-$1000.

Known as "Rescue Dog," this spill holder group depicts the heroic efforts of a Newfoundland dog in dragging a drowning child from a stream. The pictorial source of this popular figure may be traced to a painting titled "The Rescue" by Marianne A. Baker. 7.25". Circa 1850. Value: $500-$1000.

Just as crime was not an unknown to the pottery purchasing public of the nineteenth century, so too would poverty and homelessness have been ever-present threats. In response, the potters found the hero they needed in Sister Margaret Mary Hallahan, originally an Irish servant, then Dominican nun, who founded communities in Ireland and in 1851 at Longton in Staffordshire. She opened schools for the children of the poor and night schools for poor and illiterate women who worked long hours and could not gain access to education through more conventional means. Sister Margaret's community, although ridiculed for its sometimes-unconventional methods and aims, also provided food as well as housing and care for the poor, homeless, and sick of the Staffordshire communities. Hallahan's pottery portrait is the archetypal "penguin" depiction of a nun, but the figure's very existence reveals the esteem in which the recipients of her care held the good Sister.

A lithograph of "The Rescue" by Marianne A. Baker produced by R. Forse – the possible inspiration for Staffordshire "Rescue Dog" groups.

Lady Isabel Burton and Lady Hestor Lucy Stanhope, both explorer-heroes of the first stripe, were less-than-conventional Victorian women who might, by today's standards, fit into the traditional hero mold. Burton, who set out in 1856 to discover the source of the Nile, found herself in the middle of many armed skirmishes where she not only fought alongside the male members of her party, but also sustained bullet wounds, traveled extensively through Africa, and chronicled her adventures. The wonderfully eccentric Stanhope, who shook off her wealth and titles, traveled widely through the Middle East and, by 1814, adopted Eastern manners and dress along with assumed governance of a tribe of Bedouins who regarded her as a combination of prophet and queen. The pottery portraits of Burton and Stanhope depict both women in exotic and flamboyant dress and unconventional poses, in Stanhope's case, even mounted on a camel.

The Staffordshire potters' net reached wide for heroes in the world of female endeavor to include even more unconventional heroes in a lion tamer and a "cross-dressing" adventurer. Nellie Chapman, the "Lion Queen" of Wombell's Menagerie, performed with lions, tigers, and leopards. Her reputation for bravery was such that she performed by royal decree before Queen Victoria at Windsor Castle in 1847. The potters created a tableau presumably of Nellie and her wild animals looking remarkably docile by her side. After she married and retired from the ring, Nellie's replacement "Lady of the Lions," Ellen Bright, met a grisly demise when she was unwise enough to whip a tiger. The figure "Death of the Lion Queen" captures the event with a discretion and restraint uncharacteristic of the potters' usual gusto (see Chapter Eighteen).

Mary Anne Talbot (also known as John Taylor) was dubbed the "British Amazon" for her exploits disguised as a man. She started her bizarre adventure as girl of twelve when, after being abducted, she was compelled to disguise herself as a boy. She traveled through the West Indies and Europe as a footboy, a drummer boy, a sailor's lad on a pirate ship, and then with the British Navy as a powder monkey on a warship. While on the warship, a cannon exploded and shattered her leg. On landing, she was taken to a hospital. Doctors prepared her leg for amputation, but Mary Anne refused to cooperate and discharged herself. When recovered, she joined the crew of another warship, was captured by the enemy, and was imprisoned for more than a year before she escaped. Her gender was not discovered until she was press-ganged on her return to England, and her swashbuckling career was immediately brought to a halt. She was left penniless: as "John Taylor" she was eligible for a full naval pension, as "Mary Anne" she was entitled to nothing. After delivering numerous petitions to the government, she eventually received a pension under her masculine name. Un able to live within the stifling confines of the Victorian feminine role she soon resumed her daring ways and took a brief and unsuccessful turn as a "highwayman." Mary Anne died in 1804 leaving a "story" the potters eagerly seized upon to manufacture her likeness – her secret only hinted at in her earthenware likeness by a slight curvaceousness of chest and thigh.

Although war, exploration, royalty, politics, and sport provided the most fertile fields from which the potters drew their male heroes, it would be wrong to assume that there was not public appreciation of philanthropists like Lord Shaftesbury who tirelessly fought for reform of the British lunacy laws, protection of factory and colliery workers and chimney sweeps, and the expansion of "ragged schools" for the children of the poor from the 1820s to the1840s. The Staffordshire male hero could sometimes be as multidimensional and as much a reformer and humanitarian as his female counterpart. "Heroes" were a profitable commodity, so in their quest to seek them out, the potters did not draw their line at the human species. They had already crossed a previously taboo gender barrier in order to lay accolades and sell pottery, so crossing a species line to include canines in the list of heroes to be captured in clay was probably a less threatening maneuver for some scions of Victorian society. The figures of *Gelert*, drawn from a thirteenth century tale that had found renewed popularity in Victorian England, and *Rescue Dog*, based on a mid-nineteenth century newspaper story and engraving, both depict faithful hounds that have rescued their youthful masters from horrible deaths by a wolf and by drowning respectively.

Staffordshire figures of these and other heroes are rare and expensive, but they are worth the expense because, in purchasing these pieces, the collector is not only acquiring an attractive and valuable antique, but is also investing in the very best of human endeavor. Heroes have never been commonplace; they have always been apart from the mundane and the ordinary, which is what made them heroes. When assessing these figures, consider the potters' artistry, and think as well of the achievements, the sacrifices, and the legacies of these remarkable people. Some helped change the world, some helped right a wrong, some dared to challenge norms and prejudices – they all enriched the lives of their contemporaries and, in many cases, are known today because the potters recognized the merits of their contributions to human history.

Very rare group featuring the hound Gelert who, after saving his young master (a Welsh prince) from a wolf, was slain in terrible and tragic error by the boy's father. On returning home to find the child's cradle overturned on a blood-slicked floor, the king assumed the faithful hound had killed his child. As he ran the hound through, it let out a yelp that was answered from the wrecked nursery by a child's cry. On searching, the king found his son alive and unharmed; he also found the dead body of a giant wolf and realized that Gelert had saved his son's life. After making this discovery it was said that the king never smiled again. 9.50". Circa 1860. Value: $1000+.

Cast in the role of a canine hero, this faithful hound protects its mistress from a predatory eagle. 7.75". Circa 1850. Value: $500-$1000.

Watch holder depicting the philanthropist and reformer Lord Shaftesbury – the great 19th century advocate for the poor and exploited. Although there has been no source discovered to verify this identification, it is reasonable to consider it likely as the man bears a strong resemblance to portraits of Shaftesbury. 10". Circa 1860. Value: $500-$1000.

Titled figure representing "William Tell," the fabled 14th century archer and hero of the liberation of Switzerland, who is seen here with his son from whose head he was forced to shoot an apple (by order of a corrupt bailiff) as punishment for insubordination. Not only did Tell succeed in the task of shooting the apple, he loosed a second arrow and killed the bailiff. Tell went on to lead a successful rebellion against the oppression of Switzerland. The tale served as inspiration for numerous plays and spectaculars throughout the 19th century. 10". Circa 1860. Value: $500-$1000.

William Tell. 8.75". Circa 1860. Value: $500-$1000.

This highly colored figure is often referred to as "The MacDonalds of Glencoe" and may portray MacIan defending his family from the rival Campbells. Unfortunately, no source has as yet been found to confirm this identification. 10". Circa 1860. Value: $500-$1000.

"Roman Charity," "The Grecian and Daughter," and "Cimon and Pera" are all titles given to this group. The group represents the heroine Pera, a symbol of filial loyalty, who saved her imprisoned father from starvation by breastfeeding him. A painting by Rubens is believed to have inspired a late 18th century dramatization of the tale starring Mrs. Siddons and a Chelsea version of the legend. The 19th century saw the subject's popularity continue and saw the production of a table base group and, finally, this Victorian figure. The base of the figure is unusual as it is made in imitation of an earlier grotesque-footed table base version (see illustration in Chapter Five). 7.75". Circa 1840. Value: $500-$1000.

A symbol of Britain's undying heroism: St George slaying the dragon. This very unusual and rare watch holder has been claimed to form part of a 19th century gentleman's toilet set as a lidded box of very similar design and using the same manner of decoration has been identified. (Other St. George groups are illustrated in Chapter Thirteen.) 7.75". Circa 1850. Value: $500-$1000.

Not previously recorded to the authors' knowledge, this group represents countless unsung heroes who left hearth and home for the vagaries of chance. In the manner of Thomas Parr, the group depicts a young man and woman taking leave. Perhaps the young man is headed to sea for battle, or perhaps for emigration to one of the far-flung colonies. Either way this bitter-sweet parting must have struck a very familiar chord in the heart of almost every 19th century family that lost a heroic loved one to either cause. 10.50". Circa 1860. Value: $1000+.

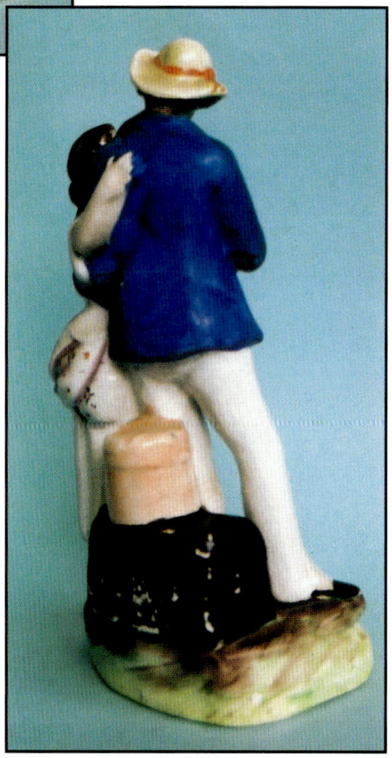

Reverse of the departure group indicating the high quality of modeling evident in this "in the round" figure.

Mary Anne Talbot, also known as Mary Taylor and John Talbot, flouted gender conventions by signing up as a sailor and earned for herself the title of the "British Amazon." Little is known of Mary Anne's early life except that she was one of sixteen children, posed as a drummer, and was abducted by a sea captain. After the captain's death and Mary Anne's own wounding she decided to pass herself off as a sailor, a ruse she successfully maintained for nearly a decade until she was press-ganged and her true gender discovered. Mary Anne finished her short, but colorful life with stints as a highway "man" and then, in a turn that can only be considered out of character, as a domestic servant. She was aged only thirty when she died. The life of the "British Amazon" was included in Robert Kirby's 1804 publication *Wonderful Museum,* Kirby having gained his insights first-hand from Mary Anne as she was his servant. Mary Anne's disguise would have had to be better than the flimsy one provided for her by the potters: her poorly concealed curves and false mustachios would have offered scant distraction from her real gender. Pugh records a version of this figure titled, "Sportsman Mary Taylor" (Pugh, 82, plate 61).14". Circa 1870. Value: $500-$1000.

"Vivandière" group of a woman providing provisions to a soldier. Without these heroines it is likely that many soldiers fighting during the Crimean War would have starved because the supply units of the allied forces were so poorly organized. 12". Circa 1850. Value: $1000+.

"Death of the Lion Queen" depicts Ellen Bright, the last "Lion Queen" who was mauled to death by a leopard in this group but in actuality a tiger that attacked her after she foolishly struck it with a riding whip. Ellen was the niece of George Wombwell (of menagerie fame) and had performed for Queen Victoria at Windsor Castle. The eighteen year-old Ellen's death in 1850 led to the prohibition of female animal trainers. (See Chapter Eighteen for details; also see the reproduction group illustrated in Chapter Twenty.)14.5". Circa 1850. Value: $1000+. *Courtesy of Susan Bishop and Darcy McGroarty, Bishop and Daughter Antiques.*

"MISS NIGHTINGALE" depicts Florence Nightingale, hospital reformer and founder of modern nursing practice, attending a wounded officer. Nightingale was superintendent of the Hospital for Gentlewomen in London at the outbreak of the Crimean War in 1853 when she was approached by the Secretary of War to take nurses to the battlefront. After arriving at Scutari in 1854, the "Lady with the Lamp" managed to revolutionize hospital practice and hygiene and saved uncountable lives through her reforms. Following a bout of fever in 1856, Nightingale was forced to return to England where she trained nurses. In recognition of her work, she was invited to Balmoral in 1856 for an audience with the Queen, and she was awarded the Order of Merit in 1907. 10.50". Circa 1855. Value: $1000+. *Courtesy of Susan Bishop and Darcy McGroarty, Bishop and Daughter Antiques.*

Figure of a fireman possibly made to commemorate the 1861 death of James Braidwood, superintendent of the London Fire-Engine Establishment. Braidwood had made fire-fighting a science and in doing so saved countless lives and properties in London. He was the hero of the people of London and, when he went to fight fires, it was not uncommon for him to be cheered by crowds en route. Braidwood was even honored in a song. His death in a fire, at that time second only in ferocity to the Great Fire of 1666, so shocked London that thousands attended Braidwood's funeral and lined the streets to see the passing of his funeral cortège. An elegant, titled figure of Braidwood is recorded with a black line running through the title, suggesting production at the time of his death. 5.75". Circa 1861. Value: $500-$1000.

Chapter Seventeen
Country Life: A Rural Romance

As hard to believe as it may seem, few, if any, urban workers of the first decade of Victoria's rein would have changed places with their agrarian equivalents. As overcrowded and polluted as cities were, the standard of living they offered their inhabitants was vastly preferable to the standards under which agricultural laborers lived. In times of fair weather the working conditions of agricultural workers may well have been preferable to the grime in which urban workers toiled, but their wages were much lower than their city counterparts, their housing conditions often as bad, and their opportunities for education far more restricted. In 1850 the average pay for an agricultural laborer was seven shillings a week with which he had to feed, clothe, house, and educate his family. Admittedly there was some supplementation available to this pittance in the form of payments in kind such as potatoes, cider, or fruits, but these "boons" did little to ameliorate the suffering.

Agriculture was a prerequisite for England's subsistence, and the nation had been a largely agrarian society for roughly four hundred years by the time Victoria became queen. At the time of her accession, approximately twenty per cent of the nation's total work force was employed in agriculture. During Victoria's reign, however, that percentage dropped by half. Industrialization and urbanization heralded a marked change for England's economy and offered farm workers increased opportunities to leave rural England and live in cities where they hoped to find better paying employment and a higher standard of living.

The sons and daughters of England's soil lived hard lives on the farms. Laborers began their day at sunrise and often worked until dusk. Women and children were used in the fields as cheap substitutes for male workers and to supplement the feeble income earned by the male of the household. Their diet was often limited to bread, bacon and cheese. Milk was only occasionally available, and most drank tea, beer, or water in which burnt bread had been soaked. Living conditions (not unlike those of today's migrant farm workers) were substandard, and during the 1850s farm laborers numbering nearly a half million lived on meager financial resources with little hope for improvement. In country areas, farm workers and shepherds (many of whom were children) occupied the lowest rungs of the social ladder – they were half starved, overworked, generally uneducated, and they lived in squalor (often in dwellings supplied by landowners that were little more than derelict lean-tos). Farm laborers existed in an oppressive feudal-type system, living and working under the tyranny of rich landowners (squires) and tenant farmers.

The raft of reform legislation witnessed during the mid-nineteenth century bettered the lives of the urban worker but left the lot of the farm laborer untouched. It was not until 1861, when the Prince of Wales turned his attention to conditions on his own estate in Norfolk and set an example by re-housing laborers in new cottages, that the eyes of the Victorian philanthropist turned critically toward the conditions in which landowners forced their workers and tenants to toil. Unfortunately, as fashionable as a social conscience had become for the middle classes, it did not reach to the more remote areas of the countryside.

In 1873, public protest led to the Agricultural Children's Act, but laborers remained unhappy and sought additional reforms. Joseph Arch's National Union was established in 1872 to contest the landowners' harsh rule, low wages, and poor living conditions. In a short time, Arch's union (which advocated non-violent, legal rebellion) swelled to 50,000 laborers and succeeded in raising the average wage. Union members also helped farm workers relocate to cities. By 1884, internal disputes brought about the dissolution of the union however, and workers continued to leave the countryside in dramatic numbers. Agriculture remained a national requirement, and industry provided machinery that made farming somewhat less labor intensive and helped cope with the exodus of workers to cities. Farmers who stayed on the farms did so by choice and, gradually, the medievalism intrinsic to British agriculture decreased. The 1860s and 1870s may be considered the "boom" era of British agriculture when growing agricultural prosperity brought improved wages for laborers. The halcyon days, however, were short-lived, cut down by the forces of Free Trade. With the removal of protective tariffs, prices for locally grown livestock and produce plummeted and even more workers drifted to the cities in search of work. Limited by their lack of education and experience, the work that faced displaced farm laborers was invariably arduous and backbreaking manual slog that offered them little chance of social or economic betterment. Although the 1880s were dire for agricultural workers, one concession to their status as "human" beings came in 1884 when males were given the vote, placing them more on the level of other workers.

Even though conditions were harsh, rural lifestyles, traditions, and customs could never be replaced by city living. It is logical to assume that the disappointments of urban dwelling conjured up recollections of tree-dotted landscapes, fields and forests, streams, clean air, and a centuries-old kinship with wildlife that were nourishment for weary spirits. In truth, for most people who replaced farm life with city life, other forms of drudgery became surrogates for the difficult working conditions they knew on the farms. It is very likely that the vagaries of memory brought the countryside's natural splendor and rustic pastimes into a sentimental focus that was sharper than the realities of agricultural labor. Remembered visions of pastoral life undoubtedly brought about an idealized perception of what had been left behind. The Victorian potters understood human psychology and produced a substantial selection of sentimental and romantic rural-theme figures and groups.

Country life is superbly expressed in these rare early 19th century figures. *Left:* group of a well-modeled shepherdess holding a basket of flowers and with a lamb at her side; 7.75"; $12,000-$15,000. *Right:* an unusual creamer in the form of a goat; 5 5/8"; $2,000-$5,000. *Courtesy of Jonathan Horne (Antiques) Ltd.*

Perhaps two of the greatest ironies in the whole scheme of Staffordshire pottery came courtesy of this category of figures. The potters perpetuated images of countrified bliss in figures and groups that the urban public purchased enthusiastically in a misplaced sense of nostalgia that bore little resemblance to the harsher realities of country living. The very subjects of these pastoral figures would likely have found purchase of them beyond their straightened means. The context, of course, was increasing urbanization throughout the nation and increasing industrialization within Staffordshire itself. Business acumen aside, the potters may have fibbed unconsciously or gently lied by omission in the very human need to preserve their own local memories and to relive Staffordshire's lost, bucolic past in the figures they made.

Rural themes had always been popular in Staffordshire and were undoubtedly defined by the original character of the region. Inhabitants lived close to the land, either farming it or working its clay in the potteries. The people, animals, and pastimes indigenous to North Staffordshire were well represented in many rural-theme figures and groups. Shepherds and shepherdesses do not precisely dominate eighteenth century rural figures, but they are noteworthy. One well-known group called *The Lost Sheep*, in which a shepherd carries a lamb on his shoulders, was produced during the eighteenth century and reprised in nineteenth century versions. Beginning during the last quarter of the eighteenth century, the pre-Victorian potters produced figures of farm and domestic animals in significant quantities. Also popular were hunters and gamekeepers, haymakers, gardeners, and birdnesting groups. Many of the latter two were modeled with bocage, the most noteworthy being a group of a man and a woman with birds in their hands and standing beneath an overstated bocage filled with leaves, flowers, and birds (Halfpenny, 215). The coming of the industrial age and an enthusiasm for urban living did not quell the tide of rural-theme Staffordshire, which remained popular among consumers through subsequent production periods.

Finely modeled pair of spill holders in the form of tree trunks beside which a man sits on a gate, as a woman and dog greet him. Left-hand figure 6.25", right-hand figure 6.50". Circa 1860. Value for the pair: $500-$1000; for singles: $100-$500.

Along with figures of familiar country animals (cows, sheep, donkeys, goats, dogs, cats, birds, deer, rabbits, swans, cockerels, and squirrels), Victorian rural figures and groups included pasture and farmyard groups, hunters (some with their kill), gamekeepers, shepherds and shepherdesses, and even Welsh and Scottish shepherds in traditional dress. Falconry was represented in falconer groups, and the less pleasant but accepted realities of nature were depicted in groups where eagles hold lambs in their claws and dogs chase down deer.

Numerous arbor groups celebrated rural courtship with much handholding and embracing beneath flowering bowers. Also produced in some quantity were pastoral groups of flower and fruit gatherers or sellers (often depicted holding baskets); harvesters with sheaves or baskets; bird nesters; groups that incorporated cows and milkmaids; beehive groups; and boys and girls sitting or standing near streams. One pair of equestrian figures depicts a boy and a girl with baskets on their arms and seated on horses that are drinking from streams that flow from rocks to the figures' bases. In one especially striking arbor group, a woman stands holding a pitcher while a man seated at her left plays a mandolin, and a deer looks up at the woman. In an equally charming group, a boy is seated on a bridge above a stream and under an arbor with rabbits placed at his sides. Another figure was modeled to depict a woman standing beside a dovecote, and a wonderful Parr Factory style group shows a young boy seated on a tree stump holding a bird nest in his right hand and a bird raised in his left. Gypsies, who were commonly seen in the British countryside, were depicted in several groups complete with campfires, cauldrons, and fortune telling – as colorful as the gypsies themselves.

Local practices were recorded in figures like *Going to Market* and *Coming Home* and in figures titled *Sand* and *Bessums*, which note the practice of rural kitchen maids who used sand and stiff brushes made of willow twigs (called bessums) to scour pots and cooking utensils. A group that underscores the geographic and metaphorical distance between country and city life is one in which a standing man and a seated woman are placed at each side of a tree-form spill vase in front of which is a milestone that reads *"London 30 Miles"* (the Hardings suggest that this group may have a theatrical inspiration but no source has as yet been discovered).

City dwellers, caught up in the hustle and bustle, and the grime and smog, were no doubt cheered by the potters' representations of rural life. The figures suggest a sense of connection among community members and to the land that was set in juxtaposition to the impersonal nature of city life. Most rural figures are pleasantly simple, serene, and cheerfully decorated. Judging by their numbers, this category of figures and groups found favor among consumers throughout the nation – those living in rural areas, those who left the countryside for the cities, and those who had never been to the country. Whether rural figures summoned up pastoral memories or stirred the imagination with images of idyllic, countrified stability, they represented a human closeness to the natural world that was pure, sweet, and perhaps even mystical.

A previously unrecorded figure of classically dressed children gathering sea shells. 7.25". Circa 1860. Value: $100-$500.

A previously unrecorded spill holder depicting classically dressed children feeding a goat. 7.75". Circa 1860. Value: $500-$1000.

Children with sheaves of grain posed beside a windmill, a unique architectural element (see Chapter Nineteen for details on Staffordshire's architectural figures). 10". Circa 1870. Value: $100-$500.

Fisherman and fisherwoman in the manner of Sampson Smith. Versions of these figures appeared in Kent catalogues as late as the 1950s. Fisherwoman 13.25", fisherman 13.50". Circa 1870. Value for the pair: $500-$1000; for singles $100-$500.

A previously unrecorded group of a woman, man, and remarkably over-sized flowers. 5.50". Circa 1850. Value: $500-$1000.

Woman in rustic dress with a basket of eggs at her feet. 7.25". Circa 1850. Value: $100-$500.

Woman with a basket of produce. 7.50. Circa 1840. Value: $100-$500.

A woman with a basket of fruit and a bird. A Parr figure of uncommonly large size. 13". Circa 1860. Value: $500-$1000.

Large and very well executed figure by Thomas Parr of a man with a basket of fruit. This size of this figure is uncharacteristically large for Parr. 13.75". Circa 1860. Value: $500-$1000.

Damaged, but still charming evocations of rural life: the brightly colored figure on the left depicting a woman, bird, and dog, while the right-hand figure of a girl and doe is in the manner of Thomas Parr, skillfully modeled and more subtle in coloration. Girl and bird 8" as illustrated, girl and doe 6" as illustrated. Value for each as illustrated: $100-$500.

Figure of a boy and dog modeled from an early 19th century Staffordshire figure which, in turn, was likely to have been derived from a porcelain 18th century original. 10.25". Value: $100-$500.

Large spill holder depicting a shepherd and shepherdess playing bagpipes and a tambourine while their dog guards their sheep. 14.50". Circa 1860. Value: $500-$1000.

Fisherman with a net slung over his shoulder and posed with his wife and child. 9". Circa 1860. Value: $500-$1000.

Arbor group of a man, woman, and beehive. Circa 1860. 7.50". Value: $100-$500.

Couple collecting grapes from a grape-lined arbor. 6.50" (length), 6.25" (height). Circa 1860. Value: $100-$500.

Man and woman posed over bridges on either side of a grain mill and water wheel. Swans glide on the streams beneath the bridges, and sacks of flour await collection at the mill's entrance. 9.25". Circa 1870. Value: $500-$1000.

Spill holders depicting a man and woman in Highland dress and standing beside waterfalls and ponds on which swans float. Both figures 9.50". Circa 1860. Value for the pair: $500-$1000; for singles: $100-$500.

"WELSH SHEPHERDS" titled spill holder, large and well executed. 14". Circa 1860. Value: $1000+.

Man in rustic costume holding a potted plant. The details of a beehive and a spill holder in the form of a giant tulip add interest to the group. 8.50". Circa 1870. Value: $100-$500.

Large group in the manner of Thomas Parr of a woman and man with a fishing net. 14". Circa 1860. Value: $500-$1000.

This figure titled "LONDON 30 MILES" has long raised conjecture as to its source of inspiration. Attempts have been made to connect the group to a popular ballad, but the clues provided by the potters conflict with those provided by the ballad's lyrics. Perhaps, as the authors suggest, it does indeed represent the sad, but inevitable exodus of poor farm laborers to even more abysmal conditions in the cities. 11". Circa 1850. Value: $500-$1000. *Courtesy of Nick Harding* (A & N Harding, *Victorian Staffordshire Figures 1835-1875*).

Unusual arbor-type group of gardeners in which the "arbor" is made by joining treetops. Note the occupational clue in the shovel propped at the side of the tree to the right. 5.50". Circa 1855. Value: $100-$500.

Country life: nothing better than a grassy seat, a basket of flowers, a pipe to smoke, and a dog for companionship. 8". Mid-Victorian. Value: $100-$500.

Chapter Eighteen
Entertainment: Streets, Spirits, Sawdust, Spotlights, and Stirrups

"The rich man in his castle / The poor man at his gate / God made them high and lowly / And ordered their estate." This verse from *Hymns for Children*, published in 1848, clearly expresses the distinction between the laboring classes and the affluent during the early Victorian period. To be rich or poor was to follow rules and restrictions clearly set out by social, religious, and moral norms, and part of the ordering of these respective "estates" were the opportunities available for the pursuit of recreation. "Leisure" time is something that we both covet and take for granted, but for the working classes of eighteenth and early nineteenth century Britain, "leisure" was something to which they had very limited access. Altruistic philanthropic pastimes might have been pursued by the elite and enlightened, but they were not for the working classes whose leisure needs were more pragmatic and escapist. Entertainment had to hold either a promise of elevation from workaday routines through winnings or knowledge or diversion through make-believe and novelty.

Industrialization, the ubiquitous driving engine of change during the nineteenth century, had deprived the newly urbanized of traditional rural pastimes and drove them into seeking out sometimes less than wholesome entertainment. Recreation, more than any other aspect of nineteenth century social conditions drove a wedge between the different echelons of society: not only between the rich and poor, but between Conformist and Non-Conformist worshipers, between tipplers and teetotalers, and between men and women. The Staffordshire potters were conscious of these divisions among the ranks of their purchasing public and accordingly cast a remarkably wide net in snaring subject matter to include in their repertoire of ceramic pastimes. Prior to the introduction of a fleet of social and industrial reforms, life for the pre-Victorian laborer was short and brutal, and many sought solace in the numbing effects of alcohol. With gin costing eight pence a pint and beer only a halfpenny to three pence a pint, it is little wonder that drinking was probably the greatest single recreational activity of the period.

Numerous Staffordshire groups like the 1820s pair *The Ale Bench* and *Teetotal* (see Chapter Five) depicted the melancholy and disruptive effects of alcoholism on family life and are possibly the only pottery depictions of both a hangover *and* the marital harmony achieved through abstinence from alcohol. As with earlier Ralph Wood figures of a drunken clergyman and his long-suffering deacon, in *The Vicar and Moses* the admonition is gentle and humorous, but the potters were fully conscious that the sector of "alcohol moderate" consumers demanded a more strident voice of approbation and such is found in the unusual Victorian figure *Gin / Water*. Figures like *Auld Lang Syne*, *Souter Johnny*, and *Tam O'Shanter* depicted drinking as a social and jovial pastime, but *Gin / Water*, an unusual figure with two "fronts" – one of a young, happy and affluent looking man, the other a ragged, wasted tramp – showed the ugliness of poverty, disease, and destitution that resulted from over-indulgence in alcohol.

Although bears were the preferred "victims" in animal baiting contests, they were expensive and not readily available, so bulls were used as substitutes. This sketch is based on a circa 1780 bull-baiting group of the type produced by Ralph Wood. Early groups like this did not fully convey the savagery of the sport in the more realistic way that later groups did, especially those in the table base class of figures (see Chapter Five). *Courtesy of Robert Buczynski.*

Other temperance figures, like *Band of Hope* and the *Independent Order of Good Templars*, were produced during the 1860s in response to the abstemious public's horrified response to Prime Minister Gladstone's

"Refreshment House Act" that granted beer licenses to eating-houses and reduced the tax on wines. The propaganda campaign to persuade merry-makers of the evils of alcohol included the installation of public drinking-water fountains in larger cities across the nation, and the potters created a related series of figures to help celebrate sobriety: beautiful young women, children, and upright handsome young men were depicted near water fountains, delighting in their untainted and virtuous sobriety. The potters were not righteous in their damnation of alcoholic drink; rather, they were astute businessmen adapting their product in response to a time of changing morals and norms.

The potters' response to the Temperance movement was only one manifestation of their genius. Completely attune with their consumers, they realized that the British public wanted to believe in a newly acquired respectability and affluence. Part of this elaborate self-deception, in which the potters were complicit, was to create an image of a preference for "genteel" entertainments.

Prior to the Victorian inclination for refined entertainments, bear baiting, a particularly savage activity, was popular among the lower classes, and was recorded by the potters in several groups. One commonly recognized bear-baiting group includes a muzzled bear with its arms clenched tightly around a struggling dog. Interestingly, similar figures from circa 1800 were modeled with political intent and depict muzzled Russian bears squeezing small monkey-like figures of Napoleon (often wearing Napoleonic hats). Bull-baiting figures appeared as early as 1760 and were made from cream-colored earthenware with underglaze oxide decoration. While bears may have been the preferred "victims," they were expensive and not readily available, so bulls were often used as substitutes. Bull-baiting figures dating to 1780-1815 include earthenware groups decorated with colored glazes and earthenware groups with painted decoration under a pearl glaze. As Turner points out, these do not convey the savagery of the sport, particularly the earlier Wood family groups, which are gracefully modeled and beautifully colored (Turner, 66). Bull-baiting groups from circa 1830 were made of pearl glazed earthenware with overglaze painted decoration. In some groups, the central figures were placed on table bases (see Chapter Five). A bill seeking the suppression of bull- and bear-baiting was introduced into the House of Commons in 1802, but it was defeated by thirteen votes. It was not until 1835 that an Act of Parliament officially banned animal baiting.

When animal baiting became illegal, people turned to cock fighting and a sport called "ratting." These sports demonstrated an analogous disposition for animal killing on a smaller scale. Cock fighting had been practiced during the eighteenth century and became even more popular during the nineteenth. Interestingly, it attracted the lower classes as well as the gentry, and cockfights organized *by* gentlemen *for* gentlemen were not uncommon. Cock fighting usually took place in a cockpit that was designed like a small amphitheater with a round platform in the middle and circled by rows of bleachers. The cocks were matched by weight; their beaks were filed down and their wings were clipped; and each was "dressed" in spurs to insure bloody combat. Ratting, popular among the lower classes, required that a number of rats be placed in a pit with a Terrier that was trained to attack and kill them. The Terriers (sometimes bred with the old bull-baiting dogs to insure ferocity) vied for status as champion ratters. Several rare rat catcher groups portray variations of a Terrier with one or more dead rats. A Terrier called "Billy the Rat Catcher" was hailed in his day as a champion who reputedly killed one hundred rats in five and a half minutes (Pugh, 1526), and some of the 1840s rat catcher figures very likely portray this illustrious Terrier.

The potters cleverly gave bear-baiting political purpose when they produced groups in which muzzled Russian bears were depicted with their arms tightly clenched around small, monkey-like figures of Napoleon (often wearing Napoleonic hats). Shown here is an artist's rendering of a typical example. *Courtesy of Robert Buczynski.*

Vicious bare-knuckle marathon boxing matches were also popular, and paired figures of the bare-knuckle fighters Cribb and Molyneux were made with overglaze enamel decoration around 1815. Tom Cribb was one of England's most celebrated fighters, and Tom Molyneux was an American who challenged Cribb to a championship fight. Cribb won the fight on December 18, 1810 when Molyneux collapsed during the 30th round. A second fight took place in September 1811, and Cribb emerged the victor again (Halfpenny, 197). In 1824, bare-knuckle fighters Tom Spring of England and Jack Langan of Ireland fought two matches that lasted over seventy-five rounds each. Spring won both but never fought again. A figure group impressed with scroll at each end bearing the fighters' names and marked by John Walton at the back was made around the time of the fights (Halfpenny, 224).

Betting on everything from animal baiting to rat catching and from games of chance to horse and pigeon racing were popular entertainments during the 18th and 19th centuries. This mounted jockey (originally one of a pair) was listed in a Kent catalog (Kent List B, no. 96). A similar, larger figure was recorded with a Sampson Smith mark on the base, and a master mold for a corresponding figure was found in 1948 at the Smith Factory. A Smith catalog lists this figure as "Champion Jockey" and it may portray Fred Archer, although no titled version of the figure has been recorded. 7.50". 20th century. Value for pairs and singles in the $100-$500 range. *Courtesy of Anita L. Grashof, Gallerie Ani'tiques.*

Prince Almansor and the Elephant of Siam, or *The Fire Fiend* provided the type of spectacle the Victorians expected in their entertainment. In this 1829 play, not only were buildings set on fire, but the action was intensified when a young and noble prince, played by Mr. Hemming, was rescued from imminent death and dastardly villains. Spectaculars based on this play remained popular until the 1850s. 6.5". Circa 1850. Value: $1000+.

H. Bentley produced a titled and signed bust of prize-fighter Benjamin Caunt (son of one of Lord Byron's servants at Newstead Abbey) in 1844. Caunt beat William Thompson in 1838 and became "England's Champion" in 1840 after beating John "Brassey" Leechman (Pugh, F452 and F464). Other popular "fighting figures" included depictions of the most famous engagement of the nineteenth century, the bare-knuckle fight between American John Heenan and Englishman Tom Sayers that was waged over thirty-seven rounds and lasted over two hours. Heenan was an American heavyweight who fought English middle-weight champion Tom Sayers on April 17, 1860. Although Sayers was over forty pounds lighter, six inches shorter, and fighting with a dislocated shoulder, he earned a draw (Harding, Book One, 74). Heenan and Sayers were depicted together on titled bases with a roped fence behind them; the portrayals, however, were remarkably restrained and bloodless.

Gambling was almost endemic among all classes and included card games ("the Devil's Handiwork"). Betting on anything from pigeon racing to horse racing, and roulette for the more wealthy, were fashionable. Horse racing has long been popular in Britain with Ascot established as the event of the year among royals and the wealthy elite. While horse and equestrian figures were produced during the eighteenth century, jockeys did not appear in quantity until the nineteenth century. Numerous jockey figures – mounted and standing beside horses – are recorded. The most celebrated jockey of the nineteenth century was Fred Archer, presumably the inspiration for many of the recorded jockey figures. One noteworthy group depicts a girl on horseback with a jockey standing in front of her rearing horse.

Portrait figure believed to represent the American actress Dianna Vernon. Miss Vernon was so popular in her home country that she had at least two steamer boats named in her honor during the 1850s and 1860s. 13". Circa 1850. Value: $500-$1000. *Courtesy of Susan Bishop and Darcy McGroarty, Bishop and Daughter Antiques.*

Portrait figure of the ballerina Carlotta Grisi depicted in her role as "Giselle," based on an engraving from a music sheet that featured famous "Beauties" of the performing arts. 9.50". Circa 1860. Value: $500-$1000.

The comedic actor Edward Askew Sothern in his 1861 role of "Lord Dundreary," a simple-minded lordling in the play *Our America Cousin*. The play's enormous success resulted in a run of over eighteen months, and it was regularly revived until the late 1870s by which time Sothern's son had taken up the role made famous by his father. This figure, modeled by Thomas Parr, bears a strong resemblance to the portrait of Sothern taken from a contemporary playbill as seen behind the figure. 8.75". Circa 1860. Value: $1000+.

Dog racing was also commemorated by the potters with titled paired figures of race dogs Master McGrath and Pretender. McGrath was an extraordinary black Greyhound (owned by Lord Lurgan) that won the 1871 Waterloo Cup against his pottery partner, Pretender.

Other organized sports may have managed to draw bets from the workingman, but in most cases they failed to elicit his participation, as opportunities for participation were almost exclusively reserved for the wealthy. Cricket and wrestling matches, the latter glamorized by the term "Thessalian games," were pastimes of the gentleman, but "involvement" in these fashionable diversions could be effected through the purchase of pottery groups of cricketers, famous batsmen and bowlers, and by wrestling groups such as the well modeled figure *The Grapplers*.

New sports included rugby and lawn tennis (invented in 1823 and 1837 respectively) and were primarily enjoyed by the upper classes. Golf was a well-established sport, and one of the most impressive golf groups is one made circa 1830-40 in which the potters depicted a golfer accompanied by a caddy. The group, based on a mezzotint by Valentine Green, was modeled in earthenware and decorated in overglaze enamels. It portrays William Innes, a member of the Blackheath Golf Club, and his Greenwich pensioner caddy. Over time, it became acceptable for Victorian women to participate in sports like tennis and cycling. Not surprisingly, however, sportswomen were not popular figure subjects.

Sanitization of leisure activities reached out to "grog shops" that became "tea-gardens" where a family man could take his wife and family, or a beau his sweetheart, to partake in the delights of tea, ginger beer, shrimps and periwinkles and other snacks, and tobacco. Sometimes enlivened with music, singing, dancing, and fireworks, these diversions led to the development of vaudeville and the music hall that incorporated the tradition of street performers with which the potters were long associated. Eighteenth century musician figures (see Chapter Four) were eclipsed by many and varied figures of children and adults either holding or playing musical instruments. Portrait figures of black street musicians Billy Walters and African Sal were quickly joined by characters from popular theatre: magicians, actors, singers, and dancers like T. P. (Tippy) Cooke. Cooke, who had been an authentic serving sailor, specialized in playing the role of a sailor. Even if the part he was playing did not call for his famous "hornpipe," the audience would usually yell until he obliged, and pottery figures of Cooke were immensely popular throughout England. Similarly, a bit of conjuring never went amiss with the Victorians, and the conjurer Rubini, who played at the St. James's, St. Georges's, and Egyptian Halls in London, was well known for his magic trick in which a lady was beheaded (Pugh, E356). The potters produced an untitled figure presumed to be of the popular magician holding a knife in his right hand and a woman's severed head in his left.

Even though strident cries of damnation rose from the more conservative churchmen of the period against such secular indulgence and diversion, dancing became popular, not only for stage performers, but also for the general populace, and by the 1850s the potters depicted couples closely clenched in happy quadrilles, polkas, or waltzes.

Mme. Alboni and her magical carriage as she appeared in the finale of her much praised role of Cinderella in the opera *La Cenerentola*. This figure, like that of Carlotta Grisi, was taken from the publication *Musical Bouquet*. 9.50" (length), 9" (height). Circa 1860. Value: $1000+.

The lovely Johanna Maria, or Jenny Lind, an operatic star known as the "Swedish Nightingale." Jenny's voice and purity captured the hearts and imaginations of European and British theater goers during the 1840s and 1850s before she became a professor of singing at the Royal College of Music in the 1880s. This figure represents Lind in her famous debut role as "Alice" in the opera *Robert le Diable* in 1847. 8.75". Circa 1850. Value: $1000+.

For the upper classes, grand ballrooms and social clubs like Allmack's in London were typical settings for dancing where dignified structure and *haute couture* attire were prerequisite. However, while their social betters took part in grand marches, observed elaborate rules of dance etiquette, and paid strict attention to dance card partnering, country folk approached dance with more freedom and greater abandon. Country and barn dances provided opportunities to leave the confines of factory and farm and to engage in the pure pleasure of music and movement. Local dances and forms of the *Contredanse* or *Contra*, from the French meaning "country dance," were popular among rural dwellers. Characterized by energetic tempos and various formations, this type of dance was the forerunner of today's square dances and line dances. A country style dance, often held in a village member's barn, usually began at sundown on Saturday night after the day's chores were completed. The festivities often lasted until the wee hours of the morning when tired revelers left for home with a few hours to spare before Sunday church services.

Staffordshire dance groups usually depict figures with crossed feet to suggest dynamic movement, a sense of dance-steps, and dexterous footwork. Because Staffordshire figures were produced for the working classes, most portray informal dance. A few, however, depict elegantly clad dancers on scrolled or oval gilt-lined bases. Some of these figures recall the waltz, a dance that was considered risqué when first introduced in England because of the way dancers held each other throughout the dance. Before the gentry accepted the waltz, adaptations of the form like the Spanish Circle (a progressive dance in which couples advance and dance with other couples) and the Varsouvianna (danced by independent couples often aligned with other couples facing the head of the hall) were acceptable substitutes. In "waltz" groups, a man wearing a plumed hat, cloak, doublet, and stockings is partnered with a fashionably gowned woman. The man in these groups is usually romantically posed behind the woman; he holds her right hand at her waist and her left extended down at her side. In one group a similarly posed and costumed couple dances beneath an umbrella. In another group, a woman dressed in a three-layered gown dances on a circular, concave gilt-lined base with a man who wears a long jacket, open waistcoat, and breeches. In a more unusual group, a man dances with a woman who holds a long scarf above her head and across her body.

Paul and Virginia is a fascinating tale about true love, hurricanes, shipwrecks, and death by drowning as a result of misplaced modesty (the heroine drowns because she refuses to take off her clothes to free herself from their restrictions so she can swim to safety). Bernadin de St. Pierre's 1787 novel saw numerous dramatic and operatic adaptations during the first half of the 19th century, including a re-write in which the heroine survives and the lovers are reunited. We can only hope she was fully dressed! 7". Circa 1860. Value: $100-$500.

Jenny Lind again depicted in the role of "Alice" in Meyerbeer's opera *Robert le Diable* in 1847. 14". Circa 1850. Value: $1000+. *Courtesy of Susan Bishop and Darcy McGroarty, Bishop and Daughter Antiques.*

Arbor group depicting trysting lovers. As yet unidentified, this group by Thomas Parr is likely to have a theatrical source. 7.50" Circa 1860. Value: $100-$500.

Most dance groups depict a man and a woman on a single base, although there are paired dance figures on individual bases as well. Often their hands are raised above their heads. Some dance groups are comprised of two girls and a boy or three girls. Many dancers wear kilts in the Scottish fashion and may be dancing the *Schottische* (the "Scottish," which was actually the German name for a dance performed in couples or pairs of couples). Plumed hats, poke bonnets, sashes, scarves, floral hoops, neckerchiefs, exposed bloomers, and various forms of country attire are seen most frequently in dance groups. In a few, stringed instruments or tambourines are included. One group, in which the characters hold castanets, is believed to be a portrait of Therese and Fanny Elssler who achieved fame for their castanet dance (Harding, Book One, 389). Especially noteworthy are Parr Factory groups of Harlequin and a dancing Columbine (produced later by the Kent Factory) and paired figures of two children who dance on circular bases with their hands placed saucily on their hips. Another group, not attributed to Parr, was based on a contemporary engraving and shows a woman (with a child at each side) dancing with a floral hoop that suggests a village fête performance.

The polka, which originated in Eastern Europe and literally means "Polish Woman," became fashionable during the early 1840s. *"Celebrated Polkas,"* a popular printed series published by Jullien and written by E. Coulon, included descriptions of several forms of the dance and featured a colored lithographed cover by J. Brandard (Harding, Book One, 350). The potters responded with several polka groups, including those based on a Jullien music front entitled *"Jullien's Original Polka Quadrilles, The Only Edition in Which 'The Original Polka' is Introduced."* A portrait group titled *"La Polka"* was based on a Brandard lithographed music front called *"The Royal Polka, Danced at the French Play by Mlle Forgeot and Madame Albert."* Another music front, titled *"Torquay Polka pour le Piano Forte par E"* with a colored lithograph cover by Carpentier De Selvier, provided the source for a portrait group of two unusual sisters who came from Alphington to settle in Torquay, Cornwall during the early 1830s. The sisters, as portrayed in the music front and in the corresponding figure group, dressed identically in odd outfits, painted their faces in a doll-like manner, and walked in step, arm-in-arm, speaking to no one but each other. When they arrived in Torquay, they brought with them two identical ponies, which gave rise to the sister's nickname "The Alphington Ponies" (Harding, Book One, 351-52). Only marginally connected to dance by virtue of the De Selvier lithograph title, this rare figure is an amusing "*foot*note" in the potters' inventory of dance-related figures.

"Masaniello." The opera *La Muette de Portici* by Auber was first performed in Pairs in 1828 and recounted the lives and loves of the Neapolitan fisherman, Masaniello, and his mute sister Fenella. When Masaniello discovers that the nobleman Alfonso (son of the Duke of Arcos) has seduced his sister, he leads the people of Naples in a revolt to avenge her honor. The revolutionaries overthrow the nobles and name Masaniello king in the nobles' stead. In regret, Masaniello helps the nobles escape, but in managing to thwart the original plans, he plunges to his death in an attempt to save another maiden from a fate worse than death at the hands of the vile duke. If the drama provided by the players was not adequate enough to captivate the audience, the spectacle of Vesuvius erupting in the background of the final scene must have impressed even the most jaded theatergoers. 11". Circa 1860. Value (damaged hand as shown or undamaged): $500-$1000.

Arbor group depicting the action from the ballet *Caterina, ou La Fille du Brigand*. This figure has been attributed to the Dudson Pottery. 8". Circa 1860. Value: $100-$500.

The fashion rage for women's bloomers, instigated by American Amelia Bloomer in the May 1851 edition of her ladies' paper, resulted in a bloomer craze that, in turn, inspired a wave of musicals and dances. Performances at the Strand and Adelphi Theaters included *"The Bloomer Polka," "The New Bloomer Polka,"* and *"I Want to Be a Bloomer."* The potters hitched their cart to Amelia's star and produced several Bloomer Girl figures, some based on an N. Currier lithograph titled *"The Bloomer Costume"* (Harding, Book One, 348-50).

"High" theatre also gained respectability and popularity among all classes during the Victorian Era as the cult of the celebrity became ensconced in the Victorian psyche. Operas, previously deemed respectable only as oratorios, through the person of the chaste and peerless singer Jenny Lind, drew immense crowds and figures of Miss Lind along with numerous other luminaries of the operatic stage portrayed in suitably dramatic pose and costume. A particularly fine and ambitious figure of Madame Alboni, an Italian opera singer brought to London as a rival to Lind, depicted her in her acclaimed role of Cinderella. The remarkable figure included a "pumpkin" coach, regal steed bedecked with plumes and ceremonial livery, and the fair singer herself in sumptuous evening attire. Ballet figures include Lucille Grahn and Jules Perrot as Catarina and Diavolino (from *Catarina ou La Fille Brigand*, illustrated in Chapter Fifteen) and Perrot and his wife Carlotta Grisi as Giselle and Albrecht (from *Giselle ou Les Wilis*). Actors, opera stars, and ballet dancers were lined up on mantelpieces with the same fervor as those who purchased them queued for admission to theatres. It was acceptable to be seen immersed in such pastimes so the production of these figures, along with swarms of unknown but glamorous performers, flourished and gave their viewers at least the feeling of better times, and a new and refined sensibility prospered.

As well as refinement the Victorians liked to regard learning as a hallmark of their time. Exhibitions like the Great Exhibition staged in 1851 and educational speakers were great draw cards for the public. Victorians were instinctive listeners, and speakers ranged from evangelists, to explorers, to academics, varying from notable to dubious, delivering their treatises. The potters obligingly responded with figures of the American evangelists Moody and Sankey and of Prime Minister Gladstone who could speak for up to four hours at a stretch. Reading was a newly emerging earnest pastime among more serious minded Victorians who were bent on self-improvement (like clerks and skilled tradesmen), and pottery figures of poets, authors, playwrights, and characters from popular literature were created to support this newly popular recreation (see Chapter Fourteen).

Country fairs were also a popular source of entertainment with Punch and Judy puppet shows an essential component. Pottery groups as well as single portrait figures of the puppet protagonists proved popular purchases for the public. But country fairs were tame when compared to other Victorian entertainment interests. Spectacles in particular fascinated the Victorians, and these came in a variety of forms (some of which were far more socially acceptable than others). A good execution was hard to beat in drawing crowds – a hanging ranked up there with a royal procession or state funeral – and a room with a view of the execution, according to one 1848 account, could command from one to three guineas for a window seat. There are, however, no recorded "hanging" figures, which is hardly surprisingly as the Victorians might have attended hangings with enthusiasm but would have balked at such morbid subject matter mirrored on their mantles: a portrait of the murderer maybe, but not his dispatch.

Another favorite entertainment that the Victorian potters *did* capture in clay was the fascination with seedy sideshows that traveled the nation presenting "freaks" and crude melodramas. Arthur Orton, the "Tichborne Claimant" and otherwise a butcher from Australia (see Chapter Fifteen), who tried to claim a baronetcy and massive family fortune, was seized upon by a sleazy impresario and ended up as a sideshow "attraction." The "Claimant" was portrayed in this "role" in a figure depicting an immensely rotund Mr. Orton. Among other sideshow-inspired figures and groups, General Tom Thumb, a dwarf who toured England with his entourage of small courtiers was portrayed kneeling and taking a bow on a large base that underscores the performer's small size. The potters even portrayed the famous Siamese twins, Cheng and Eng Bunker, although the identification of this figure is yet to be fully verified.

Lidded container in the form of a smoking man. For the poor, tobacco (along with alcohol) provided one of the few sources of recreation and relaxation available to them. 3.50". Circa 1860. Value: $100-$500.

The circus was one source of spectacle that was fully approved by polite society, and the potters produced several circus and menagerie groups. Some of the earliest date to circa 1780 and include Whieldon-type performing animals (Hall, 17). Others from the early nineteenth century were produced with bocage and on table bases for maximum effect. The most spectacular of these were groups of Polito and Wombwell's menageries (see Chapter Five for details, including an illustration of Polito's Menagerie).

Figures from circa 1820 titled *Show Man* and *Show Woman* and a group that depicts two men with a bear and a monkey riding on a dog's back suggest the British public's interest in "big top" personalities. Along with figures of unidentified clowns dressed in tunics and pantaloons, the potters produced figures of spectacularly attired animal trainers like Nellie Chapman, the "Lion Queen," Ellen Bright, and Isaac van Amburgh. These three all risked life and limb performing with lions, tigers, and leopards and were recorded excitingly, if not faithfully, in pottery form. In 1849, Chapman married and was succeeded by Ellen Bright, daughter of John Bright, a bugle player in Wombwell's Menagerie Band. Bright was just sixteen years old and performed in a cage with a lion and a tiger. During a performance at Chatham, Kent on January 11, 1850, Bright whipped a reluctant tiger, which then took her by the throat and killed her. After the inquest into her death, lion queens were prohibited with the result that, after Bright's tragic mauling, only male performers were allowed into the cages. Lion Queen figures titled *Death of the Lion Queen* clearly portray Ellen Bright (illustrated in Chapter Sixteen). Others, untitled, have been presumed to be Nellie Chapman; however, as the Hardings note, it is most likely that Bright's death resulted in the figures, and Nellie Chapman's inclusion in the potter's repertoire is uncertain (Harding, Book One, 32). Macombo, the Negro "Lion King" who worked for George Hilton's traveling menagerie gained fame and was portrayed by the potters in a spill holder group in which he is shown kneeling beside a lion and holding the lion's paw in his lap. On one occasion, Macombo was badly mauled but survived an attack by two fighting tigers. Isaac Van Amburgh (1811-1870) was a wild animal tamer/performer, born in Kentucky, who visited England in 1838 and performed at Drury Lane. Among his animals were lions, leopards, and a lamb. The Queen herself is reported to have viewed three Van Amburgh performances in a two-week period (Harding, Book One, 134). Two versions of a titled Van Amburgh group show the popular performer dressed in a gladiator's costume, flanked by lions, with a tiger on his back and a lamb or lion cub at his feet. Van Amburgh's popularity was so intense that the Duke of Wellington commissioned Edward Landseer to paint him. A man called "Manchester Jack" (the lion king of Wombwell's menagerie) challenged Van Amburgh to a competition to establish who the best tamer/trainer was. Van Amburgh refused and in 1848 added a black tiger to his act (Turner 185; Harding, Book One, 143). Figures of Sampson and the lion and a lion slayer are sometimes incorrectly identified as Van Amburgh. Another animal tamer/performer was John Solomon Rarey, an American horse trainer who toured England and the Continent with his horse show. Rarey was hailed as the trainer who broke an English stallion called "Cruiser," reputedly by tying the forelegs together and the hind legs to a collar around the horse's neck (Turner, 186). The potters produced matching paired groups of Rarey standing beside Cruiser. Some of these are titled, and the Hardings suggest that the groups were not true portraits but, rather, commercially inspired pieces commissioned by Rarey to sell at his performances (Harding, Book One, 360).

Temperance figure showing the advantages of drinking "WATER": the gentleman is clean and sober and holds a sack of money – the very picture of prosperity and propriety by Thomas Parr. The reverse of the figure holds a terrible secret – that of the consequences of drink. This figure was produced continually until the 1950s. 9". Circa 1860. Value: $100-$500.

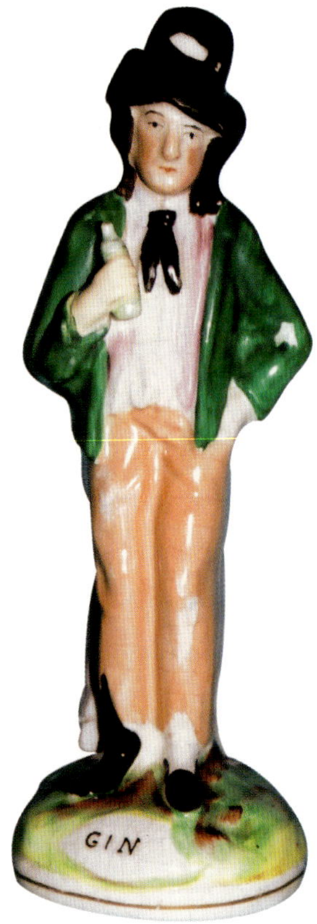

The reverse of the "WATER" figure clearly showing the evil effects of "GIN." Our young man is now dirty and disheveled and clutches a bottle of grog rather than a bag of coin. Alcoholism as a means of entertainment and escape for the poor was rife during the 19th century, and Temperance movements, particularly those enlisting the support of working class women and children, sprang up across Britain in an attempt to reduce the problem.

If animal tamers like Bright, Van Amburgh, and Rarey were popular, the fame (and resultant likenesses in clay) of a few celebrity animals cannot go unmentioned. Circuses and zoos provided a personal acquaintance with exotic animals that had previously been denied, and visitors responded with rapt attention. While earlier figures of such animals were based on printed illustrations and imagination, which rendered many figures more stylized than real, the introduction of traveling menageries, circuses, and zoos brought the common man face to face with incredible beasts from all corners of the world. The benign postures of eighteenth and early nineteenth century lion figures gave way to more ferocious feeling, and portraits of lions like *Wallace* and *Nero* added a sense of personality (Hall, 68-69). Zebras were modeled, initially from already existing horse figures but later on their own merit, including a pair in which lions are carried on their backs. Giraffes were introduced into the potters' repertoires around 1840 when the first giraffe foal was born in London's Zoological Gardens (Hall, 71). Most noteworthy, perhaps, are figures of "Jumbo," a bull elephant that came to the London Zoo around 1861 and resided in Regent's Park. Jumbo stood over ten feet tall, weighed over seven tons, and was reputedly the largest elephant in captivity. When an agent from Barnum's Circus offered ten thousand pounds for the animal, public outcry was immediate, and letters of objection flooded the media along with protests from animal protection agencies. Jumbo "mania" ensued and was manifested in pictures of Jumbo, Jumbo hats, neckties, fans, collars, Jumbo cigars, and even a music sheet entitled, *"Jumbo and Alice Polka"* by Harry Klein. The potters did not miss their chance, and elephant figures rode the wave of public sentiment. On the 1882 day scheduled for Jumbo's Atlantic crossing, the great beast staged his own form of protest and at first refused to enter the transporter. Fifteen days later, he arrived in the United States. Sadly, Jumbo was killed in a collision with a freight train in St. Thomas, Ontario, Canada on September 15, 1885.

Horse acts including Hippodramas, in which trained horses were "actors" with specific parts to play, were popular in Victorian England. Astley's Hippodrome, a distant descendant of circuses like "Polito's Menagerie," specialized in equestrian acts that often included spectacular "metamorphoses" and mechanical special effects that enraptured their audiences. Most famous among the Astley's performers were Mademoiselle Elle and Ada Isaacs Menken. Mademoiselle Elle's performance featured her entering the arena on horseback at full gallop, performing acrobatic leaps, and then vaulting onto the "Throne of Fame" flanked by two dancers. Despite her famed shapely legs and delicate feet, the fair maid was revealed to be a husband and father, but the scandal did not detract from "her" popularity and pottery figures of "her" alighting on the "Throne of Fame." Ada Isaacs Menken's most famous role was that of the Polish military commander Mazeppa who, for loving well but not wisely, was bound naked to a wild horse that was then thrashed into madness and released. Miss Menken (secured to a horse and in a state of decorous dishabille) thrilled audiences with her performance as the hero immortalized by Byron. The potters created several versions of Menken's performance; variously featuring the equestrienne lashed to a horse or, for the sake of novelty, a zebra (see illustration in Chapter Fifteen).

Thomas Potter ("T. P." or "Tippy" Cooke) in the role of "Ben Backstay" and an unidentified actress dancing the hornpipe. Prior to his stage career, T. P. was enlisted in active service as a sailor. When he brought his seafaring dances, ballads, and own brand of swashbuckling action to the stage, the Victorian public responded enthusiastically, not only to Cooke's entertainment but to its "authenticity" as well. T. P. 10.50", female dancer 10.25". Circa 1850. Value pairs or singles: $1000+.

Noteworthy horse act performers from early in Victoria's reign included the husband and wife team of Andrew Ducrow and Louisa Woolford. Variants of a figure group that depicts a man and woman (or boy and girl) standing on a horse's back may have been modeled as portraits of Ducrow and Woolford; however, the figures are untitled and an identifying source has not yet been discovered. The figure of a woman equestrian shown mounted and holding a flowered hoop strongly suggests a circus inspiration and again may represent Louisa Woolford. As the Hardings note, a pair to this figure (possibly Ducrow) undoubtedly exists although it remains to be discovered (Harding, Book One, 359). Another related group, extremely rare with only two examples recorded, depicts a man and a horse seated at a table (the horse on its hind legs with forelegs resting on the table top). The man is extending his hand to the horse, apparently offering it food. The Hardings identify the horse as *"The Learned Horse"* that was able to count, tell time, and guess a person's age and the man as possibly John Ducrow (Harding, Book One, 359). Louisa Woolford was also recognized as a tightrope walker and, although no identifiable figures of Ducrow's wife performing on the rope have been recorded, there exist two pairs of tightrope walker groups. In one, a boy and a girl stand cross-legged on tightropes with flags at each side and with the girl holding crossed flags. In the other version, a man and a woman stand on tightropes flanked by flags, and each holds a flag in upraised arms (Harding, Book One, 361).

Little Red Riding Hood on horseback, paired with an unidentified, mounted young man. As Red Riding Hood never appeared on horseback in the original fairy tale it is likely that the source of these figures was theatrical. 9.75". Value for either single: $100-$500; for the pair $500-$1000. *Courtesy of Anita L. Grashof, Gallerie Ani'tiques.*

When all these sources of entertainment are considered it becomes clear that Victorians were, essentially, a race of watchers and listeners rather than participants, but toward the latter part of the nineteenth century a change in the nature of their recreational activity started to take place. The most significant change was the holiday, a direct result of improved transport. Expansion of the railway system extended the upper and middle class habit of taking an annual vacation to the worker. Considered almost subversive during the 1850s, the workingman's right to a yearly summer vacation became more accepted with the reluctant compliance of employers. Seaside towns and popular watering places flourished through their new patronage. Towns like Brighton, Blackpool, and Southport also drew the focus of the potters to become the subject of popular souvenirs. An otherwise unrelated figure could easily be tagged with a title such as *"A Gift from..."* or *"A Souvenir of..."* and become an instant must-have as proof of the owner's ability to afford the indulgence of a holiday away.

The Victorian Era was a time characterized by contradictions, hypocrisy, and exploitation, but it was also an era of rapid and permanent social change. To be more kind is to consider it a time of self-deception aided and abetted by the Staffordshire potters who helped to set aspirations and expectations in their public that we maintain today: if we work hard, we deserve time to ourselves for rest and recreation. Perhaps we do not seek to take ourselves out of our every day reality through leisure activities as fully as the Victorian worker did but, nonetheless, we still cherish our right of escape – a universal right that the potters correctly assessed.

Often the streets provided the only affordable entertainment for many, and such entertainment was abundant as indicated by this figure of a street beggar, highly colored and gilded on a solid color base in the manner of the Dudson Pottery. 5". Circa 1840. Value: $100-$500.

Street musicians with a tambourine and unidentified instrument. 7". Circa 1880. Value: $100-$500.

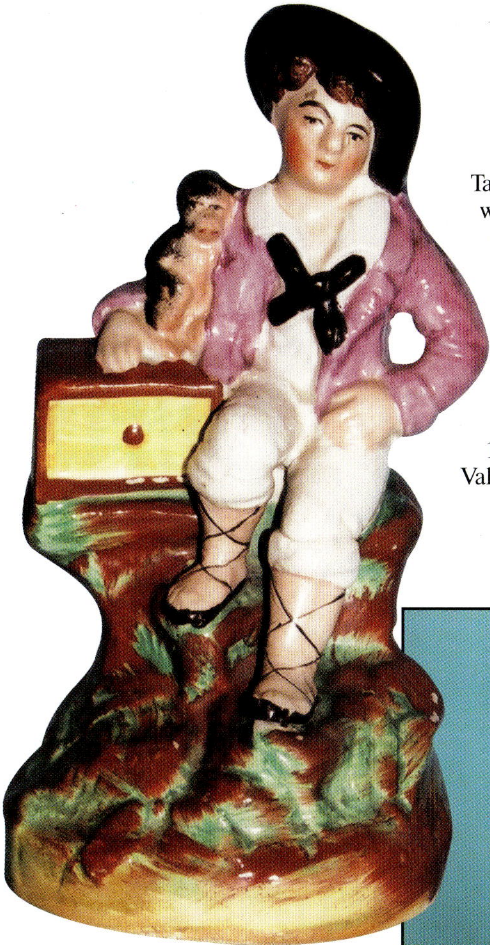

Taking music to the streets was popular during the 19th century when, for many, busking was their only livelihood. A witness to this subculture of popular street theater is the Kent organ grinder and monkey group illustrated here. 7". Late 19th or early 20th century. Value: $100-$500.

Foxhunting has long been regarded as the archetypal English sport. The potters concurred and produced a number of dramatic fox hunting motif groups. 8.25". Circa 1860. Value: $1000+.

What better way to be entertained than to catch a glimpse of your future? This young lady, produced in the manner of Thomas Parr, seems entranced by the prospects laid before her by an aged fortune-telling gypsy. 12.50". Circa 1860. Value: $500-$1000.

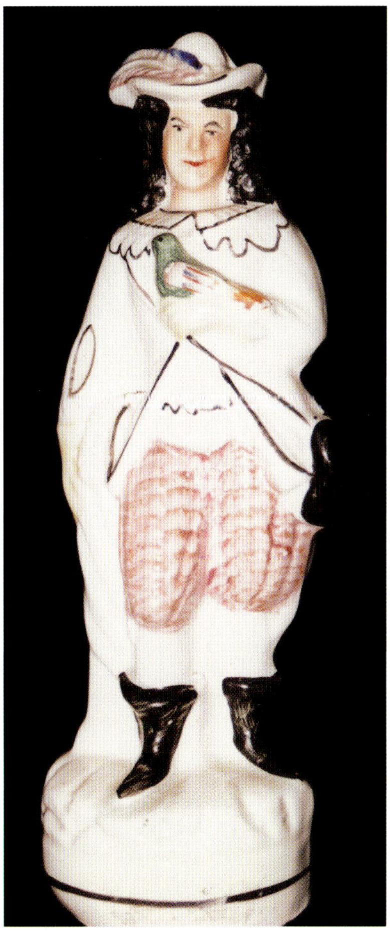

Falconry had long been popular by Victorian times, as this falconer, dressed in the clothing of a previous century, bears witness. 9.50". Mid-Victorian. Value: $100-$500. *Courtesy of Anita L. Grashof, Gallerie Ani'tiques.*

Theatrical spectacle was not necessarily confined to dry land during the 19th century as it was not uncommon to flood entire specially constructed stages in order to reenact famous naval conflicts and water ballets. The potters made sure that they covered aquatic dramas with a fascinating series of exotic boat groups as illustrated in this theatrical gondola group of two men and a woman in Eastern costume. 9.50". Circa 1860. Value: $500-$1000.

Theatrical grouping of a boy and a girl in a boat in the form of a seahorse. 9.25". Circa 1860. Value: $500-$1000.

Hunting remained immensely popular as a sport for the wealthy throughout the 19th century as depicted in this large spill holder.13". Late 19th century. Value: $500-$1000.

Circus equestrians displaying the vigor and drama of modeling for which the potters are celebrated. 11". Circa 1860. Value: $1000+. *Courtesy of Susan Bishop and Darcy McGroarty, Bishop and Daughter Antiques.*

Sleeping huntsman in the manner of Thomas Parr. 8.25". Circa 1860. Value: $500-$1000.

Woman and child quite possibly circus performers. Previously unrecorded group. 8.25". Circa 1860. Value: $100-$500.

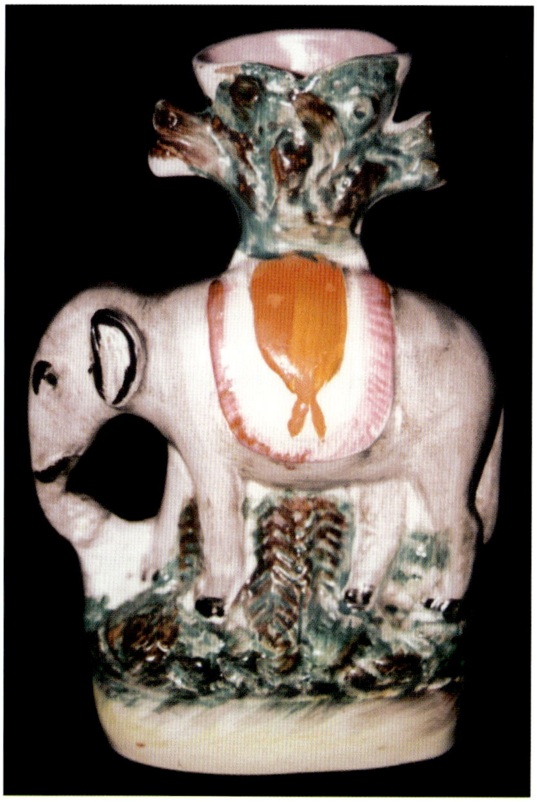

The expansion of the railway system throughout Britain during the 19th century not only fascinated onlookers, but also changed their lives. Nothing was immune to technology and progress, and improvements in train travel made it possible for thousands to journey beyond their villages for the first time. Trains were undoubtedly fascinating to children and provided increased travel possibilities for Victorians, but Jumbo, the bull elephant that inspired public protest when he was sold and sent to America, was killed in an 1885 collision with a freight train in Ontario, Canada. The spill holder shown here, like others of similar design, may have been produced in response to the early 1880s Jumbo "mania." 8.75". Value for a pair: $1000+. *Courtesy of Jane McClafferty Antiques.*

"A Present from Southport" is a rare marked souvenir spill holder from the one-time holiday destination of this group's original owner. Nineteenth century improvements to roads and the expansion of the railway system made the "holiday away" suddenly within the reach of the less wealthy, and souvenir pieces like the one illustrated became popular keepsakes that proved the veracity of their owner's claims of "time away." 4.75". Circa 1860. Value: $500-$1000.

Punch and Judy riding goats. Both figures 7.25". Circa 1850. Value: $1000+. *Courtesy of Susan Bishop and Darcy McGroarty, Bishop and Daughter Antiques.*

Previously unrecorded group of a courtier and woman in peasant dress that is possibly theatrical in source. 9". Circa 1860. Value: $500-$1000.

What better way to fill in holiday hours than to stroll along the promenade and take in a Punch and Judy show? The violent altercations of Punch, his spouse, and fellow puppets entertained children and adults alike, and booths dotted thoroughfares and beachfronts in holiday resorts. This Mr. Punch, with his dog Toby, is completely "flatbacked" with no details on the reverse. 11.5". Circa 1860. Value: $500-$1000. *Courtesy of Susan Bishop and Darcy McGroarty, Bishop and Daughter Antiques.*

Trysts were always popular "recreational" pursuits for the romantically-minded. This spill holder features a rather anachronistically dressed courtier paying suit to a very Victorian lady. 8". Circa 1860. Value: $100-$500.

Cricket was a fashionable sport in Victorian England and became increasingly accessible to all classes of players as church and factory teams were established to give working class men and boys opportunities to participate in the spiritually, morally, and physically beneficial effects of organized sports. Both figures 14". Circa 1870. Value for each or the pair: $1000+. *Courtesy of Susan Bishop and Darcy McGroarty, Bishop and Daughter Antiques.*

Chapter Nineteen

Architectural Figures: Ceramic "Real Estate"

It has long been said that an Englishman's home is his castle, and that remained the case even when the "house" was made of pottery. Although most of the chimney ornaments produced in North Staffordshire during the nineteenth century portray animals and people in numerous categories, the potters also produced various architectural figures – pastille burners, cottages, houses, castles, churches, and money banks – in answer to people's innate need to own "real estate."

Housing, like most Victorian issues, was touched by the Industrial Revolution, which brought about the availability and popularity of materials like iron and glass (as seen in the Crystal Palace built by Joseph Paxton for the Great Exhibition of 1851). During the heyday of Victorian Staffordshire figure production, the 1840s-1870s, very few workers owned their own homes. In the poorer neighborhoods of older cities like London, landlords owned multiple dwellings and rented them out to the scores of workers who required living space. While the wealthy lived in garden suburbs outside the cities, most workers lived close to their workplaces in houses owned by their employers. Employer-owned housing was generally designed to pack as many houses as possible into the least amount of space, and as many workers as possible into each house. Water and other services were not provided, there was little privacy, and, where people worked in shifts, beds were shared on a "roster" basis. Up to ten or twelve people could share the same bedroom, and up to one hundred houses used the same toilet facilities (usually a "privy," which was a deep hole dug into a corner of the yard, or a "midden," which was a heap against a wall). Some council housing was subsidized for poorer workers but, all around, conditions were substandard. Rain seeped through walls and rising damp (even in summer) was a common problem. Cellars were built in an attempt to ward off the damp; however, with housing at a premium, even cellars were sublet. In some cities, cellar dwellings were a primary cause of ill health.

There was little comfort or pride to be found living in a tenement slum or laborer's cottage, but there were alternatives for the Victorian aspirant to higher living standards. One alternative was to take up the offers of privacy and pseudo-affluence offered from the 1850s on by the ranks of cramped, poorly built, back-to-back dwellings that began to spring up on the outskirts of industrial towns with little thought to sanitation or amenity. These new dwellings, flung up by unscrupulous developers, were preferable to the cellars and hovels of the earlier nineteenth century, but not for long as these ill-planned estates were soon to become the slums of industrial areas. Even the accommodation offered by these developments was limited, so those in search of their "castles" turned to the other option that faced the aspirant homeowner: the purchase of a pottery facsimile of their dream-home, replete with climbing roses and gilded highlights, much like their gilded dreams. The Staffordshire architectural figure embedded itself in the Victorian mind-set along with thoughts of hearth and home and helped to bring about some of the most touching and ingeniously modeled figures ever produced by the potters of North Staffordshire.

Staffordshire "architecturals" were produced from the start of the nineteenth century. Most pre-Victorian architectural figures were porcelain pastille burners that were expensive to manufacture, costly to buy, and not intended for middle or working class consumers. At a time when plumbing and sewage systems were less than effective and personal hygiene was not a priority, it was believed that bad odors carried disease, and noxious smells were prevalent in cities and towns. Most upper class households burned pastilles, small cones of compressed herbs or perfumed charcoals that gave off pleasant scents when lit to diminish the stench. Porcelain containers, often in the shape of cottages, were produced to hold the pastilles and served the same function as incense burners. Most of these cottages were modeled with single-piece walls, attached covers or roofs, and openings in the back. In some cases, the cottages were designed with detachable roofs that could be lifted off. The First Public Health Act of 1848 signaled greater attention to sanitation, and odor issues slowly diminished. In time, pastille burner cottages became obsolete, but were still produced as decorative items. By the 1850s, Staffordshire's enterprising potters moved forward and created spin-off houses, castles, and churches in more affordable earthenware. Money banks in the form of small cottages and houses followed, adding clever function as consumer interest began to wane, perhaps coinciding with the increasing availability of "modern" housing estates.

Advancements in technology and a rapidly growing industrial economy signaled financial success for England's ascending middle class and greater wealth for the rich, but industrialization also resulted in intensified class divisions and separateness among the lettered upper classes and the laboring poor. As machinery and manufacturing techniques improved, England's economy boomed, and factories and warehouses demanded an increased labor force. Poor women and children provided a viable contingent of laborers that resulted in "working families" in which husbands, wives, and even the youngest children toiled long hours for meager wages. Life was focused on work and, apart from the wealthy, only fortunate middle class workers were able to rent private homes. Attempts to improve housing had been made by associations such as "The Metropolitan Association For Improving the Dwellings of the Industrial Poor" and the housing scheme established by the American philanthropist George Peabody in the 1840s, but with rental fees sometimes in excess of four shillings a week, almost a quarter of the average wage, these initiatives did little to improve the plight of the poor.

Conditions were somewhat less acute in rural areas like North Staffordshire where workers could lease and work farms to augment their factory wages. Throughout England, the voice of reform began to be heard, but for the vast numbers of workers caught up in the mainstream of industrial serfdom, change was slow in coming. While the poor continued to live in squalor (in crude rented cottages, in overcrowded rooms, and in wretched doss houses), the wealthy and rising middles classes embraced the architecture of Tudor and Gothic Revival, which developed in a return to traditional British styles as opposed to the classical styles that were fashionable during the eighteenth century. The Gothic Revival, led by philosopher and writer John Ruskin, was as much a spiritual concept as it was a school of design, and it reflected a retreat from the uniformity of mass production generated by the Industrial Revolution. Tudor, Italianate, and even medieval architectural elements were compatible with the Victorian taste for extravagance, attention to detail, and supreme embellishment. Most houses built in these styles were very large, expensive to run, and generally inconvenient to live in. Later in the era, simpler design styles heralded a return to a more "English farmhouse" architecture, which was eminently easier to decorate and keep comfortable. None of these, needless to say, was within working class means.

Staffordshire's architectural figures reflected current trends, if not in actual design then, at least, in character. In general, they ranged from the believable to the completely fanciful; many were decidedly quirky and weirdly wonderful. Castles advanced from one to several towers, and cottages were trimmed in high style through enhanced details (people, animals, staircases, multiple doors, archways, and elaborately decorated windows). When people were incorporated, the buildings took on a lived-in character and faces playfully set in tower and cottage windows provided touches of whimsy and imagination. In keeping with the ornate design elements of the mid-nineteenth century, some of the basic structures were decorated with profuse foliage, including grapevines, leaves, and slip-crafted shrubberies. Applied flowers were used in abundance, and cottages with large numbers of flowers are currently in high demand (each flower required a separate mold, making these figures more expensive to produce and therefore less plentiful). Predominant among the building colors were shades of apricot to orange in the earlier production period and minimal coloration as output and quality declined toward the end of the century. Lilac-colored buildings are very rare and fetch high prices. Along with elaborately modeled and well-colored buildings were architectural vignettes. These depict little scenes, usually pastoral, that contain one or more buildings and added details like swans, dogs, deer, shepherds, sheep, pastures, ponds, windmills, and watermills (the latter two are illustrated in Chapter Seventeen).

Decorated in underglaze colors, this rare and particularly fine example of a dovecote features an octagonal house with a doorway over which an inscriptions reads, "A New Pavilion." 9". Circa 1775. Value: $15,000-$20,000. *Courtesy of Jonathan Horne (Antiques) Ltd.*

A few pre-Victorian figure groups contained buildings and are noteworthy for their architectural elements. Two well-known groups in which buildings are present are the *New Marriage Act*, produced around 1825, and the circa 1828 *Red Barn* that records Maria Marten's murder by William Corder in 1827. While these rare groups contain buildings, they are not canonically architectural. Other early architectural figures associated with Staffordshire collecting are eighteenth century dovecotes and "Prattware" buildings produced between 1800 and about 1840. "Prattware" and "Pratt-type" are collector's terms used to identify figures distinguished by their unique style – a restricted palette (yellow, blue, green, purple, brown, and black), sponged or painted decoration, and a pearl glaze. Interestingly, there is no documentary evidence to confirm that the Pratt factory in Staffordshire ever made any figures at all, and architectural figures in the characteristic "Pratt" style were also produced outside of Staffordshire in Yorkshire, Liverpool, and Sunderland. "Pratt-type" buildings are seen infrequently and fetch substantial values. One, a fifteen-inch church with a tall spire, clock face, gargoyles, and two human figures, is rare and highly valued.

Like all Victorian-Era Staffordshire figures, architecturals of the period were mass-produced from molds and hand painted. Some were modeled in the round, especially pastille burners, but many more were made in the flatback style. Most range in size from three and a half to ten inches in height, but a few up to twelve inches tall have been recorded. Typically, the figures were decorated under the glaze, with occasional overglaze and gilt details and highlighting. As architectural figures gained favor among consumers, the innovative modelers designed increasingly imaginative buildings. Identifiable structures, modeled to represent specific and landmark sites, were usually titled in gold script. The majority, however, were not modeled to represent actual structures, and were therefore untitled. Among these were intricate castles with crenellated turrets, churches and abbeys, several-storied houses, houses with multiple chimneys, cottages with detachable bases, castles with clock towers, watch holder castles with openings designed to hold and display portable timepieces, three-tiered pagoda-like buildings, and even lighthouses.

Although not manufactured in the same quantities as other figure types, architecturals were apparently profitable. Buildings associated with royalty were popular along with those associated with the Crimean War. Another fashionable category of architectural figures included murder sites and homes of criminals and their victims produced to accompany related portrait figures. Among these were renderings of *Potash Farm* and *Stanfield Hall*, produced around 1848 when James Rush of Potash Farm killed his landlord Isaac Jermy of Stanfield Hall. Rush was hanged on a bridge over the moat at Norwich castle in 1849, and the potters responded with a model of Norwich Castle. They also issued *Palmer's House*, the home of physician William Palmer who was hanged for murder in 1856 (see Chapter Fifteen).

It is small wonder that Staffordshire's earthenware castles and cottages, which could be purchased for a few pence, brought pleasure to laborers who could only dream of owning their own homes. These category-specific figures undoubtedly represented an illusion of the prosperity and abundance that Victorian England's upper classes enjoyed and to which lower and middle class workers aspired. Staffordshire's architecturals possess the same naïve spontaneity and rustic charm of their more common figural counterparts; they are quaint and colorful, but they are also subtle reminders of a chapter in Victorian history that is the "flip side" of the glitz and glitter of England's most flamboyant age. Unique among other figures, Staffordshire's architecturals recall the story of the struggling poor. For most of them, an earthenware building was the only "real estate" they would ever own.

This large model of a church is an early "architectural." Made in Yorkshire, it was decorated in underglaze "Pratt-type" colors and features applied images of gargoyles. 15.75". Circa 1820. Value: $6,000-$8,000. *Courtesy of Jonathan Hone (Antiques) Ltd.*

Table base christening group with bocage entitled "Baptism of Mary" (repeated in elliptical panels on each side of the base front). This group features overglaze enamel decoration and a ridge footed base. The architectural detail of crenellated towers in the background is a curious "signature element" of several table base groups (see Chapter Five). 9". Circa 1830. Value: $1000+. *Courtesy of John and Barbara Gair, Castle Antiques.*

Church with two turrets. This figure is also recorded with other colored decoration and with a cross at the central peak. 9.25". Mid-Victorian. Value: $100-$500.

Back view of the "Baptism of Mary" christening group showing the crenellated towers. Courtesy of *John and Barbara Gair, Castle Antiques.*

This bizarre building features two towers, two cherubs seated on each side of a faux clock, and trailing vines. The group is common (also recorded as a watch holder); it is always badly modeled and inadequately decorated. 9.50". Mid-Victorian. Value: $100-$500

Caernarvon Castle, founded by Edward I in 1283, site of Prince Charles's 1969 investiture. 7.50" x 8". Circa 1860. Value: $1000+. *Courtesy of Susan Bishop and Darcy McGroarty, Bishop and Daughter Antiques.*

Small cottage with a cobalt blue roof and a swan on each side of the door. 7.25". Mid-Victorian. Value: $100-$500 *Courtesy of Anita L. Grashof, Gallerie Ani'tiques.*

Beaumaris Castle, currently in ruins, located in Anglesey, and founded by Edward I in 1295. 6.25" x 7.75". Circa 1860. Value: $1000+. *Courtesy of Susan Bishop and Darcy McGroarty, Bishop and Daughter Antiques.*

Oriental Pavilion from Kew Gardens. 10.50" (height). Circa 1860. Value: $500-$1000. *Courtesy of Susan Bishop and Darcy McGroarty, Bishop and Daughter Antiques.*

Pastille burner in three segments in the form of a cottage. 6" (height). Circa 1840. Value: $500-$1000. *Courtesy of Susan Bishop and Darcy McGroarty, Bishop and Daughter Antiques.*

Castle encrusted with moss (formed through the application of extruded clay) and featuring a clock tower and moat. A gilt armorial symbol hangs over the entrance, but does not provide sufficient detail to identify the building. 10.50". Circa 1860. Value: $500-$1000.

Cottage pastille burner separated to show its three detachable parts. *Courtesy of Susan Bishop and Darcy McGroarty, Bishop and Daughter Antiques.*

House with central tower. 7.25". Circa 1860. Value: $100-$500.

Small castle. 5.50". Circa 1860. Value: $100-$500.

Moneybox in the form of a two-story cottage. 6". Circa 1870. Value: $100-$500.

Unusual spill holder of a mill featuring a woman, horse, and swans (see architectural details of mill and windmill groups illustrated in Chapter Seventeen). 6" (length), 5" (height). Circa 1850. Value: $100-$500.

Bottom of moneybox indicating the degree of urgency with which a one-time owner sought to retrieve his or her savings!

Figure of a two-story house complete with a decorative archway at the left. 6.50". Circa 1860. Value: $100-$500.

Building with clock tower. 6.25". Circa 1860. Value: $100-$500.

Pastille burner in the form of a flower and moss decorated cottage. 5". Circa 1860. Value: $100-$500.

Reverse of previous figure showing the opening in the back of the figure for the sweet-scented pastille.

Moneybox in the form of a two-story house. 6". Circa 1860. Value: $100-$500.

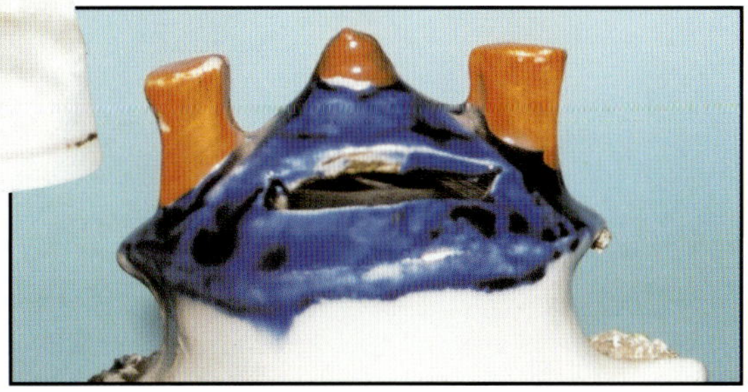

Reverse of previous figure showing the somewhat damaged money slot.

Two-story house. 4.50". Circa 1860. Value: $100-$500.

Architectural figures and groups include a wide range of castles and cottages, and the category may even be stretched a bit to include kennel groups that were produced in various styles and sizes. Shown here is a delightful group (one of a pair) in which a Poodle looks up at a bird that has perched in the spill holder tree behind its kennel. 8.50". Circa 1855. Value for the pair: $500-$1000. *Courtesy of Marla Chaikin, William Charles Antiques.*

Another charming kennel group in which a young girl sits with her Spaniel beneath a spill holder "tree;" the kennel is trimmed with extruded clay in much the same manner that other earthenware "architecturals" were decorated. 5.50". Mid-Victorian. Value: $100-$500. *Courtesy of Marla Chaikin, William Charles Antiques.*

Exotic building with stairs, turrets, and extensive "mossing" with extruded clay. 12". Circa 1860. Value: $500-$1000.

Boy and girl with rabbit and hutch. 7.25". Late 19th century. Value: $100-$500. *Gift of Mrs. Beryl Russell and the late Major Phillip Russell, 1980. Collection: Ballarat Fine Art Gallery (Acc. No. 1981.38).*

Human housing was a significant issue in Victorian England, addressed by the potters in idealized and imaginative depictions. While dog kennels and rabbit hutches were perhaps less attractive in their "architectural" reality, the potters presented them in a range of appealing figures and groups. Shown here are a paired boy and girl posed with exotic birds beside rabbit hutches on top of which their pet rabbits rest. Boy 6"; girl 6.25". Late 19th century. Value for the pair: $100-$500.

Chapter Twenty
Reproductions: Let the Buyer Beware

It has been said that imitation is the highest form of flattery, and the Victorian potters of North Staffordshire have been paid that final compliment, thrown that last accolade, by scores of eager copyists for more than a century. Staffordshire figures comprise one of the most popular, rapidly appreciating, and widely reproduced categories of collecting.

An unfortunate fact of collecting is that whenever a particular collectible becomes popular, and therefore increases in value, reproductions begin to appear in the marketplace. This is especially true of antiques and is sadly accurate in regard to Staffordshire figures. Reproductions abound, and Internet auctions alone contain an appalling number of repros that are offered for bid. The old *caveat emptor* – let the buyer beware – is particularly important as repro makers become more clever, and the telltale signs of their dubious "craft" become less apparent. Technically a "reproduction" is an item made in the manner or style of the original at a later date and not intended to deceive. In the hands of an ignorant or unscrupulous dealer, however, a reproduction is just as dangerous as a "fake" that has been made to deliberately trick the purchaser into believing the object is genuine.

Because most authentic Staffordshire figures were not marked, reproductions can be made without the need of forged signatures or factory marks. In general, some figures' simple design also makes them an easy mark for enterprising copyists.

Importantly, modern production techniques are vastly different from those of the eighteenth and nineteenth centuries. It is virtually impossible to duplicate the original qualities of molding, decoration, and glaze. Many, however, have tried, and some of their efforts have been believable. Outright fakes, that is, figures made with a deliberate intention to deceive, began to appear from around 1915-25. It was during this time that early creamware figures had reached a peak of collecting popularity, and numbers of musicians and other groups of the mid-eighteenth century style entered the marketplace. These were not reproductions of known figures but, rather, represented a body of figures made to simulate the earlier style. The original figures were produced with greater and heartier detail. The fakes exhibited narrow shoulders and their limbs were more curved than jointed. Clothing details like buttons and buttonholes, lace at the neck and wrist, and pockets and pleats were either poorly rendered or missing in the fakes. Famous potters' impressed names, including Wedgwood, Wood, and Elers were the real clues because the faked figures were not consistent with the potters' production periods (Halfpenny, 278-279). Today, these fakes are as infrequently seen as the genuine articles.

Many bocage figures and groups have been reproduced, and these *are* seen with increased frequency today. A good many have been made from old molds, but there are numerous completely new bocage pieces as well. Authentic bocage was always molded in separate sections of foliage, and front and back pieces with separately molded florets applied. The leaves on reproductions may appear with separate fronts and backs, but the florets are nearly always molded into the bocage. Some bocage reproductions are not colored on the back and many are decorated in pale colors that do not match those of the early nineteenth century. Reproduction bocages also demonstrate signs of slip molding in which an open bottom reveals a smooth interior that reflects the contours of the exterior. Authentic figures in which the bottom is open exhibit signs of press molding where the clay is pressed into a mold and smoothed, but still retains a slightly "lumpy" profile that does not reflect the contours of the exterior.

The current wave of reproductions includes everything from Victoria and Albert, to famous preachers and criminals, to castles, cottages, and pastoral motifs. Because Staffordshire Spaniels have long been a perennial favorite, there are probably more Spaniel repros available than other figure types. The range of bogus Spaniels is staggering and includes everything from Oriental knock-offs to British-made models reputedly created from original molds. Some are sprayed cobalt blue, rose, or green, and are decal decorated with flowers or French court scenes – bizarre enough to make the eighteenth and nineteenth century potters (who never made any such thing) spin in their graves, but, perhaps also share in the joke, appreciating the enterprise of their modern imitators. Fortunately, these are easily identified as new – the unfortunate thing is that they fetch prices up to $100 per pair. Several companies currently sell reproduction Spaniels. StafFisher Reproductions, owned by Curt and Jeannine Fisher in Stirling, Illinois, produces wonderful, quality reproductions of the 1850s, Number 1, classic Spaniel model in several decorated styles. For those who love the look of the genuine article but cannot afford the price, StafFisher Spaniels are the perfect alternative. Curt and Jeannine boldly mark all their dogs as reproductions, and the base rims are left unglazed to prevent misrepresentation along the line. StafFisher Spaniels may be viewed at the Fisher's web site www.essex1.com/people/fishnet.

Lidded box in the form of a miniature spotted cat on a cobalt cushion. The bright gold, the regularity of the crazing, the uniform dark discoloration, and the lack of detail around the cat's eyes and nose are clear indications of its reproduction status.

This miniature Dalmatian, made during the latter half of the 20th century, is marked at the back with a gold anchor in imitation of the mark used by the Chelsea Factory to identify its porcelain figures and groups.

Some reproductions have been made from original molds that were reissued by a few of the potteries at later dates. William Kent, Ltd. produced a number of figures from old molds, owned originally by Thomas Parr, into the twentieth century. Sampson Smith's pottery continued to produce figures, even after the time of Smith's death in 1878, until 1963. Figures of this type, while not preferred by purist collectors, retain a measure of credibility and value but, in general, they lack their predecessors' fine detail and spontaneous charm. Among the "new" figures and groups, many bear a Kent mark and appear with increasing frequency. These are identified with the William Kent firm (1894 until 1944). In 1944, the company became William Kent Porcelains, Ltd. and continued figure production until 1962. Although earlier reproductions were not marked in any way, later pieces are clearly marked "Staffordshire Ware" and "Kent" with a Staffordshire knot. Apart from these distinctive marks, another give-away feature of these later figures is the quality of their decoration. In the finest Victorian figures, especially those made by Thomas Parr, hundreds of minute brush strokes were used to build designs on clothing, while hair was produced with a distinctive "combed" effect that could not be duplicated in later versions (even those produced in the last quarter of the nineteenth century using Parr's molds).

Back view of the miniature Dalmatian, showing the gold anchor mark.

Far less desirable are figures of "last Tuesday" vintage, including those produced in the Orient (specifically in China) that are currently appearing in abundance at flea markets and in Internet auctions. Clearly, before purchasing an expensive single figure, figure pair, or figure group, both research and lots of hands-on examination (of genuine figures and known reproductions) is prerequisite.

While there is no essential guide to inform buyers, there *are* a few caveats that may be helpful in identifying reproductions:

1. All figures have inherent variations that resulted from wear on the molds and the natural character of hand painted decoration. Be wary of identical "paired" figures with painted details that appear in exactly the same places and have a deliberate, unimaginative look that lacks the guileless appeal of genuine hand painted pairs. No paired figures are ever identical – there are no twins. Pairs were designed by the potters to compliment, not duplicate, each other.

2. Most authentic figures were not marked, which makes the business of reproducing marks a "no-brainer" for forgers and reproducers. Avoid figures marked "Made in England," "Genuine Staffordshire," "Olde Staffordshire," or "Ye Olde Staffordshire." Nineteenth century potters never used such marks.

3. Staffordshire figures were decorated in a standard color palette. Whites should be a warm off-white. Reds should be rusty, never crimson. Be suspicious of very bright and very faded-looking colors. Cobalt blue was only used until the 1860s; new cobalt blue has a brushed-on look and lacks the rich texture of the original. All genuine figures have a patina, a mellowed look of age; new figures do not, and some are downright garish.

4. Look closely at a figure you are considering. Examine its surface to determine whether or not it has a patina, and do not be fooled by crazing. Fine lines on the surface of any pottery product can be achieved by using glazes and pottery bodies that cool at different rates and are not necessarily benchmarks of age. Many authentic Staffordshire figures *are* crazed, but many are not. Crazing can be, and is, intentionally created in new pottery to simulate a look of age. Watch out for dark craze lines that may have been color enhanced through the application of a coloring agent such as boot-polish to heighten the effect. Many of the reproductions made in China (there *are* many in the marketplace) are treated with color-enhanced glazes and have a grayish, sooty look. Often the gray is darker in folds or in corners. Some Chinese-made figures actually have an Oriental look about the eyes.

Like the Dalmatian figure previously illustrated, this 1.75-inch micro-miniature spotted dog, also made during the latter half of the 20th century, bears a gold anchor on its back.

This late 20th century 7" reproduction of the "Death of the Lion Queen" group produced during the 19th century (see illustration of genuine group in Chapter Sixteen) was purchased in 1997 from a wholesale importer; it bore a paper "Made in China" sticker and sold for $7.50. The underside of the base is concave and has a small release hole; there is moderate, but not color-enhanced, crazing over the body of the group.

5. Facial details (and animals' muzzles) should be well defined. Genuine figures often show a measure of fine brush strokes, but most repros show evidence of spray-painting or dabbing with sponges or brushes. Authentic figures were all hand painted, and each is unique.

6. Best gold, soft and rich, was used on older figures. It required burnishing and is impossible to duplicate. The gold used on newer figures is either mirror-bright or very dull.

7. Old figures, except those with natural openings like spill vases, had release holes in the back or bottom to allow gasses an escape "route" during firing. These were usually smaller than the diameter of a pencil. Larger holes suggest slip molding, which was not often used for figures made prior to 1900. Large release holes and open bottoms have long been suspicious; regrettably, the repro makers "caught on." Today's reproductions often have small release holes and require additional "tests." Older figures have rough, uneven holes, and while repros may have small holes, they are often perfectly rounded with no rough edges.

8. Genuine figures were glazed over the entire body. If a base is unglazed or if the rim feels chalky to the touch, be suspicious. Look for scratch marks on the base that might indicate an abraded mark (sometimes unscrupulous dealers will use abrasion to remove a new factory mark). Some repros are sprayed with a grayish glaze or are dusted with dirt that gets into the crevices and glaze to create a phony "old" appearance – be wary of figures with smudgy gray areas that are obviously not part of the painted decoration. New glazes cannot compare with those created in eighteenth and nineteenth century Staffordshire. The old glazes, into which figures were hand dipped, contained lead and arsenic that achieved lustrous glazing; these chemicals are restricted from use today, even in the Orient, and new glazes are distinctly different from the originals. Old glazes have a telltale discoloration that can be seen in the crevices of figures: a slight blue stain from the cobalt that was added by the potters to give figures whiteness that was intended to mimic popular and more expensive porcelain figures of similar vintage.

"Olde Staffordshire Ware" mark, which appears on a number of 20th century figures – the 18th and 19th century potters never used any such mark! *Courtesy of Marla Chaikin, William Charles Antiques.*

9. Check the weight of a figure in question. If it feels unusually heavy or light, closer inspection is warranted. Figures repaired with plaster take on additional weight, and a black light is a wise investment to insure detection of restorations. Slip cast figures are comparatively light. Some repros are light in weight, but others are plausibly heavy.

10. Bocage figures and groups should be carefully assessed as numerous items in this class of figure have been reproduced. If the leaves are not applied in separate, back-to-back pieces, the figure is suspect. The florets must also be separately molded and separately applied – florets molded into the leaves usually indicate post-1835 (and often much later) manufacture. Authentic bocage figures were decorated in the round, many repros have uncolored backs. Note, too, that the oldest bocage figures were pearl glazed, and white areas should exhibit a slight but discernable bluish tint. If an investigation of the underside of a figure reveals a smooth interior, indicative of slip casting, authenticity should be questioned as original figures display "lumpy" and uneven interiors resultant of press molding construction.

11. Deliberately faked figures are usually noticeably smaller than originals especially when they are cast from molds taken from original figures. During the process of taking molds there is considerable shrinkage from the original and, for example, a figure of dimensions like nine inches high by six inches wide can be reduced by as much as a half to three quarters of an inch all round.

Reproduction Spaniel head tobacco jar. This style of Spaniel has been widely reproduced and examples have been seen that are less well made. Similar reproduction book-end Spaniel heads are also recorded.

12. Restorations must also be taken into consideration when purchasing figures. Although not so dramatic a trap as that of the reproduction or fake, restoration must be carefully assessed, as a damaged and repaired figure will never be worth as much as an undamaged, near-mint figure. Damage should not stop a collector from purchasing a figure that might be very rare and represent a once- in-a-lifetime opportunity to enhance a collection, but the damage or repair must be factored into the price. Figures might be more than 150-200 years old: at such an age they should be permitted to show some marks of the generations of appreciation they have undoubtedly experienced. Ultra violet lamps may be used to detect repairs, but a trained eye and sense of touch (repaired areas will feel less smooth than original surfaces) are usually just as reliable for detecting restorations to figures. The "nail test" is another simple method for detecting repairs. Simply draw your fingernail gently over the surface of any suspicious areas on a figure to detect any changes to the surface that would indicate the presence of repairs.

There are, of course, exceptions to every "rule," and it is easy to fall into the trap of thinking that a low price for a credible-looking figure means a real bargain. Despite whatever warning signs may exist, it is human nature to want a particular item to be the "real thing" and under priced. With Staffordshire figures, that does not happen very often, and buyers are far better off paying a fair market value for an authentic figure than to fall prey to ignorant or unscrupulous dealers who will capitalize on any buyer's blind enthusiasm. So remember, *caveat emptor*, and do not be afraid to ask questions. Legitimate sellers will be happy to discuss their merchandise with you. Needless to note, it is best and wise to buy only from reputable, experienced dealers. However, at flea markets and similar venues, it is a good idea to note the seller's degree of knowledge as well as behavior. Some repro sellers are very convincing and are good at "moving" their wares, but none is as good as a well-prepared and educated customer who knows what and where to buy.

Common reproduction Whippets on cobalt blue bases. Whippets have been reproduced in various models. All are dreary imitations.

StafFisher mark, which appears on the base of every StafFisher product.

A trio of 20th century white and gold recumbent Spaniels. These have a more believable look than those made in China, most of which are produced with a sooty glaze, color-enhanced crazing, and decidedly bland facial expressions.

Purchased in a large department store in 1996, this papier-mâché Spaniel is a novelty – clever and cute – but never intended to impersonate a real Staffordshire Spaniel.

Twentieth century sheep with bocage in which the florets are not separately molded – a lackluster attempt that misses the spontaneous liveliness of authentic bocage figures.

Paired red and white StafFisher Spaniels (one of several available styles), handmade in Sterling, Illinois by Curt and Jeannine Fisher; 2003. *Courtesy of Curt and Jeannine Fisher.*

Sugar and creamer in the form of Staffordshire Spaniels decked out with holiday wreaths and bows at their necks. Bottoms marked © FF 1992. 4.75".

Novelty Spaniel salt and pepper shakers, 3.50". Late 20th century.

Reproduction (left) and real (right) "Elijah and the Ravens" groups. The real group is earthenware with overglaze enamel decoration and was possibly made by Enoch Wood, c. 1810-30 (Halfpenny, 202). The reproduction was made during the 1990s.

This late 19th or early 20th century begging Spaniel pitcher is an example of the scant decoration and bright gold highlighting typical of its production period. Made earlier in well-colored models of several styles, these jugs are currently widely (and poorly) reproduced in red and white, black and white, and white and gold, and may be purchased for as little as $15.00 each from wholesale importers.

Big, yes. Bold, yes. Dramatic, yes. Authentic, no! These large, paired red and white Spaniels were purchased from a wholesale importer in 1997 for $15.50 (for the pair!). They mimic the excellent examples shown by Pope (p. 97, fig. 42), have small release holes, do not have color-enhanced crazing, and their painted decoration has not been applied identically in the individual figures. However, their facial features, glazing, unglazed base rims, and "static" presence are clearly "red flags" indicating that these Spaniels are "not right."

Conclusion

The End of an Era and the End of an Art

For well over a century the Staffordshire potters "figured" large in the homes of Britain, the colonies, and, to some extent, the Continent. For much of that time, a small woman ruled over one of the largest Empires the world had ever known. By the end of the nineteenth century, however, figure production, the queen, and the Empire itself were all failing. Queen Victoria was old and bereaved, the Empire was fraught with conflict and economic instability, and the Staffordshire figure's supremacy as ornament of choice was challenged across the nation by new styles and cheap ceramics from overseas. The age was changing. The sun effectively set on the British Empire with Victoria's passing in January 1901, and it effectively set on the production of Staffordshire pottery figures. A small number of figures were manufactured until the end of World War I, but most of these were the product of a new age: more sophisticated and internationalist in style than their earthy and uniquely English predecessors.

Illustration from a Godey's Ladys Book entitled "The Figure Merchant," showing a Staffordshire vendor with a tray of figures on his head. Figures were often sold door-to-door in this manner for a few pence each. Other venues for sale included "charney" or "toy" stalls at fairs, outside theaters, and at other public places and events; in cities, they were sold at "china" warehouses, specialist "china" shops, and "fancy goods" stores.

Victoria's reign neatly coincided with a period of unparalleled change in tastes, beliefs, habits, and ideals, as well as in science, technology, and economics. It was a time of self-congratulation and self-satisfaction, and it was a time self-deception. It was a time of humanitarianism, and it was a time of great economic disparity and exploitation. It was a time of progress and affluence, and it was a time of poverty and privation. It was a time in which the individual began to shake off the bonds and restrictions placed on him by the yoke of the "everyman" and started out on a search for the "self" that still preoccupies philosophers today. The Victorian era was a time when individuals could aspire to better themselves, either through education or economics, and one of the most common and desirable hallmarks of this betterment for the under-classes was the Staffordshire figure.

An 1851 British census revealed that nearly forty thousand persons were involved in the manufacture of earthenware, and an additional six thousand were occupied in its marketing. Pottery was big business. In the more remote regions of Britain, figures were sold by hawkers, "hand sellers," and "cratemen" from wagons and packs, at fairs through "Charney" or "Toy" stalls, and from trays that were carried door-to-door.

Detail of the Godey's Ladys Book illustration showing an assortment of figures: busts, military, and religious.

In towns and cities, figures were sold through "china" warehouses, specialist "china" shops, and the more general "fancy goods" stores. They were even sold in stalls outside theatres, on public occasions like the Great Exhibition, and at funerals of the famous. The figures were freighted from the potteries to their eager public in carts, by rail, and by canal. They were sent around the world in sailing ships via the luggage of hopeful émigrés and in commercial quantities via the holds of freighters (archaeological evidence of figures in nineteenth century shipwrecks off the coasts of England and Australia confirms their commercial freighting). In short, Staffordshire figures were the vanguard of British colonization, a far more effective, and lasting, occupying "presence" than the British military ever managed to be.

This tintype of a little girl and her Jackfield-type Spaniel bears witness to the high regard in which Staffordshire figures were held during the Victorian Era. Photography, a relatively new science and art at the time this image was made, allowed common folk to record their likenesses with the accuracy of permanent mirrors. Given the high infant mortality rate, photographs often outlived their subjects, as did the Staffordshire figures they included.

The Argus-eye of the potters captured in clay most of the significant events and prominent personalities of their time, but there were some interesting omissions. Why, for instance, did the potters ignore the effervescent operettas of Gilbert and Sullivan, the effete aesthetic and parody-inviting icon posed by Oscar Wilde, the social commentator of the era Charles Dickens, and the Poet Laureate Alfred, Lord Tennyson while figures paying homage to Milton, Bryon, and Shakespeare were struck? Where are the Pre-Raphaelites (and their "stunner" models, lovers, and wives) who took the art world by storm, whose lives and liaisons were as colorful as their canvasses, and who exemplified the Victorians' propensity to dream? Why does Jack the Ripper cast no shadow across the field of pottery ghouls and miscreants when the Red Barn Murder continued to drip gore long after the perpetrator was taken to justice? Why was Dr Livingston ignored? These are mysteries worthy of Sherlock Holmes from whose popularity, too, the potters averted their eyes. The potters recorded real history but, sometimes, their reasons for potting the figures they did are enigmatic, and the enigmas are part of their mystique. Today's collectors may attempt to enter the potters' world, but can never manage to completely do so: puzzlement adds to appeal. Along this line is the preoccupation of some collectors with assigning definitive identifications to figures. The chase is challenging and the intellectual exercise stimulating, but to be preoccupied by attribution diminishes the magic present in every Staffordshire figure.

There is much to be learned from Staffordshire figures – they invite collectors to study and understand their incredible history and the history of their time. Spontaneity, vitality, and passion went into the creation of these figures and it should be with the same qualities that we approach them to best understand and appreciate their legacy – a legacy that speaks to generations of beneficiaries in wordless testimony to the people, places, and events that helped shape our modern world.

Further testimony to the importance of Staffordshire figures in Victorian life, this tintype of two men includes a Spaniel positioned between their hats. The people in early photographs like these are long gone but, because of images like this, they are not forgotten; and, happily, their Staffordshire figures may live on, treasured in 21st century collections.

Figure of Wallace from a time when the golden age of the Staffordshire potters had become a thing of the past. Modeling and decoration had been simplified, and figures lost their vitality and individuality. Cheap and novelty imports from the Continent had made the figures produced by North Staffordshire's potters less tempting to the public as tastes and fashions had moved on, leaving the Staffordshire figure stranded at the edges of the Victorian Empire. The few stragglers that made their way into the 20th century were sad and embarrassing reminders of a past age. 17.50". Late 19th century. Value: $100-$500.

These musicians are examples of later Staffordshire figures and display the reduction in detail indicative of their production period. 10". Late 19th century. Value: $100-$500.

Fewer well-colored figures, lack of attention to detail in modeling, the inclusion of glass eyes in some animal figures, and spray painting were all characteristics of late 19th and early 20th century figures and groups as seen in this recumbent lion. 11". Early 20th century. Value single: $100-$500; pair: $500-$1000. *Courtesy of Anita L. Grashof, Gallerie Ani'tiques.*

The inclusion of glass eyes may have boosted waning sales for a time, but the end of an era and the end of an art were near when these Spaniels were produced. 12.50" Late 19th or early 20th century. Value: $500-$1000. *Courtesy of Marla Chaikin, William Charles Antiques.*

Previously unrecorded figure of a sleeping girl. Like this girl, the appreciation of Staffordshire figures lay inert for many years, seen as an artless reminder of an age obsessed with ornament, sentiment, and propriety. If it seemed an age completely at-odds with our own, the assumption could not have been more wrong. Staffordshire figures speak of real people and their everyday lives: their dreams, their beliefs, and their sufferings. These wonderful earthenware figures help us realize that the condition of being human is one that is timeless, and the potters' passion and sincerity in making these figures remain as relevant to 21st century collectors as they were to their first proud owners in the 18th and 19th centuries.

Bibliography and Suggested Reading

Anthony, Evelyn. *Victoria and Albert*. New York: Thomas Y. Crowell Company, 1958.

Antique & Collectors Reproduction News. "New Staffordshire Figures from China," July 1996, Vol. 5, #7.

———. "On the Trail of Staffordshire Dogs," February 1995, Vol. 4, #2.

Balston, Thomas. *Staffordshire Portrait Figures of the Victorian Age*. London: Faber & Faber, Ltd., 1958.

———. *Supplement to Staffordshire Portrait Figures of the Victorian Age*. London: John Hall, 1963.

———. *Victorian Staffordshire Portraits*. Country Life Annual, 1951.

Bedford, John. *Staffordshire Pottery Figures*. New York: Walker & Walker, 1964.

Bennett, Scott. *Victorian Periodicals: A Guide to Research* (J. Don Vann and Rosemary Van Arsdel, editors). New York: Modern Language Association, 1978.

Bentley, Nicolas. *The Victorian Scene: 1837-1901*. London: George Weidenfeld & Nicolson, 1968.

Charles, Geoffrey Stafford. *Christies' Collectibles: A Connoisseur's Guide: Staffordshire Figures*. Boston: Bull Finch Press (Time Warner), 1998.

Drabble, Phil. *Staffordshire*. London: Robert Hale, 1948.

Earle, Cyril. *The Earle Collection of Early Staffordshire Figures*. London: A. Brown & Sons, 1915.

Fisher, Stanley. *English Ceramics*. New York: Hawthorne Books, Inc., 1965.

Gaston, Mary Frank. *Collector's Encyclopedia of English China*. Paducah, Kentucky: Collector Books, 2002.

Godden, Geoffrey A. *An Illustrated Encyclopedia of British Pottery and Porcelain*. New York: Crown Publishers, Inc., 1966.

———. *Antique Glass and China, A Guide for the Beginning Collector*. New York: Castle Books, 1966.

———. *British Pottery An Illustrated Guide*. London: Barrie & Jenkins, 1974.

———. *British Pottery and Porcelain 1780-1850*. London: Arthur Barker, Ltd., 1963.

———. *Encyclopaedia of British Pottery and Porcelain Marks*. New York: Bonanza Books (Crown), MCMLXIV.

———. *Jewitt's Ceramic Art of Great Britain 1800-1900*. London: Barrie & Jenkins, 1972 [revised edition of Llewellynn Jewitt's book, *The Ceramic Art of Great Britain,* first published in 1878 with a revised edition in 1883.]

———. *The Concise Guide to British Pottery and Porcelain*. London: Barrie & Jenkins, 1990.

Grashof, Anita (Gallerie Ani'tiques), personal communications, Scotch Plains, NJ, 2002.

Haggar, Reginald G. *English Pottery Figures 1660-1860*. London: John Tiranti, 1947.

. *Staffordshire Chimney Ornaments*. London: Phoenix House, Ltd., 1955.

Halfpenny, Pat. *English Earthenware Figures 1740-1840*. Suffolk, England: Antique Collectors' Club, 1995 [1991 reprint].

———. Personal communications, Winterthur Museum, Winterthur, Delaware, 1997.

Hall, John. *Staffordshire Portrait Figures*. New York: The World Publishing Company, 1972.

Harding, A. and N. *Victorian Staffordshire Figures 1835-1875, Book One*. Atglen, PA: Schiffer Publishing, Ltd., 1998.

———. *Victorian Staffordshire Figures 1835-1875, Book Two*. Atglen, PA: Schiffer Publishing, Ltd., 1998.

———. *Victorian Staffordshire Figures 1835-1875, Book Three*. Atglen, PA: Schiffer Publishing, Ltd., 2000.

Harding, Kit. *Miller's Staffordshire Figures of the 19th and 20th Centuries* (Collector's Guide). London: Miller's (a division of Mitchell Beazley), 2000.

Hodkinson, Malcolm and Judith. *Sherratt? A Natural Family of Staffordshire Figures*. London: Chisquare, 1991.

Horne, Jonathan. *A Collection of Early English Pottery* (catalogs), Parts V (1985), VI (1986), IX (1989), X (1990), XI (1991), XIV (1994), XV (1995), and XVI (1996).

Howe, Bea. *Antiques from the Victorian Home*. London: Spring Books, 1989.

Hughes, Bernard. *Notable Earthenware Figures*. Country Life Annual. 1957.

Huxford, Sharon and Bob (editors). *Schroeder's Antiques Price Guide*. Padukah, Kentucky: Collector Books, 2002 and 2003.

Kenny, Adele. *Staffordshire Spaniels, A Collector's Guide to History, Styles, and Values*. Atglen, PA: Schiffer Publishing, Ltd., 1997.

———. *Staffordshire Animals, A Collector's Guide to History, Styles, and Values*. Atglen, PA: Schiffer Publishing, Ltd., 1998.

Kies, Kenyon Charles. *Collecting Victorian Staffordshire Pottery Figures*, 1989.

Latham, Bryan. *Victorian Staffordshire Portrait Figures*. London: Alec Tiranti Ltd., 1953.

Latham, Jean. "A Zoo of Staffordshire Animals," The Antique Dealer and Collectors Guide, 1965, vol. 20.

Lewis, Griselda. *A Collector's History of English Pottery*. London: Studio Vista, 1969 and New York: Viking, 1969.

———. *A Collector's History of English Pottery*, Fourth Revised Edition. Woodbridge, Suffolk, England: Antique Collector's Club, Ltd., 1981; reprinted 1992 (first published in 1969 by Studio Vista Ltd.).

———. *A Picture History of English Pottery*. London: Hulton Press, 1956.

Logan, Thad. *The Victorian Parlour*. Cambridge, Cambridge University Press, 2001.

Miller's International Antiques Price Guide, 2002 and 2003 (Elizabeth Norfolk, General Editor). London: Miller's (a division of Mitchell Beazley), 2002 and 2003.

Mingay, G. E. *Rural Life in Victorian England*. London: Lund Humphries Publishers Ltd., 1976.

Moore, Hudson. *The Old China Book*. New York: Tudor Publishing Company, 1903.

Oliver, Anthony. *Staffordshire Pottery, The Tribal Art of England*. London: Heinemann, 1981.

———. *The Victorian Staffordshire Figure: A Guide for Collectors*. New York: St. Martin's Press, 1971.

———. "Victorian Staffordshire Pottery Animals," The Antiques Dealer and Collectors Guide, January 1971.

Pearl, Cyril. *Victorian Patchwork*. London: Heinemann, 1972.

Pope, Clive Mason. *A-Z of Staffordshire Dogs, A Potted History*. Oxon, England: Classic Press, 1990.

Pugh, P. D. Gordon. *Staffordshire Portrait Figures of the Victorian Era*. Suffolk, England: Antique Collectors' Club (revised edition), 1987.

Rackham, Bernard. *Animals in Staffordshire Pottery*. London: Penguin, 1953.

Ray, Marcia. *Collectible Ceramics*. New York: Crown Publishers, Inc., 1974.

Sekers, David. *Popular Staffordshire Pottery*. London: Michael Joseph, Ltd., 1977.

Stanley, Louis T. *Collecting Staffordshire Pottery*. London: W. H. Allen, 1963.

Theus, Will H. *How to Detect and Collect Antique Porcelain and Pottery*. New York: Alfred A. Knopf, 1974.

Thomas, John. *The Rise of the Staffordshire Potteries*. Bath: Adams and Dart, 1971.

Turner, H.A.B. *A Collector's Guide to Staffordshire Pottery Figures*. London: MacGibbon & Kee, 1971.

"Victorian Staffordshire Figures." The Collector, p. 15, June/July 1994.

Williams, Peter. Wedgwood, *A Collector's Guide*. Radnor, PA: Wallace-Homestead, 1992.

Wills, Geoffrey. *English Pottery and Porcelain*. Garden City, New York: Doubleday & Company, 1969.

Woodhouse, Charles Platten. *The Victoriana Collector's Handbook*. London, George Bell and Sons, 1970.

Index

Names and/or page numbers of Titled and other important figures appear in *italics*.